*Dedicated to myself,
for all that was and all that will be.*

THE BAGMAN

i. endings

Vinegar. Why did it always smell like vinegar in here? Squinted eyes, shrivelled up nose; I was doing my best to ignore the foul scent. Somehow it kept finding its way to my lungs, so much so that the task at hand was hard to focus on.

A man squabbled before me, drool leaking out of his mouth as tears lined his pathetic eyes. Maybe the smell was coming from him. Maybe it was piss.

So I rolled my eyes and spat at the ground. My hand firm against the steel. My finger sharp against the trigger, ready for any sudden movements.

"I'm not going to ask you again, James."

Making him cry made me groan.

"I p-p-promise," James blubbered, the tears rolling into his fat mouth.

"Tell him the fucking truth!"

That was my associate: my dumb, fucking associate.

"Didn't I tell you *not* to talk?" I hissed at the associate.

Who the fuck was this kid? I specifically told him to *shut up* before we walked through the door. If it had been my choice, I would've walked into this crack den alone. However, I'm stuck following orders and sometimes the orders are completely unjustified. If I had it my way, I wouldn't be the

1

one showing the newbie how we like to do things around here.

"James, you know Daddy wants his money," I reinstated, trying so hard to concentrate.

"I know! I know!" He cried harder, unable to keep up eye contact with me.

James had his hands behind his sweaty head as he knelt before me. His knees pressed into the unidentifiable goo and mould that clung to the cracked floorboards. I watched as his tears rolled from his rugged cheeks to the ground onto what I could only assume was an old blood stain. I raised my boot and stomped on his sad little tears. The squelching sounded over his blubbering. The muzzle of my gun soon rested on his forehead.

"Don't make me ask you again."

"I don't have it!"

My associate's rage resurfaced, "Bullshit!"

I was ready to shoot him too. I tensed, trying not to snap again. I needed to pay attention… James… The gun… I pulled back the hammer and the sound shot a flicker of realisation across his eyes. I was one pull away from ending everything.

"Are you sure about that, James?" I politely asked.

"Okay! Okay!" James whimpered and I smirked.

I drew back my revolver and stepped back from his pitiful presence. I fell back in line with my associate. He was being surprisingly silent for the time being.

James slowly rose from his uncomfortable position, hands in the air as a sign of peace now. He was still trembling and crying as he waddled to his kitchen counter. We watched him, guns still pointed at his bruised and breaking body. He bent behind the bench and opened a trap door that easily blended in with the mouldy, grotty tiles that I thought may have once been white.

James came back into vision, cautiously lifting a raggedy brief-case to the counter. He placed it on the surface, over the dead flies and moths that littered its dusty display. James' house was always so disgusting. All throughout the week he was busy with his gang, prodding diseased needles into his limp arms and burning his throat with homemade ale. When he wasn't here in this oasis, he was out gambling. He gambled a lot. He gambled with Daddy and he thought he could get away with cheating.

James grabbed a plastic bag then opened the brief case and I could smell it. Dirty money.

"Five thousand, right?"

"Don't flirt with me, James," I jested, walking over to him, gun in hand.

"S-s-sorry…ten," he stammered.

He started pulling out the wads of damp green currency. He counted them, the piles in his arms growing fatter. Eventually he asked me to double check, still quivering and scared for his life. I counted and nodded. He pushed it all into the plastic bag which I grabbed with a smile.

"Thank you for your co-operation, James," I grinned.

"Why don't we just take the whole brief-case?" I was heading to the door but my associate appeared glued to the sticky floorboard. He was furious.

"Take all of James' savings and let him die? A boy has got to eat! Come on, let's go."
We bid our farewells to the dank little house and its dank little tenant. As any good dungeon away from society, the front door took us straight into a dark alleyway. I adjusted my blazer before walking along the cobbled ground, my associate finding it hard to keep up.

"Why were you so nice to him?" he screeched. I rolled my eyes. This kid was never going to learn. I stopped and turned to him with a stone cold face. His act was getting old although I had known him for no more than a week.

"James is a regular client. We like to keep our clients' brains within their skulls and not all over the floor. We couldn't continue our little business transactions if all went south, could we?"

"You had your gun to his head though?"

"Did you see me pull the trigger? I don't kill people."
I continued walking, trying to find my way out of this concrete maze. I got a couple of steps ahead of

him before he jogged back to my pace. He seemed unnerved. There was something bugging him like food stuck in between his teeth.

"Are you telling me you've never killed anyone in your life? Surely... You're Daddy's nephew... You've been in the business for so long... Never?" I almost laughed, "I don't like resorting to violence, newbie."

"You can call me Temper."
This comment also had me fighting back a chuckle, "I can see why. You could barely hold it back there."

"I'm not used to this, any of this. The smell in there... I promise I won't do it again."

"Who's to say you're ever going to come with me again?" I scowled.
I definitely didn't want him to. His arrogance was a star on the verge of implosion, it would only hurt him in the end but I didn't want to be around to witness it.

"I'm still learning and Daddy said..." He swallowed, afraid by my intimidating stare, "He said *Chop Suey* was the best in the business and that you'll train me up and... And..."
This wasn't an after school special. This over-the-top act of a boy trying to do right by his family wasn't doing as well on me as it would of in front of a live studio audience. In fact, the performance reminded of some other actors I knew.

5

"Oh, so you're a cop."
He stayed silent. Terrified. He totally was a cop.
All the newcomers these days were cops. I wanted
to argue that nobody wanted a life of crime
anymore; but when has anybody wanted this life?
We weren't born to play the part of criminals like
some were born to be heroes. Rather we were
adopted into it, raised on crime and taught to adapt
to the world's darkest shadows. No, nobody truly
wants a life a crime but those groomed by it are
unsure how to step into the light. So when
somebody so sheltered pretends they have
grappled with the traumas we have faced, it is so
easy to decipher them just from the smoothness of
their skin or the furrowing of their brows.

"How dare you!" Temper regained his, well,
temper, after a stifled silence.
I kept walking, ignoring him.

"Fuck you! How could you even say that? I was
the only one ready to blow his brains out and you
just stood there, cracking jokes. If anything you're
the cop, fuck the force man. Fuck you. I can't
believe this-"
I threw him against the wall. I held him against the
graffitied bricks with my hands fastening on his
collar. He was definitely taken aback as I was
much shorter than him and the suit I was wearing
did well to hide my muscles. His feet dangled
above the ground like a child on a swing. My eyes
were piercing his for a while until I looked down

6

to his chapped, pink lips. I kissed him, quite violently. His breath caught in his throat, talking about surprise. My overwhelming frustration had turned to lust. He wasn't an unattractive man despite his anger and dishonesty.

I detached our embrace and dropped him to his feet, he almost toppled over. I stood back, taking a deep breath to regain myself and he did the same. I brushed off my blazer, cleared my throat and began on my journey again. He blindly followed.

"What are we doing now?" He innocently asked.

"I'm taking you to my motel room."

ii. beginnings

Sheets loosely lapped around my thighs, covering my naked body as I sat on the edge of the motel bed. My feet were firm on the carpet, my toes mindlessly playing with the fabric as I took a drag of a cigarette. I blew out the smoke between pursed lips, the toxins leaving invisible stains on my lips.
There was a shuffle behind me, the sheets rustling and the bed squeaking. I flicked my head back to notice Temper was awake. I looked at the time, it was barely witching hour. Shame, I thought I had worn him out enough for him to sleep through until late morning.

"What are you doing?" He lazily cooed.
He rolled over, propping himself up on one elbow so he could stroke my back. I flinched away from his hand and immediately stood up. I took another drag of my cigarette to calm down. I didn't bother to answer his glare from my reaction. All I did was put out my cigarette and start to get dressed again. The moon was taunting me through the slits of the window blinds, as if discouraging my actions. However, this was definitely not the first time I'd ever broken somebody's heart. I licked my lips and fixed my fly. My lover sat up, still naked in the bed.

"Do the other boys know... About you?"

I stopped to laugh which startled him. I looked back at him, maintaining his glare.

"Do the other boys know? I've *had* all the other boys."

"All of them?"

"Nearly," I grinned, buttoning up my shirt.
He grumbled, throwing the sheets off himself and reaching for his phone.

"I never told you that you should feel special," I rolled my eyes, this always happened.
A ringing disrupted our little spat. I thought it was his phone at first, considering his face was so glued to the screen. Then I saw mine vibrating on top of the bedside table, with 'Daddy' flashing on the screen. I picked it up without another moments notice.

"Hey, hey."

"Simon, we have to talk," his voice was stern, low, serious.
I was used to three in the morning calls to knock down someone's door who double crossed us or reclaim money somebody stole from us but not to talk; never to talk. People feared me because I was so close to Daddy that the need for formalities was long gone. We could read each-other's minds. Our relationship was purely based on action. The only talking we needed to do was give and take orders.

"I'll be right there," I confirmed, now was not the time to ignore whatever it was he had to say.

"Who was that?" Temper's voice mumbled from behind me but I didn't bother to look back.

"Your boss," I bluntly answered, fixing my tie.

"What did he want?"

I laughed again and took a glance back at him to catch his agitated eye roll. I wasn't a dumbass, though I'm sure he thought I was.

"You're a cop."

So many officers of the law had tried prying into the family business. So many of them specifically hoping to dismantle mine and Daddy's life. I had become quite privy to their attentions and although cursed with a big mouth, and learnt when to keep quiet.

"So this was a one time thing?" He asked.

I noticed his sudden change of subject the same way I noticed his black curls falling over his grey eyes as he sat himself up more. I was intrigued. He knew I was onto him but he didn't seem to care. I had fucked him into submission.

"And I guess I should keep my mouth shut..." He bitterly continued.

I don't bother answering these trivial questions.

"Whatever. I won't say anything. Don't want to ruin your image," he bitterly scoffed and I could tell he was hurt.

He turned around as if to go back to sleep and I left without saying another word. Daddy didn't like waiting. I tipped my head to the tired receptionist when I reached the lobby before entering the

10

carpark. I drove away from what was a sure night into an unsure day.

I never intended on being a Bagman. I was only sixteen. I came home one day after school with my four sisters to find the house empty. It wasn't unusual, my stepdad had to work late sometimes and my mum was always out with her friends. I had put the girls to bed as I was the oldest and stayed up watching television, but my eyes kept flickering to the door. I kept checking the time, midnight, one, two... My eyes were starting to droop but anxiety was choking me, I couldn't sleep even if my body was compelling me too.

At three in the morning the door opened but it wasn't who I was expecting. My eyes did not meet with the friendly eyes of my parents. They were greeted with stern, darker ones which hastily narrowed onto mine, making me almost swallow my tongue. He wasn't expecting me as I wasn't expecting him. Tension filled the air and grazed my knees, my knuckles, my heart. I swallowed, still unable to speak as this intruder continued to glare.

He lifted his arm, an object in his hand. I almost jumped out of my skin. What was it? Was it a knife, a gun, a ninja star? My little boy paranoia was racing through my blood cells. Alas, it was just a phone. He punched in some buttons and raised it to his ear and all I could do was silently stare.

11

"Yeah... there's a kid here, Daddy."
His voice was sharp. My hands clenched the fabric
of the couch. All I could hope for was that he
would leave without any knowledge of my sisters.
As young as I was, I was still their protector.

"He looks about twelve, are you sure?"

"Sixteen."

I had corrected him out of offence. He repeated
what I said back into the phone and cackled. I
swore that was the end of my life as I knew it.
They were going to kill me, whoever he was
talking to was demanding I should die regardless
of my age and then they'd take my poor sisters too.

"How would you like to be part of our little
family?"

Traumatic childhoods are often the leading causes
of fucked up adulthoods and although it feels like a
cop-out to blame my past for my behaviour today,
I can't deny that it definitely influenced the rest of
my life. My step-dad was a deadbeat, I hated him
from the start. Sons always have some protective
complex when it comes to their single mothers but
I genuinely wanted what was best for her; he
wasn't that. He hit us when he was mad and she
did nothing about it. The denial was so thick inside
her blood that she was running off of sludge. He
was a good man, she'd always say, a police officer
who could do no wrong. That officer, as if hitting
his step-children wasn't enough for moral
ambiguity, often broke the law anyway. His vice
was illegal poker tournaments. One night, he
screwed Daddy over and so he ran. He ran and left
his wife and her children behind like a coward. He
knew Daddy had complete power to trace him
back to his family, to kill us and still, without
shame, he vanished, Somehow, I came out on the
better side of the whole ordeal. Daddy did not kill
us but granted us, myself in particular, a life I
couldn't have imagined.
I pulled up at the normal meeting spot. It was
approaching six in the morning now. Daddy was a
family man through and through. His house was
one you'd see in a red-blooded American

13

magazine. It was a two-storey house with red shutters, a white picket fence and hand-painted garden gnomes. Illegal didn't have to mean inhumane. I got to the porch and raised my hand to knock on the red door but I paused, still reminiscing on how this all came to be.

It was a day like today that I had met Daddy. After the intruder broke in, he arranged a flight for me to America. Daddy had recently relocated on terms I still wasn't too clear on and I was to have an interview with him to consider being recruited. If the meeting hadn't gone well, I was sure I'd be dead. The flight was dull and long and painful. Heathrow to LAX for a teenage boy basically felt like travelling by molasses. Upon arrival, a man I didn't know but had to blindly trust picked me up and drove me to this very same house.

Coming out of my pointless memories, I knocked on the door which was slightly faded now and waited until it swung open. I had to drop my eyes however, as the smallest person I knew answered with the sweetest smile.

"Uncle Simon!" She exclaimed, holding her chubby arms up in the air.

It was my signal to pick her up and I did just that. The toddler buried her face into my neck and I gave her a big squeeze. I kissed her temple and put her down to find her mother strolling along the corridor to meet us.

"Mrs. Gideon," I greeted, as her daughter grabbed hold of my hand.

"Seikatsu has missed you," she grinned, swooping down and picking her child up who clung to her side.

"I missed her too. I'm assuming Daddy is in his study?"

"Daddy! Daddy!" Seikatsu chuckled.

"That's a yes," Sakura Gideon nodded.

She could've fooled anyone into thinking English was her first language. She knew nothing when I first met her. I gave her a polite nod back before making my way down the corridor. I knew this house better than my own, I knew this family better than my own.

I knocked on the study door and a hoarse 'come in' was bellowed from the other-side. I opened the door and saw him there, in his big office chair behind his big office desk. It was exactly the same as when I met him, even the smell of tobacco and the way his black ponytail was drooped over his shoulder.

At sixteen I was intimidated by his presence. Although he wasn't what I was expecting, movies had ruined my perception of people like this, he still had a certain air about him that made me feel cold.

Daddy was Italian, I didn't think he would be allowed the run the family if he wasn't. He had that slight olive-skin glow and big blue eyes. He

15

was skinny, lanky almost, but well-dressed. That day he was wearing a grey suit with a pink hyacinth poking out of his jacket pocket. His goatee was surrounded by stubble he was yet to shave, accompanied by bags under his eyes. I could tell he was exhausted.

The man who had taken me there sat me down in the chair opposite and then left the room. I was alone with this powerful man and he had my life in his hands. For a few minutes, nothing was said. We were both examining each-other. I noticed his rings, he wore so many on both fingers and that lead me to his bruised knuckles. I realised one of his eyes was bruised too, concluding it wasn't just sleep deprivation.

"I remember being sixteen," he was the first to talk, and sheepishly too, as if he was more nervous than I, "Lots of hormones, lots of questions. Let me be the first to tell you that the rage and the constant horniness never really subsides."

He brushed a strand of his midnight hair from his eyes, looking into mine.

"What do you want from me?"

I did have a lot of questions and I did want them answered. I was frightened as he stood up but he made no move towards me, he just paced back and forth with his hands behind his back in deep contemplation.

"I need someone I can trust."

"And that's me?"

He turned and coyly smiled at me, "It could be. I figured the closest bond is that of a child you've raised."

"You haven't raised me. I'm sixteen! I'm an adult!"

He had laughed at me, if I was him now I would've laughed at me too. Sixteen year olds are the epitome of naivety.

"You remind me a lot of me at your age," he walked over to my side of the desk and sat on it, watching me closely.

"I don't want to be you."

"Good."

He had gone back to looking serious. I didn't know how to analyse him or his answer. He was a closed book, even then. He wandered over to his side of the desk and sat back down, still watching me.

"I've already told people you're my nephew."

"Why?"

"So I can raise you without any questions. We used to be based in England, it's where my family raised me after we left Italy, no-one will question our relation. I want you to be my prodigy, Simon, to be my eyes and ears."

I shuffled uncomfortably in my seat. I didn't have the whole picture and I could tell he was being intentionally vague. I didn't have the authority to demand answers, however I was still going to try.

17

"Why?"

"Let's just say I am new to my role as the head of the family," he shrugged, still vague, "Look, you must be worried sick about your family but don't worry, I arranged for your mother and your sisters to be flown here to Washington, they've been put in safe-house. However, you won't be allowed to visit for some time, you see, I need to gauge your loyalty."

I had forgotten all about my family and that made me guilt-ridden. As much as I had tried to hide the existence of my sisters, Daddy was relentless in background checks. I was so paranoid about my own wellbeing that theirs suddenly didn't matter. I think he noticed, I think he could read my mind and I think he liked that I was more concerned for self-preservation.

"So… What is this family? What do we do?," I gulped, already somehow knowing the answer.

He gave me that coy smile again and reached into the drawer of his desk, pulling out a book. He handed it over to me, saying only, "read this."

It was 'The Godfather' by Mario Puzo.

iv. the moths

A hug from Daddy was something I took for granted. He believed affection was the height of masculinity and a symbol of our friendship. Every time I walked into his office, I was greeted that way as a reminder I wasn't alone in this life. Yet this time he didn't raise from his seat at all. I could tell he had been crying. Peaking out from his un-ironed sleeves was a row of razor-thin cuts along both of his arms. The combination of oily hair and poor body odour told me personal hygiene was out the window too. Something was seriously wrong.

"Want a drink, Daddy?" I asked, playing it cool as I walked over to his drinks cabinet.
He didn't answer. I grabbed the crystal tumblers and bottle of aged scotch, and silently poured us each a drink. I walked to the desk and put his down first for emphasis. His face looked like it would melt right off, all he was doing was staring at his lap. I assumed I had to start the conversation.

"Does Sakura know you've been cutting yourself again?"
As soon as I said that, he grabbed his scotch and downed it in one.
When I was nineteen, I was promoted to Bagman. Not that I really knew what that meant. Reading one book (and then later the movie adaptation) about a fictionalised family like ours wasn't

enough for me to know the ins and outs; certainly not the terminology everyone threw around either.

"It's a big role, lots of responsibilities," Daddy had to clarify, seeing as I wasn't as impressed as he wanted me to be, "You'll be collecting and sometimes delivering payments for me, as well as being a bit of muscle."

"Payments?"

"How do you think I keep this family afloat? A nine to five day at the factory?" He was starting to get impatient with my ignorance, "Poker, Simon." I had known he played poker, I just didn't realise it was our whole income.

"I'll need you to come with me to games now, watch over me, make sure nothing that shouldn't happen happens," he added.
As far as I was concerned, a Bagman was just an accountant who doubled up as a bodyguard. It was definitely a step up from the computer work he had me doing previously.

"I'm also going to let you go visit your family." I should've been resentful for him making me wait three years but when he said that, I hugged him for the first time and our relationship grew from there. Charlotte, Michelle, Catherine and Carol. I was saying their names over and over in my head as my hand grasped onto the cold steel of the doorknob. My sisters names, the sisters I hadn't seen in three years. They had been held here, in this neighbourhood, in this house. They were with my mother. They went to school like normal children and they had friends and celebrated holidays. My mum had a job, my mum cleaned the house, my mum looked after her daughters. They were a normal family who continued being normal after being moved to another country under the strangest of circumstances. The only weird thing was they had a guard; multiple. Daddy's soldiers took shifts. Soldiers was another term I had learnt, they were basically hitmen. One cared for them during the day and one watched over them during the night. They had to be protected at all costs, for my sake. They weren't just there to ensure their safety though, it was to ensure there were no rats. I opened the door. I wasn't a soldier but Daddy scheduled me on for a shift. It was time I saw them. It was time I looked after them. When I saw their faces and heard their gasps, my heart fluttered. I was hugged and kissed and drowned in affection. I apologised, over and over, for my abandonment. I apologised for my corruption. I apologised for ruining their lives. They forgave me with joyful tears in their eyes but it wasn't enough. I promised them I'd visit every week. I promised them I'd be a better brother, a better son. I promised them from now on I would protect them. You're meant to protect your family.

Jumping back to present day, I realised Daddy was my family. Daddy was my closest family, if anything.

"Can I trust you?" Daddy spluttered, tears springing to his eyes.

"You jump, I jump, right?"

"We've been set up," he said ever so nonchalantly, as if he knew for a fact.
Panic.

"I'm going to die at the Benefit," he continued, shaking his head,
Suddenly he was sobbing. The only other time I had seen him cry like this was when his daughter was born. His tears then were out of love but this was out of fear. I pursed my lips, unsure how to comfort him. He sniffled, burying his red face in his hands and all I could do was stare.

"My family…" He blubbered, his bloodshot eyes shooting up to me.
I couldn't tell if he was referring to *us* or Seikatsu. I could tell that he was afraid to lose whatever he meant. I offered him some tissues and he blew his nose. None of this felt real.

"I'm sorry, my boy," Daddy gulped, he truly was scared and he truly was convinced he was going to die.

"Do you have any more details of the set-up?" If I was going to help him, he needed to help me first. I couldn't save him from certain death unless I knew why he thought he was in so much danger in the first place. He pushed forward a letter address to 'Daddy'. They knew his address, which wasn't a good sign. When I took it out of the ripped envelope I was surprised to find nothing but a stamp of some sort of winged insect.

"It's them. It's the Moths."

v. murder

"The Moths?" I raised an eyebrow.

I had never heard of them. I couldn't say I was big on knowing mobs other than our own but the fact these so-called 'Moths' had shaken Daddy up this much by a mere stamp... I felt I had failed by my sheer lack of knowledge.

"They were around a long time ago, they were after anyone they could get their hands on. They attempted a kidnapping of the President but failed and then ultimately disbanded."

"I had no idea..." I continued to study the letter, I was no detective but maybe there was something I was missing.

"There's been sightings, here in America. That symbol on government buildings or on sidewalks near jobs we've carried out. Weapons and people disappearing without a trace. They're back but I don't think it's just me they're after. I'm just the beginning."

"You've thought about this a lot," I mumbled, not really buying this whole 'movement'.
He scoffed, trying to hold it together and not break down again. I gave up on the letter, there were no hidden messages beneath the red ink. I stared at Daddy. I wanted him to be strong again, it felt ridiculous to me to be brought down by something as silly as a drawing of a moth.

24

"They might not even be after you, they might want the President and they know we're on good terms with him," I tried to steer the conspiracy elsewhere.

"They probably do but that doesn't mean I'm not also on the list," he groaned, not lifting his eyes.

"You know I'll always protect you, Daddy but I'm not a troop. Send in one of your soldiers to guard you..."

"It'll look to suspicious if I have people with guns following me around and watching my every movement. I'm not meant to look important. The story is I'm an old friend of The President's who runs a local business and who happened to get back in touch after settling down with my family in this great country. I have a plus one, I was going to take my dear wife but now I'll be taking my nephew."

"Daddy..."

He didn't say anything else. He took my glass and drank the rest of my scotch. I wasn't going to persuade him.

"What if nothing happens?" I asked, convinced nothing would.

"Then it's a job well done," he cockily retorted as I grimaced.

"And if your crazy suspicions are true? If somebody attacks you? What am I supposed to do?"

"Kill them."

I wasn't a murderer and he knew that. Sparrow made me realise that…Sparrow. That was his name. I had been struggling to remember that for a while. Well that was his code name, he never told me his real name. I couldn't even remember his face anymore. I was trying hard, I could see blue flecks in his eyes. I remember he was bald, older than me…

I was twenty, almost four years ago now. Sparrow was important. Sparrow was always going to be important in my life even if I couldn't remember his nose, his cheeks, his ears, his chin... He was tall. That's right, he was tall and fit. Sparrow sparked two things inside of me. He taught me two things about myself I was unaware of until that moment. One, as mentioned, I wasn't a murderer. One of Daddy's poker games was the setting for this realisation. Tachivana, or Tachi as we called him, was a Japanese businessman who was in America for a few nights and had money to blow. He was a well-known CEO in the land of the red sun, so gambling had to remain hush hush to keep up appearances. Daddy invited him for a one on one game with him, promising discretion as well as fun. Daddy's games had a reputation even in Japan so it wasn't hard to convince Tachi to come on over and verse a man who statistically speaking, rarely ever lost.

People were so stupid versing Daddy with odds like that. I didn't know how he did it, there was only three routes he could take; bluffing, fate or fraud.

Tachi had brought a woman, Sakura. She was beautiful and definitely caught Daddy's eye; maybe she was the reason he was off his game that night. It was a one hundred grand buy in and he lost all of it. Hand after hand he was folding or getting his bluffs called or thinking he had a good hand only to see Tachi had a better one. By the end of the game, Daddy was furious. He was convinced something was up, he couldn't let it go. He took out a gun and shot the dealer at point blank range which Tachi found distasteful, cussing him out and threatening to besmirch his name if he carried on this way. Daddy was filled with rage but he dropped the gun anyway, finally accepting he had lost.

As Tachi was leaving, bowing goodbye as is his cultural custom, all it took was one card to slip out of his sleeve and fly as light as a feather to the ground. The rage resurfaced and before any orders could be ushered, Tachi turned around, slipped a hidden knife into his hands and cut open the belly of his mistress. Daddy gaped in horror. I couldn't comprehend it. Tachivana took our shock as a means of escape and bolted out the door. Daddy didn't run after him but to Sakura, kneeling down and raising her numbing body onto his lap.

"Get Sparrow!"

Sparrow. I can remember his scent too, arrogance and gunpowder. My legs started running before I even comprehended my orders. I was at the front door and running into Sparrow's broad back before reality struck me. Sparrow's orders that day were to guard the door, keep this game a secret. It quickly turned into hunting down the bastard who thought he could cheat our boss.

"Tachi cheated," I blurted when he angrily turned around.

He nodded, trained for this exact situation. He started running and I had to keep up. He must've seen Tachivana leave the house, assumed nothing was wrong but luckily memorised his direction.

I followed Sparrow as he pursued the damned. My feet glided over the hot gravel, the sun beating down on our blurs of bodies. My hands fumbled over my pockets as I ran, equipping my gun and keeping it steadily in my hands. My breaths were short and clammy, my ribs were hurting as we continued to run. I couldn't tell what direction we were going in, I couldn't even see Tachi. Sparrow's fast manoeuvring blocked my line of vision. I had to trust him.

Suddenly he was leading me into a faded building. There were cracks in the windows as well as graffiti smeared up the walls. It looked relatively abandoned. I didn't have time to pay attention to detail as I stormed in after Sparrow, his gun was

28

pointed and ready for action. We slowed down and I was grateful, my legs were burning and I was out of breath.

Sparrow cautiously paced up the cement steps leading to the next floor. I gulped, my hands shaking as I became his shadow. We could hear Tachi, always one staircase ahead of us. His steps were obnoxiously loud as we chased him to the top floor, my lungs imploding. I held it together. I had to keep composed for the sake of cornering him. I couldn't pant or sweat or stammer or tremble. I licked my dry lips, took small breaths from the nose and clenched tightly onto the handle of my gun as Sparrow and I entered the last room where Tachivana had gone.

Chaos. The first thing I saw was his silvery hair not his smug face or same coloured gun. He fired upon seeing our faces. He missed. Sparrow rolled across the floor but I stuck back behind the wall for protection. Sparrow shot back but nothing was pierced. A gun fight. Bullets went back and forth until eventually, Sparrow had shot Tachi's leg and Tachi had ran out of ammo. Relief washed over me, I stepped back into the room. Sparrow dropped his gun, bolted to Tachivana and knocked his empty gun from his wrinkled hands. He wrapped around behind him, pushing the man to his knees. Tachivana cried out in agony, dust and glass remnants infecting his open wound. Sparrow gripped his hair back as the other hand harshly slithered around his throat to lock him into place.

"Shoot him!" Sparrow had screamed at me. We had the grub exactly where we wanted, on his knees and looking down the barrel of a gun. All I had to do was end his miserable life. The weapon shook as my hands trembled, trying so hard to keep it aimed at his head. Shivers ran down my spine and crept into my tear ducts. My face grew hot and red as I puffed and puffed as though I had ran a marathon. How could I be so exhausted? I was just standing there, my gun rattling with my trembles producing no real physical exertion at all. My eyes lined with hot, shameful tears quick to run down my flustered cheeks. Tachivana was smiling as he watched me sob, as he watched my body go up in flames at Sparrow's request. I was burning, every inch of me was on fire and I could do nothing about it. I wanted to scream and flail and succumb to the pain and die. Yet I stood, pretending I couldn't smell the thick black smoke consuming me or that I couldn't see the flickering orange about to attack my glistening eyes.

"For fuck sake," Sparrow screeched after watching me cry.
He pushed Tachi to the floor and buried his face in the rubble of the ground. With his hand firmly against the old man's neck, he snapped back the hammer of his gun and placed the muzzle to Tachivana's greasy hair. One shot.

I spat, unable to control my tears anymore. I crumbled. I fell to my knees and cried louder and messier than I ever have in my life. As Tachivana lied motionless, his brains on the floor and his blood covering Sparrow, all I could do was break. Sparrow rolled his eyes at me, at my weakness, at my pathetic nature. He rose from the ground and over to me, yanking me up from under my arm. I squirmed underneath his grip, my face soaking and my teeth chattering. He stared at me with a certain ferocity and gave me no sympathy as I tried my best to swallow my tears. He opened his mouth as if to speak but gave up. I'd give up on me too. These memories made me feel guilty which gave me no other choice but to accept Daddy's request.

"Okay," I agreed and got out of my seat.
This time I wasn't going to be weak.

vi. intentions

Two, I was interested in men. More than interested, I was attracted, I was compelled to them, I was in love with them. I was in love with one.
Sparrow didn't talk to me for a while, not that I cared. We didn't ever do missions together, he was never one of the soldiers to escort me on my Bagman assignments. He was usually by Sakura's side since the incident, even after she had healed. Daddy had taken to Sakura and demanded she had security. She didn't speak English but Sparrow spoke Japanese and could translate. As well as being a translator for Daddy's newfound crush, he protected her and escorted her anywhere she had to go. She mourned Tachivana's death and was cold towards all of us in the beginning. She soon realised she would not survive if she hated us and started to warm up. She bunked in the spare room but found being in there all day was a bore. Sparrow was paid to take her out; to the park, by the lake, to go grocery shopping, to dinner. Sparrow started teaching her how to speak English, starting with reading picture books and eventually through the classics. He got her to read, write and speak our language within eight months. Daddy loved watching her learn. His eyes grew with fondness as she read to him. Every night at six o'clock her homework was to read a chapter of

a book of her choice to Daddy. Daddy was so infatuated, her voice giving him goosebumps and taking his breath away. He would reward her with whatever she wished, whether it was more books, more money, more makeup, more clothes… One night Sparrow translated that she wanted an easel, canvas and paints. She got these one by one, it took her over a week to collect all she required on Daddy's rewards based system. Sparrow took her by the lake every Sunday morning with her new materials and watched her paint. Her brush strokes were insanely beautiful, that mellow mixtures of greens and yellows captured the environment around her completely.

The art paradise didn't last, sadly. Sakura had taken to painting portraits of Sparrow and when Daddy found these in her room, his rage resurfaced. He was jealous, envious. He wanted this woman to be his. He wanted her to fall in love with him as he had with her. She had brought colour to his life. She was the pink trapped in his cheeks that was prominent no matter how hard he tried to suppress his blush. She was the blue in his eyes that were as clear as a spring sky and held the same hope and bloom the season did. She was the whiteness in his knuckles that he clenched when she was near, that he hoped to caress her face with. I couldn't imagine being in love with your captive. That's what she was. A prisoner they had claimed once killing her previous master. I couldn't imagine if

33

she was in love with him, such Stockholm
syndrome, such insanity. On top of that, English
wasn't even her primary language and it was
difficult for her to even communicate, for *them* to
even communicate. The whole situation was
difficult. So Daddy took her belongings away and
she screamed and she cried and she cussed and she
called him a monster. As the soldiers stole the
creative things from her room, she clawed at
Daddy who stormed through the house to find
Sparrow. Sparrow was in Daddy's office with me.
We were both waiting to get orders with tension
lingering between us. He still refused to
acknowledge my existence since I couldn't kill
Tachivana.

When Daddy entered the room we both turned
around, curious to find Sakura sobbing as she tried
to rattle her captor. Daddy firmly grabbed hold of
Sparrow's shoulder and didn't miss a beat as he
punched him straight in the eye. Sparrow stumbled
back from the harsh impact, gripping onto the desk
behind him to prevent toppling over completely.
He cussed, raising a hand to his eye and staring at
his attacker. He knew hitting Daddy back would
get him as far as kneeling in the gutter with his
hands cuffed behind his back and a gun to his
head, so he restrained himself. Sakura cried in
horror and I stepped between them, pushing Daddy
back slightly.

"Calm down," I hissed at Daddy.

34

"He stole Sakura from me!" Daddy hissed back.

"What?! Don't be ridiculous," Sparrow grumbled, stepping forward and I had to push him back as well.

"Ridiculous?! It's not ridiculous. Explain the paintings! You've had plenty of time to win her over. I was practically sending you on dates with her! All throughout the week, every second of the day, you're with her. I should've been more careful, I should've given it more thought. She's in love with you and I'm sure you're with her. How dare you... You knew she's all I've ever wanted. I trusted you!"

"Fuck off," Sparrow grumbled.
Sakura was still sobbing in the background, unable to speak up to confirm or deny anything.

"Just admit it!" Daddy was still yelling, my ears were starting to ache.

"Admit what?"

"That you two are together."

"We're not," Sparrow spat.

"Sure," Daddy growled.
I was getting sick of this debate.

"You're barking up the wrong tree, Daddy," Sparrow argued, carefully feeling his swelling eye.

"How so?"

"I don't love Sakura... I couldn't."

35

"Why not?" Daddy continued to yell, as if he was offended Sparrow couldn't love the girl that he did.

"Oh for fuck sake," Sparrow hissed, defeated. He pushed forward and grabbed my shoulder. He spun me around to face him and took hold of my hips. He pulled them into his, bringing me closer to his chiselled body. He clashed his thick lips onto mine, passionately tangling them to prove his point. I was in as much shock as his grip was tight. His eyes were shut but mine were wide open. He was putting his all into this kiss and eventually, I reciprocated.

He was the first to pull away and I stood staring at him. I wasn't alone, Sakura and Daddy couldn't take their eyes off of him either.

"So no, I haven't been fucking Sakura. Read her diary. You're the only thing she writes about. Excuse me," Sparrow declared, rushing out of the room.

Daddy did read that diary. It was part of her English writing practice. Although faced with a couple of grammar and spelling mistakes, Sparrow was correct.

So they got married. They got married and not long after Sakura was pregnant.

I was still thinking about Sparrow. I wanted to see him, I craved it. He was never at his regular post or in Daddy's office when I was. It got annoying. Days went by and still the taste of him was on my lips. He spent less and less time out with Sakura, so I couldn't ask her. I was going insane until one day, our paths crossed again. I was doing my duties as a Bagman at some filthy hotel and he was in the lobby. I soon forgot my job and strolled over to him without thinking. He was at the counter, asking about something. I wasn't considerate. I pulled him aside.

"Simon? What do you-"

"Where the hell have you been?!"

"Excuse me?"

"Everyday I go to Daddy's house and hope that you're there. I hope to see you either getting orders or helping Sakura or protecting the house. I don't hear from you. I don't see you. I'm freaking out because all I can think about is you. You're this big, annoying brute of a man and I was never interested in you before you kissed me but now you've plagued me. And I want you. For fuck sake, I want you."

He looked angry. I gulped as if to swallow back all the words I had just said. He grabbed onto the scruffs of my collar and dragged me down the corridor. I thought he was going to kill me. His eyes might as well have been red. He pushed me into one of the rooms and continued to let me squirm beneath his grip, although I wasn't fighting very hard. He let go, pushing me back and I fell over and onto a bed. I frowned, the mattress supporting my back. He quickly hovered over me, his arms beside my head as he swooped down and ravenously kissed me. I guess he wanted me too. We couldn't get enough of each-other. We met three times a week, at the same hotel, at the same time, in the same room. I was in love. I couldn't hide it anymore. I didn't want to. I wanted the world to know.

"What are we?" I whispered into Sparrow's ear, giving it a soft nibble before I pulled away.

"What?" He grumbled, turning on his side to face me.

We rested under the mass of stained hotel sheets, the moon creeping through the tattered window as we laid naked beneath both the fabric and the moonlight. I remember looking at him and thinking I had to memorise his face. I had to learn every every pore, every indent, every eyelash, everything but I guess that didn't go to plan.

"I don't do boyfriends," Sparrow said so matter-of-factly, no emotion to it.

"You do now," I kissed his jutting jawline and giggled, my head returning to his bare chest.

He groaned but didn't object, entwining our hands as if to confirm it.

We didn't really come out to anybody but we knew we were each-other's and that was enough for me. People had their suspicions and I was sure Daddy knew but it didn't bother us. We did everything together. Although we were opposites, nothing in my life felt more right. He was the easily angered, stone cold, pessimistic, violent type and I was the happy, almost sensitive, flamboyant, out-going type; Yin and Yang. He took me out a lot; ferris wheels, picnics in the park, skinny-dipping in the lake... We were domestic. He'd stay at my house a lot. I'd cook for him, he'd make the bed. We showered together, shopped together, sung in the early hum of the morning together. I remember one time, we were both in Daddy's office. We hadn't seen each-other in a week because he had been off galavanting with the other soldiers on an important mission. The tension was unbearable. Daddy was giving us our instructions for the next week but we weren't even listening. I kept looking at him, trying not to drool. It was pathetic.

"Anyway, I have to attend Seikatsu's dance class. Chop Suey, man the office."
I manned it, alright. I manned it all over the desk, the floor, against the bookshelves... I'll always remember it. If anyone caught us we would've been shot but it was part of the thrill. I was happy. I had a secured and easy job, I had good income, I had a great family with Daddy, I had my very own apartment and I had Sparrow.
We were happy.
Were.

vii. benefits

I had to stop thinking about Sparrow, it wasn't
good for me.
I climbed the dewy steps of the city hall, my
tuxedo catching the light of the early dusk stars. A
line of people were queuing behind a table, their
ball gowns flowing alongside the wind. There two
men in charge of marking off names for the
Benefit. I wasn't lining up for anybody, however. I
strode past the multi-coloured flock of big
spenders and showed my presidential pass to one
of the men. He nodded and I proceeded into the
building without a second wasted. Daddy had
given me the pass after our talk; only him, the
President, the President's personal assistant and
bodyguard had ones the same. We were the
important people. We were the stars of the event.
As I strode inside my vision was blurred with
decadence but I wasn't bothered. I stood on the
mezzanine balcony, looking below at the marble
floor and the mass of people dancing and chatting
amongst themselves. I could see Daddy, he was
with the President. I put on my mask, this was a
masquerade ball after all, and climbed down the
spiralling staircase, my hand tracing the golden
railing. The crystal chandelier hung above my head
as I approached the duo with a smile. The
bodyguard stiffened as I stood before them but

Daddy brushed them off recognising me even with the porcelain wrapped around my face.

"Evening," I bobbed my head in acknowledgement.

They weren't masked. Who would mask the President of the United States anyway? Well, if Daddy's suspicions were correct, The Moths will. Apparently they had a habit of masking people in black bags right before they killed them or so he informed me. The more I learnt about this gang, the more fictional they sounded.

"This must be your nephew," The President grinned and held his hand out.

I shook it, it was smooth and soft. The texture caught me off-guard as I always imagined his hand to be tough. There was no basis to this assumption though seeing as he had never done a day of manual labour in his life. He was a blue blood through and through. A basic and generic old, white, rich male. A typical American voted in by people who could've been his carbon copies. If anybody knew how entangled he was with our family, however, his reputation would be ruined.

"It's nice to finally meet you, sir," I lied and pulled my hand away.

This meeting was long overdue but Daddy didn't want many people associating with his biggest client, not even his 'nephew'. He nodded and so did I before parting ways. Daddy wouldn't want me lingering; too suspicious. So I'd watch from the shadows.

Sparrow left me, in the end. Three months of my life were dedicated overseas on irregular orders and the missions I carried out weren't exactly agreeable. I didn't see the problem with the work Daddy sent me to do, at least I wasn't murdering anybody. I still had that close to my chest, something Sparrow lost long ago. He knew exactly what my orders were but he never mentioned having a problem with it. He continued loving me until the morning of my departure to Thailand. The night before was bliss. My fleshy, tanned body slotted into his muscular temple of a body so perfectly. It was his way of telling me he'd miss me. Although no words were shared, not even whispered, I knew. The minute I walked through his door with a saddened smile flickering across my face and his hands found my hips, I knew. The only thing I didn't know was that the sex wasn't just for the three month goodbye but for a lifetime goodbye. I should've guessed it. There were so many hints. The biggest being I wasn't left with a trail of purple love bites across my chest and my neck like he always decorated me with after engaging in the activity. It was his way of branding me, of claiming me as his own. This time my skin was blank. He didn't want me anymore.

He didn't come to the airport with me, he couldn't. In the morning we kissed goodbye and I saw the glimmer in his eyes that shone purple like the love bites I missed out on. He looked so sad and I was so naive. I asked him to promise to wait for me but I couldn't tell if he was nodding or bowing his head in shame. He never looked up, I never looked down.

As the plane took off I thought to myself how lucky I was. The sky was as purple as Sparrow's eyes that morning.

Three months later and the plane was in Washington again. I had hoped to see his face at the airport but there was no sign of him. Maybe he thought it was too risky. I was feeling anxious. Under strict instructions from Daddy I wasn't allowed to contact anybody for the three months I spent away. It felt like eternity and I hoped he hadn't forgot about me.

Daddy had been paying off and caring for my apartment so I wouldn't worry about it. It felt good to come home and be in a forgiving and familiar environment after all that time. The only thing I hated about my unit was that it was empty, it was lonely. Sparrow wasn't there waiting for me like I had imagined. He didn't have a champagne bottle or a bouquet of roses to greet me with. I couldn't see his toothy grin, his open arms or purple eyes. Did he even have purple eyes? I was losing my mind. I retired to bed but the next day I called him.

I called him and I called him but I got no response.
I gave him hours to return the calls and still, I was
left in the dark. I decided to visit his apartment,
paranoia lurking over my shoulder. It was locked
but I had a key. I attempted to get in but it dawned
on me the locks had been changed. The paranoia
soon leaked into my chest and spread like wildfire
across my entire system. My last hope was Daddy.
It was getting late but I desperately needed to see
my soaring bird. It had been too long.

I rushed to his house without calling first. It was a
stupid thing to do with Daddy who was married
and had a toddler who needed to sleep. I was in
distress. I was impatient. He opened the door with
his messy raven hair, electric eyes, pursed lips and
gun behind his back. He breathed a sigh of relief
after seeing my face and put the gun in his pocket.

"Where is Sparrow?" I didn't give him a chance
to respond to my arrival.

His face became solemn and I wanted to puke. It
was bad news, "Has he been sent on a special
mission? Where is he? When is he coming back?"
He ushered me inside without replying but I shook
my head. I needed to know that second. I didn't
want to go inside. I didn't want tea. I didn't want to
chat. I wanted Sparrow, I needed Sparrow.

"Simon..."

"Tell me," I spat, gritting my teeth.

He crossed his arms and gulped, darting his eyes to
the ground. He didn't want to tell me but he had to.

"After you left for Thailand he came to me and asked for permission to resign. He knew if he tried to run it wouldn't end well. I was considering it because he was only a soldier, he didn't know our secrets but he did know our faces. He knew your name... He knew everything about you. I couldn't let him go when he held such valuable information, so I rejected the idea."

"Why did he.."

"I'm not finished," Daddy interrupted, "Then a week later he bursts into my office in the middle of a meeting. He made such a commotion even my fellow friends were shocked. He was a blubbering mess. I had never seen him so vulnerable."

"What did he say?" I muttered, barely able to breathe.

"He said that he loved you. That he's loved you more than anything he's over known. He said that's why he had to leave. He had to go because you were worth more. You deserved more him. Someone who spoils you with gifts and isn't afraid to kiss you in front of everyone. Someone who doesn't kill for a living and someone who looks at you like you light up the room. I agreed with him. No matter how much you loved each-other, it was for the best. So I gave him my permission, I let him sell his apartment and hand in his guns. I don't know where he is but I trust him not to tell

anybody about you. He loves you too much,"
Daddy sighed, "I'm sorry, my boy."
I nodded even though I knew he was lying. Daddy
held out his arms and I folded into his chest. I let
myself wail, convulsing against his body. He
stroked my matted hair and kissed my forehead
like any caring father would.

"You deserve someone who lets you in on their
thoughts even if they're just trying to protect you
by not doing that," Daddy whispered and I cried
harder.
Although I can barely remember what Sparrow
looked like, I could definitely remember the pain
of him leaving.
At the Benefit, a cute Irish waiter offered me a
drink from a silver platter but I refused. I didn't
like drinking anymore. After Sparrow left it was all
I did. When he left, I drank and fucked my way to
recovery. Not that I ever fully recovered. I became
harsh, crude, demanding, sleazy and impatient. In
a way I turned into him, all but the murdering. I
wanted to feel what he made me feel again. I didn't
care if it meant drinking so much it swelled in my
lungs and burnt holes into my throat. I didn't care
if it meant having sex with almost everybody in
the family. I wanted to feel him again.
I gave up drinking a couple of weeks ago when I
realised it didn't get me anywhere. So there I sat,
sober and alone.

viii. a dance

"Excuse me?"
My head shot up and my eyes were greeted with
two giggling blondes.

"Would you like to dance with us?" One of
them asked, her lipstick grin widening.
I smiled, this always happened. Although radiating
with beauty, I was not attracted to them but there
was no harm in letting them think I was. I nodded
and took their hands. They lead me onto the dance
floor to a mass of other stunning girls in glittery
gowns and masks. I'm sure they all wanted to kiss
me as we danced and talked like we'd been friends
for years. Laughter was echoed throughout the hall
as one held onto my hand so tight I thought she'd
break it. I kept my eyes flitting back and forth
between their pearly teeth and Daddy, who was
way off in the distance. Everything was going
well. I was enjoying myself and nobody was dead
yet.
Yet.

"So Mister Gideon, is there a Mrs. Gideon?"
One of the drunker ones asked after a while, a
pitiful attempt at seduction.
There was a chortle from behind us. I frowned,
looking around to find the culprit but the girls kept
bugging me for my attention, I couldn't dare look
at anyone else.

"No, there is not," I finally responded, winking at the one who asked.

The girls oohed and chuckled but somebody was still being cynical near us. I looked around for the deep laugh and my eyes found a man. He sat close to us, a long and pointy black mask perched on his pale face and long sweeps of brown curls rested above his shoulders. He had a cocky smile playing about his face and it unnerved me. Not only that, but the mask reminded me of a Witch Doctor. He seemed so out of place.

"Oops," he murmured after seeing my agitated state.

"Hi," I passive-aggressively greeted him, "Wouldn't happen to have a problem with us, sir?"

"No, no. Carry on," he smirked, hiding behind his eerie mask.

I turned back around, deciding to ignore him. Taking one of the girls hips in my hands and pulling her closer, as if to prove a point to this interruptive stranger.

"Is there any chance of one?" The one in my arms enquired, batting her eyelashes at me.

The curly-haired man laughed again and it took all I had to block him out. He was being so rude and unkind. He didn't know me or these girls. Probably just some rich asshole who was jealous of the attention I was getting.

"My career is too demanding right now to even think about that sort of thing," I brushed them off, losing all interest in keeping up the flirtatious charade.

The man was cackling again and I clenched my fists. Before I could turn around and snap at him, he had seemingly got up himself and tapped on my shoulder.

"What is it that you want?" I grumbled, facing him, hands on hips like an annoyed mother.

"A dance," he abruptly stated and I was taken aback.

Apart from his obnoxious and inherently rude nature, he was somewhat *charming*. I could see his emerald eyes peaking through his inappropriate mask and his taunting lips seemed almost tempting now. I wish I didn't fall in love with pretty boys so easily, especially ones like this.

"I'm not interested."

"Are you sure?" He pressed, holding out his hand.

I hesitated, staring at his long fingers and open palm. The girls were devastated. I ignored them, trying to make my own decision. I could feel the tension brewing between myself and the masked man; it was steaming, boiling, thick. I took a quick glance at Daddy, he seemed to be managing himself fine. I had time.

Lust was at my fingertips when I let them glide into the stranger's hand. He quickly took hold and

dragged me away from the frothing ladies. They had no chance at all against such a beautiful man. He took my waist and I wanted to whimper, it felt so nice to be touched there again. When our feet started to move I felt like we were gliding.
I missed this.

"So, Simon-"

"How do you know my name?" I interrupted in a panic.

"You mentioned it to your posse over there," he replied, bobbing his head to the sad women.
I didn't recall ever stating my first name but I let it slide, maybe I slipped up. I wouldn't let paranoia consume me. I wanted to enjoy this. It had been a while since I last had fun especially with a man who initiated things first.

"So Simon, what brings you to this fine event?" His language was so formal and on top of that his accent was British. One of my own. I was liking him more and more.

"I'm with my Uncle, he's good mates with the President," I replied, "They go way back."

"Uh-huh."

"You?"

"Let's just say a couple of my friends were looking for something to do," he shrugged.

"It's bit expensive for just something to do," I doubted him.

"Well two of my mates are actually doing service jobs here tonight. The rest of us decided to tag along," he explained further, "They got us discounted tickets."

"If you say so."
We continued to sway to the slow tempo, eyes glued on each-others. I was so captured. They were so green, so vivid, so alive. I thought I had become sick of eyes until I saw his. He really had swept me off my feet so easily. Sparrow had to kiss me before I got the point and all this man had to do was hold out his hand. Maybe I was getting desperate, willing to be with anyone for the slightest bit of affection.

"Why were you laughing earlier?" I asked which brought back his smirk.

"*Is there a Mrs. Gideon*?" He mocked the girls and I had to suppress my own giggle.

"They were interested, leave them alone," I tried to defend them but the truth was I couldn't care less, I liked that he had been listening.
He laughed that same hearty laugh as before and I grumbled, it was hard to stay mad when he could make a noise like that.

"Oh you're so precious!" He emphasised, sweeping my fringe out of my eyes.
I tried to suppress a blush, almost swallowing my tongue. I darted my eyes to the floor but he delicately lifted my chin back up with two fingers.

"You're beautiful too."

The playful mood had dropped. He meant it. I didn't know him but I felt him. I felt for him. I believed him. I trusted him. Who was he? How was he doing this to me? I felt goosebumps. I felt ill.

He cleared his throat, returning his hand to mine. I didn't even realise we had stopped dancing until he started to move his feet again. I tried to recollect myself but all I could think about was what he had just said and his piercing eyes that transcended the limitations of words and said more than I ever could.

"You're clearly gay," he cleared his throat, continuing our early conversation.

"You don't know that," I rolled my eyes at his assumption.

"If you're not... Then why *isn't* there a Mrs. Gideon here tonight?" He tried to contain his immature laughter.

"Work is demanding."

"Are you saying women are too?"

"No," I panicked, "I just… don't have time for these things."

"Love makes time."

"You're so pretentious," I say through laughter.

"You could learn a lot from me," he chuckled, spinning me and then pulling me back into his lanky body.

"Like what?" I breathed, looking up at the taller man.

"Your sexuality, for one."

"I'm not gay!" I argued for the sake of it.

"Prove it," he sniggered, that same doubtful tone in his voice.

"How?" I gulped.

"Kiss me."

"I think that's the opposite of what I'm trying to achieve here," I scoffed, even though the thought of kissing him had been on my mind since we started dancing.

"Just do it," he barely whispered, his hot breath stroking my face.

Fuck.

I licked my lips, my heart racing and a semi poking at the fabric of my pants. It was embarrassing how much this stranger was effecting me. Nonetheless, I stood on my tippy-toes, my hands against his chest as his hands grasped onto my hips. I tilted my head, dodging the long porcelain nose and leant in close to his face. I pressed my lips against his and I think we both stopped breathing. His lips were so soft but his hands so firm as his nails dug into my hips. I moaned slightly into his lips which made him reciprocate the noise and dig a little deeper. He passionately tangled our lips and I felt like a teenager making out in the hallway of school when we were meant to be in class. I loved it. Our bodies

were so close and our breaths were so hot and I
was so turned on. He pulled back and I gulped
hard, returning to my normal height. He chuckled
under his breath, shaking his head as I bit my lip.
He leant in near my ear with a smile.

"You so are," he whispered.

"What am I?" I teased.
He paused, looking at me as if he was searching
deep within my eyes for the answer.

"A Bagman."
My heart stopped.

"What?" I barely uttered, the whole world
turning upside down in a single beat.

"Don't drink the champagne."
And like that he disappeared.

ix. losing the game

Frozen. The smell of vinegar attacking my nostrils again. My breathing was sharp, short. My eyes began to water. How did he know? How the fuck did he know? There was only one answer but I couldn't bring myself to spit it out. Bile found its way to my throat but I forced it back down. I was a mess.

I had to get to Daddy, I had to alert him before it was too late. I began shuffling through the crowd in a hurry, barging past the disguised faces with no remorse. I couldn't see him. A weight fell heavy on my chest. I wanted to fall to the floor. I didn't give up, no matter how out of breath I was. My frantic state was not being put to rest.

A hand gripped me and I tried to struggle free. When their grip was too tight to escape, I turned to see who was restraining me. The waiter from earlier with the Irish accent, his mask crooked now as he clenched hard.

"Sir, no running."

"I have to find somebody, I have to tell them…"

"An announcement is about to take place, I'll ask you now to stand still and wait to find your friend later on," he insisted.

I swallowed, trying to recollect myself. He had to be in on it. He was hovering, no chance of escaping him. I hoped so much that Daddy was safe, that he was okay. The waiter finally released me and faded into the crowd. I wanted to start bolting again but I knew I'd be going in circles if I even tried, he was nowhere in sight.

Suddenly there was a screech of a faulty microphone and a boomed apology for the horrid noise. Everybody turned to face the stage that sat beneath the twisted stairs of the hall. Feet perched on the floorboards, I turned to see who was making the announcement. It was him, the curly-haired man who knew so much.

"My apologies again but this time for the abrupt disruption of your fine evening."

The music had stopped and not another sound was echoed except for him. He had everybody's attention, even The President. The world was his.

"I must turn your attention away from the charity of the night for a few minutes as I wish to shed light on another subject worth caring about," he explained, his mask still tauntingly sitting over his face, "Although, I wish not to take your donations for this cause but your acknowledgement and thirst for justice."

My palms were sweaty, what was he blabbering on about? What was he leading up to? I felt so faint. I was bathing in the idea of failure and disappointment; or more-so drowning in it.

"Good evening, Mr. President," he beamed at the powerful man in the very front row who's security guard had mysteriously gone missing.

The President did not smile back, he was confused like the rest of us. It was clear he had no idea who this man was. Surely, there would be back-up. He was the President, the most important man on the planet and he only brought one body guard? I was furious at the circumstance, rummaging my brain for logic. Back up had to be on the way, it had to.

"Don't let my English accent put you off, I've spent most of my life here in the United States now. While I was here I learnt a few things. One being how corrupt this system is, in every single way. It's time you all step up to the plate and take action. It's time you stop turning a blind eye and learn the truth about your own politics. It's time you all learn the truth about your own country," he exclaimed, his tongue curling up as he spoke as if he had tasted something sour.

The waiter from earlier and another were hauling something up to the stage. Not something, someone. They weren't delicate at all as they dragged this person up the small steps with their knees scraping along the floor. The two men threw the person at the curly one's feet. They were handcuffed, hands harshly secured behind their back. Not only did their hands not have freedom but over their head was that famous black bag. The audience gasped and I forgot how to develop my own thoughts.

"Behind this hood is the man who is running your country. Behind this hood is not the man you voted for, it is not the man you elected to be your voice but the person who works behind closed doors. Behind this hood is the man who is controlling what this political party fails to. Behind this hood is the man you'd never want in a million years to be so close to our presidential leader and help him do his job because he can't do it on his own. Behind this hood is a con, a man made from bribes and coercion. Behind this hood is a man so pathetic he goes by the title 'Daddy' to maintain the image that he's in charge, that he's calling the shots and to trick his workers into thinking he cares about them like a father. Behind this hood is a man who's name isn't important but his career is," he harshly spat, knowing all eyes were on him.

The President jolted forward as did I. We both knew exactly what was coming next. He looked around in search for his bodyguard but his face grew grave to find he was nowhere in sight. I watched him reach a hand in his pocket and then another pocket and another, unable to find what he was searching for. I assumed no back-up was coming. As for me, I didn't need a bodyguard, I was one, and I had failed. I had failed because the man I was supposed to protect was up there on that stage and I had no idea what was going to happen to him.

"I present to you the real President, Mr. Gideon! The head of an illicit and extremist criminal organisation that begs on the phrase, the *mafia,*" the Speech-Giver cried, yanking off the black hood.

I gulped to see the spotlight landing on Daddy. He looked so weak, his eyes were bruised, his hair was matted and his mouth was gagged. His eyes were wide with fear as sweat dripped into them, darting around asking for help from all the disturbed faces.

"Since your President was elected, this scum has been calling the shots. You think you can trust our government? They accept bribes from the *mafia* and give your taxpaying money to them to run things you'd throw up at the mention of. The mafia are gambling, murdering cockroaches who feed off our government. Ask The President himself, you're happy aren't you, sir? You think giving in to this kind of criminal activity is okay because they give you security? Because they offer a sense of safety? The Mafia are backstabbers and eventually, although you may not see this yet, they will stab you too. They will get sick of sitting in the sidelines and coaching you. They will want to do things themselves, more so than they already have been."

I reached for my gun, I had to end this. I had to, I had to, I had to.

"The Mafia have been reading your conversations, killing innocent people, stealing your money, corrupting secured files, meddling with the media and watching your every movement. The Mafia are cheats, they are liars and your President is too. If you can't trust them then you can't trust him," he elaborated, "If my words are not convincing the evidence is in the papers, it's online, it's between the lines. If you don't believe me it's because you haven't looked hard enough. You don't want to look because ignorance is bliss. Out of sight, out of mind. Bullshit."

My gun was rattling in my slimy palms. I raised it, aiming it at the lunatic who had my family at his fingertips. I bit my lip, my hands weren't steady and the gun kept shaking. My vision was blurring because of the thick sheen of sweat falling from my brow and into my eyes. I pulled back the hammer, my trembling finger on the trigger. *Pull, goddamnit.*

"As much as I despise people who ignore the wrongs and don't even attempt to make them right, I made a vow. I made a vow to bring it to you lazy Americans' attention to everything that is wrong in your world. I made a vow to show you the corruption and how to discipline it. I made a vow to protect you and the first step of doing that is to minimise the threats," he screeched, "If we start with the head of the snake the rest will falter shortly after."

60

Soft music started played as he pulled a knife out of his sleeve. He was so close to killing my family and yet I was too weak to kill him first.

He yanked Daddy's raven hair, his neck snapping back and his eyes torn from our faces to the ceiling. I could tell he was crying, his reddened face was soaked with tears. It was unbearable to see Daddy in this situation as the man brought the blade to his neck. This was so performative, an indulgent display of radical violence just to prove a point and would any of these people listen? Or would he make them more afraid?

"I don't do this out of hate but out of redemption. This society can redeem itself once we stop drinking the poison that is fed to us. Sometimes it takes a more immune person to fight back on behalf of themselves and everybody else. I don't do this alone, I stand here with all of you as we take the first step together," he persuaded, as if he thought this audience was on his side.

I was surprised nobody was screaming or trying to escape. They all stood still, their eyes glued to this madman and this victim. They didn't try to save him and they didn't try to stop the madman either. They stayed in a state of shock while I was close to puking.

"I made these vows when I started my movement, *The Moths* and tonight we make our official debut. This is only the beginning," he smirked, revealing the real reason to this show. Quick-fire. It was like tasting burnt cocaine sniffled through a filthy one dollar bill. It was like the sinking feeling you got as a kid when your parents pushed you too high on the swing set and you swore you could see God. It was like being trapped in a dark and empty room; the smell so dank, the walls so moist, the toxins making you want to rip your eyes out.

I wish I had shot but instead I dropped my gun when I saw the blade sweep across Daddy's neck so elegantly as if it were some kind of dance. His neck was painted with the thickest and darkest of reds which splashed onto his nice suit. His eyes rolled back into his head, his mouth wide open and his body going limp. The leader of the Moths pushed his lifeless body to the floor which clunked almost as loud as my knees when I collapsed beside my gun. I tried not to wail. I didn't want attention brought upon myself. I wanted to be invisible. I wanted to dissolve into the floor. I wanted to dissipate into the air and because of that I hardly noticed everyone else around me had fallen to the floor as well. I passed out.

I had just lost everything.

x. the morning after

My ears twitched at the sound of a cackling fire. I
could smell it, the ashes with a hint of evergreen. I
didn't know where that forest scent was coming
from but I had bigger issues at hand. My head was
aching, a stinging pain in my crown was
accompanied by a headache that roared through
my mind. My eyes flickered open, curiosity
overwhelming my desire to remain asleep.
I could see the gentle flames I had pictured tucked
safely in a fireplace on burning wood and I
understood the evergreen scent when I looked
outside the glossy window of this compacted
room. Rows and rows of towering trees and their
vivid green leaves surrounded the place and made
for a beautiful natural view. The room was entirely
made of wooden logs like an abandoned cabin
from an old campsite. The room was so alive.
I looked beside me to find him, the leader. He was
kneeling down to my level and rinsing out a damp
cloth over a bucket of water. He smiled to see me
awake. I propped my elbows up to gain a bit of
height. I on a futon, a thin blanket loosely over my
clothed body. I was down to my undershirt and
jocks, I could see my dress pants and blazer
hanging up beside the door.

"Morning," he chirped and pressed the cloth to
the back of my head.

I cringed at the pain. He pulled away, giving me time to recuperate. I sighed, unsure how to respond. He proceeded with the cloth and I bit my tongue. I was in pain in all senses of the word.

"You hit your head pretty hard when you fell. We did clean and bandage it last night but it's still bleeding. So I'm re-cleaning and re-bandaging to prevent infection. How did you sleep?" He causally asked.

I shrugged, feeling a bit uneasy. I had no recollection of anything after Daddy died.

"Any dreams?"

I shook my head and sat up properly. I turned away from him to make his job easier and awkwardly rubbed my arm. He rinsed the cloth back out after removing the dried blood. He put on a bit of antiseptic powder before wrapping it in a bandage. Once my wound was ready for time to heal it, I sighed once more.

"What's wrong?"

"I hope you're kidding," I retort.

He didn't reply and I turned around to face him with angry eyes. How could he be so cold?

"You murdered the person I care about most. He was my family, my closest fucking family and now he's dead!"

He smirked and got up, placing his medical items aside. He walked across the room to draws perched in the corner and pulled out a folder. He returned to me, opening the folder and reading the document inside.

"Simon Gregory Sullivan, aged twenty four as of October. Born in England but migrated to America at the age of sixteen. Career as a Bagman to the infamous Daddy figure who is head of the Washington based Mafia. Simon was coerced into the mafia due to his step-father's mistakes. Forced to do Daddy's biddings to ensure the safety of his immediate family, one distant mother and four younger sisters, he stayed with the family for years. Although Daddy and Simon have no biological link, the pair claim to be uncle and nephew."

I bit my lip as he continued on.

"I don't give a shit if your forged driver's license, apartment lease and bank details have Simon Gideon all over it, I have copies of your original birth certificate and early paperwork. Legally your name is Simon Sullivan and biologically you and Daddy are not family. Don't lie to me, I've been studying you two for months now."

"I still loved him," I protested, although the regret of speaking hit instantly.

"That's only because he was all you ever knew. He raised you in this filth and so filth you became. His way of living was the only way of living for you until now. Can't you see? You're free of him. You're free of his lies and deceit. You're free of his secrets and his demands. You're free of him and you're free of that filthy life. I've saved you," he earnestly tried to convince me.

Solemn but still in the mood to fight, I snapped back at him.

"Maybe you're right. Maybe it was just Stockholm Syndrome but it still hurts. I don't care if he kept secrets or if he lied to me. He wasn't just the head of the family, he was also my friend. He was practically my father. He raised me when he didn't need to at all. He caught my tears and he shared my laughter and when I was hurt he was always there. I've lost that... For the second time I've lost someone who I could go to no matter the situation."

Sparrow.

He said nothing. He sat down in front of me and crossed his legs, raising his fingers to his lips in thought. His eyes were watching me, trying to read my mind. I gave him nothing because that's all I could feel at the time.

"What about his wife and his child?" I asked after a while, "They loved him so much."

"They'll be safe. Eventually they'll understand."

"You can't say that. A daughter doesn't have a father anymore and a woman has lost the love of her life because of you. Even if he was as evil as you say, they won't understand. They won't ever understand."

66

He shook his head in pure disagreement. He was frustrated that I couldn't see reason. Did he not expect me to be a little biased?

"A daughter now has a chance to be raised in a world of hopscotch, lollipops and sunshine instead of blood, guns and torture. Maybe you're right and maybe they won't understand but I know I've done good by them even if they don't see it," he retaliated.

"So now what? Why am I here?" I changed the subject, feeling sick.
He nodded his head, knowing this question was coming. He was still examining me, though, as if questioning himself whether or not to answer me. He took a deep breath and clapped his hands together, looking directly into my eyes with sincerity.

"I want to enrol you in my little troop," he smiled, standing back up and reaching out his hand.
I didn't take it this time.

"You want me to join The Moths? That's why I'm here?"

"Yes. Please."
I folded my arms. He retracted his.

"Why on earth would I want to join *you*?"
The word tasted like poison and I couldn't wait to spit it out. I was mad at the world, true but mostly mad at him.

"When was the last time you did something stupid for the sake of infatuation?" He joked, playing at my heart strings.

"Infatuation?" I questioned, hoping my inappropriate crush wasn't that transparent.

"Love can change the world," he teased and I wished he would be more straight-forward in his answers.

"What would I even do?"

"Listen and follow instructions."

"You're no better than Daddy," I scoffed, finding this all so hypocritical.

"I'll be your new Daddy," he winked. Flirtation could only get him so much. I had already given him a dance, I wasn't ready to impart him my whole life just because he gave me butterflies.

"Look, The Moths stand for more meaningful things than money and gambling. We want to save the world by letting the world recognise its threats and save itself. We do a lot of different things, meet a lot of different people and we go to bed with our conscience clean. I can't say more than that but your Bagman skills will come in handy and you're wild, opinionated personality will be a great addition to our team. Join us because you could think of a thousand better things to do than taking my hand now and betraying your dead 'uncle'. Join us because despite all that, you almost feel compelled to. Join us because it's everything you could've been before Daddy tore you away from the good life," he gracefully spoke, holding out his hand again.

I was hesitant.

"Join us just because you want to know how soft my hand is right now," he cheekily added and I couldn't help but smile.

This man had just killed my friend, my mentor and yet I was willing to overlook it because he made me feel things I hadn't felt in a while. Would I have done the same for Sparrow?

"Can I trial?" I enquired.

I wasn't ready to fully commit myself but I was curious as to what all the fuss was about. He laughed but nodded and I took his hand and it was soft. It was really soft.

xi. cillian, maria, tara, nicholas, fetch, sarah, liam

We exited the confined cabin room after I had gotten dressed, with our hands still connected like sleeping otters in a stream not wanting to stray too far from each-other. The sense of betrayal still lingered in my stomach but the butterflies were doing their best to overcome it.

"Let me introduce you to the team," he smiled, gently and eagerly squeezing my hand.
We walked down the dimly lit hall on creaky floorboards. My heart was racing, what had I signed up for?
We turned a corner into an office to find the Irish waiter, Cillian, with what looked like reading glasses on. He was pouring over documents, clearly distracted. He seemed jittery, not even noticing our entrance into his study.

"Cillian O'Conner, twenty two as of September last year. One of the youngest but best psychologists America has seen. Originated from Ireland but has since studied psychology here in Washington and is still attending his college classes even now. Cillian, I believe you and Simon have met," the curly haired one announced and I felt I was in a movie.

Cillian jumped in his seat and tore his body away from his work at his sudden backstory. He looked at us, spinning his chair around and leaning back. He sighed, taking off his glasses and giving a half-hearted smile.

"I don't think I made a very good first impression," Cillian sheepishly chuckled.
He got out of his seat and held out his hand. I hesitated before shaking it and he nodded with gratitude for what he assumed was my forgiveness. Though I felt he had done nothing wrong.

"Simon has officially joined The Moths," the leader stepped in once more.

"Pleased to have you on the team, I'm sure you'll be a great asset. Have you told Liam yet?"

"No."
Cillian laughed which made me nervous but I tried to keep a straight face.

"Good luck, you'll need it."
The leader ignored this and dragged me out of the room again. I had forgotten we were holding hands. We snuck further down the hall, stopping at a closed red door. He knocked and I didn't have time to comprehend the Irish psychologist before I was confronted with more characters.

"What have I told you before about the door being closed?"
A woman answered this time, keeping the door as shut as she could without cutting us off. She had a black, silken dressing gown covering her pale

figure. Her blonde, wavy hair flowed over her breasts and highlighted her guinea pig face. Her lipstick had been ruined and smudged around her lips. It became apparent to me that gown was her only means of covering up and she probably wasn't alone in there.

"Maria Scarlett, aged thirty seven as of December last year. Maria went travelling to Russia after graduating art college. In the sovereign she was kidnapped and sold into sex slavery against her will. A couple of months into the torture, which almost killed her, Maria was sent to have sex with the slaver's closest associate. After the deal was done Maria was about to fall asleep when she found herself eavesdropping a phone call where the associate talked about killing the slaver. Maria told the slaver at once and saved his life," he explained and Maria yawned, she had heard this all before, "Impressed with her loyalty, as others would have just let him die and then run away, he pulled her out of the trade and gave her the chance to work for him as a spy. They formed a bond but years later the slaver had died and there was nothing left for her in Russia. Maria fled to America, finding herself the richest spy in Europe after the slaver left millions of euros for her in his will. Maria continued her spy work in America under a new boss who was close to the slaver until she met Tara."

Maria raised her eyebrows, waiting for the rest of it. This was some strange routine they had. The leader smiled and pushed the door completely open. Exposed was another woman, no, a girl. She lied down on a mattress on the floor of the room, the blankets brought up over her bust to cover her naked body. She was frowning with lipstick that wasn't hers all over her lips. Her red fringe was falling into her dark brown eyes and long eyelashes. She was beautiful in the sense of her youth.

"Tara Scarlett, aged nineteen as of January this year-"

"Australian. Trained assassin. Daddy killed my parents. Maria took me in. Blah blah blah," Tara immaturely interrupted.

"I was getting around to that with a little more detail," he grumbled.

"Leave us alone, please," Tara demanded.

"Tara's not feeling well," Maria attempted to diffuse the situation.

"Tara knows the rules," The leader insisted, "All new recruits have a right to know about your past."

"Not the ones I don't trust," Tara retorted. Tara sat up slightly, the grimace on her face cutting right into me. I had never heard Daddy talk of her or her parents before. Tara got out of bed, her nude body exposed to all before she could grab a dressing gown and cover up. She glared at me as

73

she stormed past us, leaving her lover to defend for herself.

"After rescuing Tara from Daddy, I got a job for the government which is where I found out about the Moths. Tara didn't think they were real but I did my best to assure her. I told her I would marry her if she came with me. I can remember it, all the hitching-hiking and backpacking but we're here now. We're here and we got married as soon as she was of age," Maria continued the story, obviously feeling a sense of guilt about her partner.

"Thank-you, Maria," The leader sighed.

"You don't have to humour me if you don't like me," I decided to chime in, "I can appreciate your resistance to the infiltration of your cause."
This made Maria smile. She glanced at her leader and then back to me. She placed a hand on my shoulder, leant in and gave me a kiss on the cheek.

"Welcome, Simon," Maria continued to smile, "Consider it from the both of us."
Then she shut the door. I turned to the leader and he rubbed his forehead, avoiding eye contact. I still didn't know *his* name.

"It's okay, I understand," I said to relieve his stress and I squeezed his hand which was still clasped onto mine.
I finally got his eyes to fall on mine. I hoped for a smile but I only received a nod. I'd have to settle.
We reached the end of the hall, arriving at a rumpus room in the cabin. It was full of natural

sunlight as large glass doors were present in all three walls, one which lead to a porch outside. I could see the vast terrain of trees beyond it. The whole cabin was enclosed by such a vivid green forest. It stretched on for miles, the trees so tall and so full of life.

He tore my eyes away from the scenery and brought to my attention a man who was sitting at a computer. His ebony skin was rich in colour as were his sparkling blue eyes that were shielded by heavy blue glasses. He turned to us before the leader could even open his mouth and he stood up from his chair. I frowned as he moved towards me and grabbed the sides of my arms. I thought he was going to hurt me but he pulled me into his body for a gentle embrace instead.

"Nicholas Kite, aged thirty as of June last year," the leader began to tell me his tale.

Nicholas continued to hug me, patting my back as if to comfort me. I shakily brought up my arms to hug him back, unsure how else to respond.

"Nicholas was born in South Africa but moved to America to pursue his dream to be a surgeon. He spoke French at the time but learned English for the sake of his dream. He eventually graduated college with honours and moved into the best residency programme in America. He was fantastic at his job, he was really going to make it as an Attending Surgeon. In his fourth year of residency he fell in love with a patient. The patient was

75

unable to get insurance from her bank because of a minor misunderstanding on a form she filled out ten years earlier. Thus she was unable to pay for her treatment and died. Nicholas was willing to pay for her surgery and even went to the chief of the hospital to declare his love and offer to pay the bill because of that love but in doing so he lost his job," he continued, watching us, "Luckily the day he returned to the hospital to reclaim his things from his locker, I was in the waiting room. I grabbed him thinking he was still a doctor. I befriended him, I talked to him about The Moths and how we could use a doctor. He said it's what she would've wanted."

"Her name was Rose. Blonde with rosy cheeks... They were the reason her parents named her so. She wanted to travel. I taught her to speak French and we were going to visit France together. We were going to live there... She was always smiling even in the face of death. I miss her everyday and I'm sure you miss Daddy too. I was against his murder to begin with. I'm here for you," Nicholas shakily said, clearly getting emotional.

Nicholas stepped back, ending the hug and he stared at me, waiting for a response. My lips went dry as I observed the sad doctor. His eyes were so glossy. I found it strange for him to tell me he was against Daddy's murder, like he was throwing his colleagues under the bus. However, I did appreciate his honesty and could tell he liked talking about Rose.

"How long did you have with her?" I breathed, wanting to let him relive his memories.

"Four months. She was lucky to have survived so long but I was unlucky to have such little time with her."

"What was your favourite thing about her?" I continued to indulge him.

"She had a purple tint in her eyes," he glumly spoke.
I smiled but it reminded me of Sparrow.

"Where's Fetch and Sarah?" The leader asked. Nicholas bobbed his head to the couch in which two heads popped up over the cushions in wonder at the mention of their names.

"Thanks Nick."

"Anytime. Hey Simon, I hope we get along," Nicholas grinned.

"I hope so too," I replied, a certain lightness swamping my eyes.
We walked to the couch, still hand in hand. Two people sat on the small lounge, their legs entangled as they played on their handheld gaming devices. They had lost interest in us quickly.

"Excuse me," the leader cleared his throat. They sighed, switching off their devices and looking back at us. It was like they were in sync; two bodies, one person.

"I thought maybe you'd like to tell our newest member your own files."

"Why?" One arrogantly spat.

"I apologise for my twin, Simon," The other one said, her eyes glowing with kindness, "they appear to be going through a punk phase."

"The less I look and act like you, Sarah, the better," the other twin grumbled.

It was true, although in sync, at first glance they barely looked like friends, let alone related. One had bright blue hair and dark makeup and wore rugged clothes. The other had a hijab covering her head, leaving only her soft complexion and brown eyes to view.

"What do you want to know? I'm non-binary, she's trans. She's a hacker, I'm an acrobat. What else do you need? Just leave us be."

"Fetch, please, Tara already gave me enough strife…"

"We joined because we grew up with Zach, because he was our best friend and-"

"Fetch!" Sarah hissed louder.

Fetch stopped and solemnly gulped, looking up to the leader whose face had grown grave. Zach appeared to be a topic worth avoiding but the reaction of the name made me curious. I pondered if it was the leader's name or someone not in the group anymore. I tried not to show my interest as my eyes flitted amongst the three of them. Nobody was speaking and the tension was tightening and the leader looked on the verge of tears.

"What are your pronouns?" I decided to ask, trying to develop a bond.

"They, them. Yours?"

"He, him. Thanks for asking."

One of the glass doors slid open and there was a thud against the floorboards. All eyes shot to the west of the room to find your all American boy; tall, tanned, muscled, brown hair, brown eyes, camouflage clothes and a shotgun in his hand. He entered the room and it was as if everyone else was afraid of him.

"Liam Plum, aged-"

Liam, realising what his leader was doing, grunted and stormed right back out of the cabin, making an effort to slam the door behind him. It reminded me of Cillian's warning chuckle.

"Don't worry about Liam," Fetch said, "He's an asshole."

xii. revival

Democracy. The Moths appeared to be a democracy. Well they liked to think they were a democracy but the curly-haired, green-eyed, frat boy appeared to be making the shots. He was like Daddy, a man he loathed so much until he managed to slaughter him but he couldn't slaughter the part of Daddy that rested inside himself.
I turned on the tap of the bath that sat lonesome in the middle of the room. It had been a long and rough day and I felt so filthy. They didn't have showers, just one bath. A bath in a room with no other furniture other than an open window to look out on the greenery and reflect. The perfect setting to get a little too philosophical.
They really liked getting in touch with nature. There was something about being naked and exposed to the wilderness that made you feel connected with the Earth.
I turned off the tap and slowly eased myself into the tub. I heaved a sigh, my speckled eyes following the sound of birds outside. Finally, a moment of tranquility in the never-ending chaos of my life.
I was here because of a kiss. If Daddy were here right now as a ghost haunting me for failing him... If he was hoping I was infiltrating their team, their system, their trust in order to avenge him... He'd be disappointed. I was here because that man kissed

me and I liked it and I'd hate myself every day because of it. I was a hopeless romantic on the quest for true love, for someone to spend the rest of my days with. I thought I had it before but I was tragically mislead, so now I was searching for love in all the wrong places. I hated love but I was one of it's biggest victims, that's for sure.

There was a knock on the bathroom door. It creaked open without waiting for me to reply. I was relieved to see the man who kissed me. Funny that, I was more comfortable with the murderer seeing me naked than anybody else I had met today.

"Can I come in?" He asked, only his head peeping in.

"If you must."

He wasted no time entering, shutting the door behind him and clambering to the side of the bathtub. He brought soap and a loofa and a smile.

"We wash each-other here... It breaks down the walls of discomfort and builds ones of trust and friendship. It might be uncomfortable at first but it's rewarding. You truly get to know a person when washing them and that's what we're trying to achieve. We need to be able to know each-other so we can work with each-other."

Sounded like a load of garbage to me but I wasn't going to object; even if his sense of building a team was a misguided way to soothe his horniness.

"Will I have to wash anyone?"

"Not for the first week, I'll roster you for next Monday. Okay?"

A roster was a strange way to go about this convoluted washing system. I wondered if anyone else on the team found it odd rather than rewarding.

"Okay."

"May I?" He asked, raising his eyebrows and the bar of soap.

I nodded and he got onto his knees. He pulled up the sleeves of his buttoned shirt up to his elbows and tied his long hair back. He was beautiful.

"Is the water warm?"

He dunked the loofa into the water and rubbed the soap against it. He began to scrub my arm with it and I tried to keep a straight face.

"I know everybody in this cabin's name but yours," I coolly mentioned as he washed off my soapy arm.

"It's Phoenix. Phoenix Jackson," Phoenix finally introduced himself, extending an open hand.

I playfully shook his hand. Afterwards, he continued washing me but I wanted to know more than just a name.

"Do I get your backstory too?" I coyly asked.

"Not today," he cockily objected, scrubbing my chest.

"Why not?"

"Because you haven't been playing this game for very long and to unlock the tragic backstory you need to be at least level eight," Phoenix joked, "You're not even level two."

"It's hard to level up when the controller isn't even in my hands" I scoffed.

He lifted my leg up and started to scrub it down, washing away the sweat and grime and the memories of death. We stayed silent as he did the other leg and I dropped them both into the water, accidentally splashing him, which made us both laugh. He squeezed the loofa clean and put it aside, bringing out a flannel from his top pocket. He soaped it and dampened it and brought it to my face.

"Close your eyes," he breathed.

I obliged and I felt the wet cloth conform to the contours of my face, the only thing keeping his hand from caressing it. The dead skin fled and I felt revived. He began to scrape the cloth against my neck and behind my ears, also.

"I don't think it's fair, you read mine off a file."

"I read a textbook retelling of your life, it's hardly the same," he grumbled, removing the material from my face.

Upon opening my eyes, it's like he knew I was about to object. I shut my mouth as soon as I opened it, waiting for him to go on a big rant.

"I know an outline of you. I know your relationship with Daddy and the childhood he robbed of you. I know your career and your limited ability to visit your real family. I know what high-school you went to and I know your birthday. I know what I read off a piece of paper but I don't know you, Simon. I don't know what your favourite colour is, I don't know what you're like when you wake up, I don't know what song means the most to you or why, I don't know what makes your heart skip a beat, I don't know how many people you've kissed, I don't know how many people you've killed, I don't know your biggest secret, I don't know your saddest memory nor your happiest, I don't know if you prefer inside or outside, baths or showers, I don't know if you have issues with identity, I don't know if you hate yourself, I don't know if you're capable of hate, I don't know what makes you cry, I don't know what you fight for, I don't even know if you've ever been in love…"

I gulped. I was seeing this man for the first time. I was seeing Phoenix; without the mask, behind the mask. Suddenly his face was so visually noisy. His hair, although swept back in a tangled matted mess of brunette locks, had loose ends falling over his sweaty forehead. His jawline was jutting as were his plump pink lips. His nose was straight, almost chubby in feature… But his eyes, oh, his eyes. The crystal green delicacies that stared threateningly

84

into my fragile blue ones were almost too surreal to be true. As I said, I hated eyes and all they represented... Until I found it hard to comprehend his.

The silence consumed us. I had swallowed down every word in my vocabulary, not that words were vital in this situation. They weren't needed nor was I, really. I didn't know why he wanted me around so badly. I didn't know why he wanted to know all these things about me either. These thoughts induced by the silence continued on as Phoenix went on to wash my hair with the shampoo he had stashed underneath the tub. As my head went underwater for a split second, all I could think was have I been in love? Did I even know? Was Sparrow the love of my life?

"What are you thinking about?" He asked as I came back into the air.

"Sorry, pal, you have to reach level fifty before entering my brain," I laughed and he rolled his eyes.

"Simon, I'm not sorry for what I did but I am sorry for hurting you," Phoenix admitted, breaking the playful mood.

I wiped the water from my eyes and ran a hand through my soaking hair. He was behind me, above me, waiting for me to forgive him.

"The more you and your friends talk about Daddy the less I like to hear."

85

"I know you trusted him…"

"It was a lot more than trust," I sighed.

"He did more harm than good, Simon."

I turned around in the tub, feeling compelled to face him. I crossed my arms on the edge of the tub and laid my chin on them, looking up at him as he looked down at me.

"He gave me the codename Chop Suey... Was that in your pamphlet of my life?" I mentioned before he could say anything else to ruin the image I had of Daddy.

"No."

"A funny anecdote about an Asian restaurant turned into my family name. I bet you didn't know that. I bet you didn't know not just that but that we had those moments at all, Daddy and I, full of hilarity and fondness," I glumly reminisced.

"I said I was sorry, Chop Suey," he mumbled and I was unsure if he was using the name to mock me or make me feel at home.

"Will Tara?"

He paused for a moment. Before responding he felt the urge to reach out and stroke my cheek with his bare knuckles, collecting the water droplets that had been sitting there. I closed my eyes and enjoyed the touch, wishing I didn't.

"Maybe. Tara's different. A good different. A special different. Daddy took her life away too," Phoenix cautiously replied, dropping his hand back down.

86

"It lead her to Maria though," I was trying hard to understand him.

"Consequence can lead to good, we're all aware of that but it doesn't justify the damage that was done," he explained.

"You killed Daddy and that lead me to the Moths and shelter and security and not having to be alone but that doesn't justify the damage you've done," I snapped, re-evaluating my position with the movement.

Another pause.

"She'll warm up to you," Phoenix ensured, ignoring my remark, "so will the rest of them." Phoenix gave me a smile before rising from his knees. He wiped his arms down on my ragged towel, leaving it on the floor for when I wished to use it. He took his bathing equipment and strode to the door, opening it but looking back to me. Our eyes connected once more before his lips parted to speak.

"Welcome aboard."

xiii. outside

Fetch didn't want to be a token. They felt
Phoenix's crafting of the group felt very in-
genuine. It was as if they were all collectibles and
he was marking them off a grocery list; one black
man, one lesbian couple, one muslim, one non-
binary person. Fetch made this opinion they had
clear to me my next wash day - apparently we
were only allowed a wash three times a week.
Although Fetch and I had gotten off to a rough
start, I was realising Fetch was just an outspoken
person who didn't bow down to anybody. Fetch
was actually becoming a good friend and I could
trust them because I knew they wouldn't do
anything to compromise the truth. I asked about
Phoenix and they didn't seem to like him at all,
hence the whole tokenisation debate.
I was undergoing what was known as a 'rest'
week. A week of exploring the ideas of the
movement before getting too involved. After the
third day, I felt I was getting cabin fever. Stuck
inside all day with nothing to do and only Fetch to
talk to. Fetch took me to their room to ease my
nerves and that's when I asked them about their
gender identity. I had nothing against it, I was
simply having trouble wrapping my head around
it. They told me it didn't matter if I understood it,
only that I respected it. That was the end of the
conversation and that's when my appreciation for

Fetch grew even more. They didn't owe me an explanation for their identity and I didn't owe anyone for mine either.

Dinners were the only time the whole group would assemble and even then I barely talked to anyone but Fetch. Nicholas was the cook of the group and he was damned good too. Phoenix was there despite being mysteriously absent during most of the day and he'd sit at the head, of course, ignoring me. Nothing serious was ever spoken about. I started to think the politics of the movement were purposefully being hidden from me.

At the end of the rest week, I sat in my dimly lit room on my bare mattress, leant up against the log walls. Fetch had given me a journal as a present for initiation. They said that when their sister and them-self had finished rest week they presented each other with gifts. They said it was small but that I should be thankful, that sometimes your thoughts can get lost in this movement and that writing them down could help keep track of them. I was thankful but staring at an empty page at five in the morning made me feel nervous. I wanted to write down how it was getting increasingly harder to sleep through these lonely nights with no clue as to what would happen next. I wanted to write down how I felt about Phoenix, his eyes and his orders. I wanted to write about how Tara and Liam hadn't spoken to me at all. I wanted to write down the nightmares I had about Daddy and his family who repeatedly yelled at me for abandoning them. I wanted to write about my biological family, my mother and my sisters, who I had left in the wreckage and I had no hope of seeing again. I wanted to write but my hand kept freezing up. Lost in thought, my door slammed open and I dropped my pen in alarm. Liam had stormed in wearing a camouflage-vest and steel-capped boots and a backpack secured on his shoulders. He was holding his gun as well.

"Wake up, Sully," he demanded.
He ignored my already awakened self as he crossed the room. He yanked open the curtains, letting rays of natural light spring into the room. I watched as he looked out the window as if he was in a hurry. He grabbed onto one of the straps of his backpack and turned to me. He was surprised to see me awake and propped against the wall, staring at him.

"Good, you're up. Now get dressed."

"Why?" I questioned, very clearly annoyed. Liam scowled at me and I scowled right back. The searing hatred becoming obvious between us.

"Because your honeymoon period with Phoenix is over and you've been assigned to me."

"I haven't even been with Phoenix, I've been with Fetch all week," I hissed, even more annoyed.

"Yeah, whatever. Now you don't have to deal with her ogling at you. Get up and get dressed."

"*Them,*" I corrected, rising from my bed, not just annoyed but furious.

He ignored me as I reached the set of drawers. Phoenix had purchased a multitude of new clothes for me to wear whilst I stayed with them. I had no idea how long I was meant to be staying but by the amount of new t-shirts and pants, Phoenix was hoping for a while.

"What do you mean when you say that I've been assigned to you?" I asked as I pulled out some appropriate clothing.

"It means for the next couple of weeks, you're my responsibility," he bluntly explained, checking his watch to indicate I was taking too long.

I frowned, still unsure what entirely that answer meant. I waited for him to exit the room so I could change but it became clear he wasn't going anywhere. I grunted, tearing off my shirt. He started to blink rapidly as he watched me undress before he became aware of exactly what he was doing. He cleared his throat and turned around, allowing me a small level of privacy. When I was done, including putting on some sneakers, I threw my dirty clothes in the hamper in the corner and tapped his shoulder to gain his attention. He turned back around, his gun still by his side like a loyal dog.

"Liam, what are we doing today?" I asked almost cynically.

"You'll see," he assured, "Now move it."
He pushed me out the open doorway and I
groaned. I had to keep thinking that at least the
muzzle of his gun wasn't lodged into my back. We
walked down the corridor and into the rumpus
room. It was the first time I had seen it so empty. I
assumed everybody was still asleep, drooling over
sheep and catching some z's. I wished I had that
luxury.
Liam guided me to the glass door and into the back
porch of the cabin. This was the first time I had
exited the confined and lively shack. I wasn't
allowed to go out for even two seconds of fresh air
and yet Liam was demanding I walked down the
steps. I took a deep breath. The air was so new, so
crisp, so fresh. It wasn't like the muggy, sweaty,
stuffy air inside. I enjoyed it, taking my time to
devour it as I took those first few steps and walked
onto leaf litter. I wasn't meant to feel like a
prisoner there but having my lungs fill to capacity
with nutritious, clean oxygen and to watch it
become visible before me made me realise how
restricted I had been. We walked across the fallen
leaves, delving into the forest I had spent so much
time admiring but not being able to explore.
I was excited, very excited. My fingers tapped
against my sides and my lips twitched up into a
smile. Liam rolled his eyes at me when he saw me
look up to the blue sky which was shrouded by the
vivid canopy of the forest.

"C'mon Pocahontas," Liam couldn't help himself, patting my back.

I probably looked like a child in a chocolate factory. I couldn't help but reach out and touch the bark of every tree we skipped passed. I couldn't help but savour the air. I couldn't help but stomp extra hard to hear the crunch of the leaf litter. I couldn't stop smiling. We continued to walk further into the natural wonderland. In my happy mood, I appeared braver than I was and decided to talk to Liam while we ventured.

"Why do you hate me?" I enquired.

He couldn't dislike me that much if he was smiling at my reaction to the wilderness. So what better time to ask when we were both somewhat elevated.

"I don't hate you," he scoffed, "I just don't like you all that much."

"I think I know why."

"Oh yeah, why?"

"It's one of those situations where you cover up a crush by being excessively mean," I teased, in a good mood.

He laughed, shaking his head at my arrogance, "You're cute, I'll give you that."

"No but seriously, tell me," I begged, halting and grabbing his arm so he couldn't run away from the problem.

He faced me with alarm, almost scared we had stopped. He sighed and ran a hand through his hair, clearly no-one had told him to express his feelings before.

"I don't think you deserve to be on the team," Liam admitted with a casual shrug.

"Why?"

"I don't know… You're from the mafia, it feels wrong," Liam tried to elaborate, clearly struggling, "I don't believe you have anything to fight for. We all do. Nicholas has Rose, Tara has Maria and vice versa, the twins have each-other, heck even Phoenix has his past… We're all here fighting for something, feels wrong to have someone join just because somebody else told them to."

For some reason, it made me angry.

"Why does everyone use that word? The mafia? We weren't the mafia, we were a family," I spat, "You don't anything about it. You don't know anything about me."

I knew, deep down, that he was right. I didn't deserve to be here. I couldn't let him know that, I couldn't let him see my inner conflict or the war inside my mind.

"Simon, I-"

I didn't even know if I *wanted* to be here.

"No. I didn't even hear about your past, I don't even know if *you* deserve to be here when I don't even know what *you* fight for."

Liam stared at me, he was taken aback from my uproar. I took a deep breath, trying to calm down my reddened cheeks and reopen my shaking fists. He took a step back, rubbing the back of his neck and awkwardly looking to the ground.

"Liam Plum, aged twenty two. Joined because somebody told me to."
I wanted to stay mad at him, at the hypocrisy but I burst into laughter. I laughed and laughed until my tummy ached. He cracked up too and I figured we'd get along just fine.

xiv. take the shot

We started the hike back up with stupid grins plastered on our faces.

"Well... who told you to?"

"Phoenix, obviously. I met him years ago with Cillian. Felt like I knew the lad my whole life though. We all met him that year, actually. Not that we ever really got along with... You know what, never mind that. The point is Phoenix is a very good friend of mine and I appreciate all of his views no matter how much he exaggerates them. When he started The Moths, Cillian and I were the first members and we haven't left his side since," Liam happily answered.

"So really you do have something to fight for, it's Phoenix."

"You could say that. I fight so he has a better world to live in, Cillian and Amy too," Liam shrugged.

"Amy, aye?" I raised my eyebrow at him.

"Girlfriend."

"Of course," I nodded, "Although judgemental as hell, you're also hot as hell."

"I'm not cheating on my girlfriend with the fairy mafia boy. I'm not cheating on my girlfriend with the fairy mafia boy. I'm not cheating on my girlfriend with the fairy mafia boy," he jokingly repeated under his breath.

I laughed, blushing as pink as a fresh crop of summer strawberries. He was blushing too. I had to stop making people fall in love with me. Flirting probably didn't help. I was about to ask him how often he got to see his girlfriend under these odd circumstances when he latched onto the side of my arm.

"Don't move and be quiet," he whispered, his eyes glued ahead.

I turned to see what the fuss was. I was expecting police scouts or a bear on a rampage but instead I was faced with a harmless doe. It was beautiful. Her coat was a light shade of amber, the belly side pure ivory. Her eyes matched the colour of the tree trunks surrounding her and her nose cute and petite. She was the perfect picture of peace. Liam started to gently push me aside so I obliged. We slowly got to the floor behind some loose bushes, the deer still in sight. We watched it as it lazily chewed on some forest grass in a clearing. I licked my lips, wondering why we were observing such a domestic creature. It seemed very unlike a movement like this to be stalking such innocence.

"Take my gun," he quietly breathed, offering it to me.

I glared at him, it all becoming clear to me. We had been sent out to hunt, to collect meat, to *kill*. This wasn't a special mission to make the world a better place, it was a not-so-special mission to satisfy our own selfish needs.

"No," I hissed.

He stared at me in confusion as our bodies laid amongst the dirt and leaves for nothing now. I refused to take away an innocent life regardless of the food chain. This was wrong.

"What do you mean?"

"I'm not taking your gun and I'm not shooting that defenceless animal."

"You eat meat don't you?"

"I'm a vegetarian but that's not the point," I angrily whispered.

"Of course you are," he grumbled, still eyeing off the prey.

Now he thought I was one of those pushy vegan activists when in reality this had nothing to do with politics but my own cowardice. There was silence for a while before he returned his gaze to me. We frustratingly stared at each-other for a while before he spoke up again.

"You don't have to eat it, just kill it. Please. Your first official day on the team was to get you to provide for the team. Now take my gun and provide," he insisted, shoving the gun into my side.

"I have never killed anyone or anything in my life and I'm not about to start for a bit of meat," I declared, "If I wanted to start it would've been

Phoenix to save Daddy's life. Now if you'd excuse me."

I stood up, not caring about scaring it away. I wanted it to run, I wanted it to be free. I wanted to be free with it. I turned my back on the scene, hoping he'd follow as I made my way back to the cabin. Yet as I took my third step, I couldn't hear the crunch of the litter but a bang; a loud, deafening bang from behind me. I flinched, shutting my eyes and feeling my heart shatter.

"Liam..." I croaked, turning on my heel.
I opened my eyes and to my horror there was Liam sauntering over to the still and lying body of the deer. I gulped hard, trying not to cry. I always cried. I had to stop. I picked up my weak feet and slowly walked towards the two. As I stepped into the clearing, the bleeding bullet hole between the deer's eyes became apparent and it made sick.

"Come here and let me teach you how to dress a deer," Liam ushered, eyes on the dead prey.
My feet subconsciously ended up behind his crouching figure. He had whipped off his backpack and pulled out a rope. He wrapped a noose-like knot and slunk it around the deer's upper neck. He tightened it and handed me the end of the rope.

"Hang it from that branch over there, I'll help you."
I swallowed my pride and lifted the animal. We hung it from the sturdy branch and watched it dangle with it's hooves not far from the ground.

Liam removed a Stanley knife from his bag and stabbed into the deer's abdomen. With only the tip of the blade inside the carcass he swiftly manoeuvred it down the length of the body.

"You have to be careful about not rupturing the stomach or intestines. You don't want to spoil the meat," he mentioned.

Liam reached inside the abdomen and began removing the organs. I had to look away after his hand came out red with blood. He noticed I wasn't watching so he started to describe his actions to me.

"After the organs are gone, you have to remove the bladder. It looks like a golden sack, full of urine. Now when cutting it out you have to be careful and you make sure the urethra is closed."

I heard a pop, worried he had burst it and ruined the meat which meant the doe had died for nothing. I turned around but he had it in his hand, smiling as he chucked it away, the liquid spilling onto the grass.

"Now to cut out the anus and intestines…"

"Liam, can I leave?" I interrupted, unable to handle this anymore.

He looked up to me, his bloody hand tight on his knife.

"I suppose," he sighed, "Go get Fetch, they'll help me carry this back for skinning and collecting. I'll be here stripping it of organs."

I nodded. I started heading back to the cabin, unable to form coherent thoughts. My breathing was uneven as I muttered to myself profanities in relation to what I had just witnessed. I would've liked some warning. Just a 'Fine, don't kill it, Simon, but don't mind me as I do the job for you' would've sufficed. The air didn't feel the same, the crunch of the leaf litter frustrated me and I didn't feel the need to stroke the bark. I wanted to sit in my room and pretend this day never happened. I wasn't watching where I was going and only steps away from the cabin, I ran into something. I ran into someone. I grumbled, apologising profusely before stepping back and looking up at the victim of my incapability to pay attention to anything other than my own pathetic thoughts. It was Phoenix, of course it was Phoenix.

"Woah there," he playfully bellowed, eying me off.

"We're gutting a deer," I blurted out.

"So I've heard."

He was smiling but his eyes were still trying to read me, confused about my jittery and agitated state. He must've known I wouldn't have enjoyed it.

"I have to get Fetch," I answered his eyes, "because I'm too weak."

"Weak?" He raised an eyebrow.

"It doesn't matter. Look... You send the orders , right?" I asked.

"We're a democracy…"

"You send the orders, right?" I repeated, ignoring his bullshit.
He folded his arms and nodded, not attempting to object again.

"Why this? On my very first day, for my very first mission, to be my very first memory of being an active Moth member... Why this?" I cried, my face getting flushed.

"So you understand that killing for survival is a normal part of life,," he said and I realised this was all still a ploy to forgive him for Daddy's murder. It made me even angrier. Killing an innocent animal for the sake of symbolism didn't sit right with me. I knew he was right, though. They grew all their own fruit and vegetables too. It's not like these highly wanted people could duck down to the supermarket for the food they needed. Although angry and feeling absolutely disgusting, ready to break their three times a week wash rule, I found myself exhaling into a peaceful physical state. Phoenix noticed my body language change and looked even more confused.

"Okay"

"Okay?"

"I think I'm going to be okay," I vaguely elaborated, not wanting to get into it anymore.

"So you're going to help bring the deer back and harvest it with Liam?" Phoenix asked.

"Yeah."

"Okay," he smiled.

"Okay," I smiled back.

xv. new friends

After a month of being assigned to Liam, I was
still no killer. Despite that first week at his side
where everyday we went down to the forest to
hunt, I never once pulled the trigger. I did help
dress and skin the deer most of the time, although
the first time I threw up. It was mostly observation,
taking notes and getting in touch with that survival
instinct.

Hunting wasn't the only thing we spent that month
carrying out. He was teaching me how to survive.
He taught me how to filter dirty water and urine to
restore to drinking quality. He taught me what
plants were poisonous and what berries would kill
me open consumption. He taught me how to set
camp and hitch a tent. He taught me how to treat
all types of wounds and scrapes. He taught me how
to use the gun on targets as I would have to get
over my heroism if I wanted to eat and stay alive
when abandoned in a forest, at least so he said. He
taught me how to climb a tree the right way and
use the view to my advantage. He taught me how
to make a fire pit and start a fire without matches.
He taught me a lot of things but most importantly
he taught me how to handle being alone.

"Wake up," Liam screeched.

I jolted forward in my bed, being taken from my
slumber abruptly. I looked up in the dark room at

the intruder who held a candle-lit lantern in his hand.

"What the fuck, Liam?!" I hissed back, throwing my pillow at his face and lying back down.

"Oh no you don't."
He rushed over and yanked the blankets off my body. He started hitting my leg and I hit his hand away.

"It's like midnight," I whined, wanting much needed rest.

"No, it's eleven thirty and so technically you're still assigned to me and have to do everything I say. Get up," Liam corrected, not taking 'no' for an answer.
I sat up, running a hand through my messy hair. I rubbed my eyes and yawned before I crawled out of bed. There was no point arguing with him when he was like this. He helped me to my feet and slammed a vest, slacks and worn-in sneakers into my chest.

"Get dressed, I'll be on the porch."
I grumbled after he exited and shut the door. I pulled the pants on over my briefs and the vest over my white pyjama tee. I quickly chucked on the shoes and hurried out of my room and down the corridor. I wondered what could be so important that he had to wake me up for just a half hour.

I clambered out onto the porch. Although it was Spring the air was still as harsh as winter. My arms grew goosebumps, my breath was visible and my fingertips were beginning to numb. Liam turned to face me after he heard my rapid rubbing to warm my arms up. He laughed and started heading down the steps and into the forest. I reluctantly followed, not paying attention to the time. Even if the half hour clocked out, I wasn't following him because he was my teacher; I was following him because he was my friend. I guess he was my friend.

As we travelled further, my body began to warm but it wasn't because my blood was pumping. It was because the further we went, the closer we got to something producing heat. Soon enough, I could hear it too, that purr and crackle of a fire. Eventually, we were standing in front of a rather large bonfire. It didn't smell the nicest but it sure felt good against my near-frozen stature.

"I'm in charge of disposing of all our waste every month. I pile all the rubbish up until it's time, throw on some logs and light it up. I'm usually alone but tonight, this bonfire is yours," he explained, propping his lamp on a hook embedded in the nearest tree.

"Ours," I corrected, smiling at him.

"Yeah, ours," he smiled back.

We walked around the blazing fire to a long and smooth log; Liam had arranged as a seat for us. We sat down, it wasn't too close to the fire but close

106

enough to feel the heat light up our faces. He took off his backpack and put it between his thighs, opening it up. He pulled out two long metal sticks and passed them to me. I frowned at the cold poles in my hand. I was going to ask what they were for when the answer came out of the bag. Liam clutched a packet of marshmallows and grinned at me, I couldn't help but roll my eyes and chuckle.

"Genius," I barely muttered, snatching them. He put his bag on the ground and we both set up our poles so marshmallows were impaled on the ends. We put our snacks into the fire and watched them cook.

"In five minutes, you'll officially be out of my care," Liam said and I couldn't tell if he was being cocky or if he was sad.
We ate our crispy marshmallows, creating more as I developed a response.

"Hopefully I won't forget anything you taught me," I replied, deciding to take the light-hearted approach.

"Let's go over some things now then, shall we?" Liam liked to quiz me. He did it quite often. I think he just liked being a little know-it-all and boasting if he knew something I didn't. Regardless, I gestured for him to fire away.

"How long should you age freshly killed deer meat?"

"For a week, in a moderately cool place," I replied, that one wasn't hard.

"How do you treat a bleeding scrape wound?"

"Wash it with water, put powder on it and bandage it," I answered, this was too easy.

"How do you stop a bear from charging at you?"

"Pepper Spray."

"Top five things to have in your backpack..." He raised his eyebrows, trying to trip me up.

"Knife, compass, matches or lighter, rope and a first aid kit."

"How do you appease 'The Knights who say Ni' of the forest?"

"You buy them a shrubbery," I laughed, even acing the pop culture question.

"I've taught you everything I know," He smiled, this time I could tell he was sad.

There was silence for a while. Well, not complete silence. We still had the roar of the flames and the cooing of birds and the rustling of the leaves in the wind and the sounds of us chewing our marshmallows but it felt like what silence sounded like.

"Simon, I love you," Liam blurted, nervously staring at me.

I turned to him, my brows burrowing into my eyes and I licked my lips. Again, to take the serious approach or light-hearted approach?

"I'm sorry, old chap but I'm afraid I have far too much emotional baggage than you could handle. Besides you have a girlfriend, don't be a slut," I teased, hoping he would laugh and not get upset.

"Shut-up, not like that. I love you in the way I love Phoenix and Cillian. I didn't think I was capable of it and yet… you're the only person to sit with me on bonfire night. You're the only person who's gotten an invitation before."
I felt a little relieved.

"I love you too, Liam."
He had more to say but he was working up to it. I gave him all the time he needed, relying on the company of stars for entertainment.

"Three months ago I asked if Amy could join the gang. Phoenix said no. He straight up refused. He had two reasons. The first was that having couples in the movement was complicated. He already regretted having Tara and Maria on the team. They refuse to be apart and if one of them were to die during a game... Well... The other one would become a ghost as well. The second reason was that, you guessed it, she had nothing to fight for. She apparently had no passion, nothing drawing her to the Moths but me," Liam explained, going shy and looking to his feet.

"Liam, I had no idea-"

"I was so mad," he interrupted my pity, "I yelled at him 'Am I not enough?' and I yelled it over and over until it physically hurt. He didn't answer. He's such a hypocrite. Everybody else is here for somebody else, even he is. Then you come along to prove he's a hypocrite even more. You guys kissed once and then suddenly it's okay for his crush to join but not my girlfriend of two years... I haven't talked to him since. I mean, he's given me orders but I don't talk back. I want to talk to him, I love him like I said but it's so hard. I haven't seen Amy in six months and she doesn't know where I am. She doesn't know about the Moths at all. She thinks I'm pursuing a career in India..."

It took me a second to realise he was crying. His stubbled cheeks were drenched in a sheen of regretful tears and his eyes were becoming red with pain. Watching him cry made me cry and I put my hand on his knee for comfort, letting him talk it out.

"Simon, I'm sorry for hating you over trivial things. It's been a privilege teaching such a compassionate person like you. I hope everyone else falls in love with you as well. You deserve to be here, hell, you deserve to be here more than me. I'm so sorry for everything."

I hushed him, wrapped an arm around his shoulder and brought him into my chest. He began to sob even harder and I kissed his crown. He had been so strong, so brave, so pulled together this entire time. I should've assumed he'd eventually fall apart.

"You are enough. You are enough of a reason to fight in this movement," I assured him, "If Amy isn't allowed to fight for you, I guess I'll fight for you enough for the both of us."

He sat back up, staring at me with glossy eyes and a half-hearted smile, "Is there nobody else you want to fight for?"

"Sparrow."

"Sparrow?"

"I fight to remember what he looked like before he left," I mumbled, looking at my feet, "At the same time I fight to forget about his purple tinted eyes."

Liam nodded, realising I wasn't going to say anything more about the man. He swallowed his tears and shifted further from my body, picking up his stick and pushing a marshmallow onto it.

"You should head back, get some rest before you're woken at the crack of dawn to take somebody else's orders," he suggested, dipping the marshmallow into the fire.

I nodded, heaving a sigh as I stood up from the log. I pushed my hands into my pockets, knowing they'd start to feel like ice pretty soon and began walking out of the clearing.

"Oh and, Simon," Liam called as I reached the edge of the trees.

"Yeah?" I shouted, flicking my head around.

"Tell anybody I cried and I will literally kill you."

"Yep, got it."
I didn't doubt him. I'd seen him gut and skin deers,
I wasn't about to cross him even if he said he loved
me.

xvi. patience

There was crust digging into the corners of my
eyes when I woke up. The wind was blowing the
curtains away, letting the obnoxious daylight in
and it had rudely woken me up. I had gotten such a
good sleep, as if Liam's words last night were a
lullaby. I checked the time, realising it was noon.
My first reaction was panic, thinking I may have
missed my next assignment, until I saw the note
stuck to the door. I got dressed and dawdled over.

'When you're awake, come see me in my office
- Nicholas.'

It appeared my life was now in the palm of the
doctor's hands. I was satisfied with that but it didn't
mean I wasn't going to miss Liam. I missed him
already.

I walked out of my room and down the corridor to
the second last door on the right. It was such a
long corridor but such a small house. I knocked on
it and my action was greeted with a soft 'come in'
from the other side. I entered but the surgeon didn't
look up, fiddling with his laptop as I took a seat in
the chair in front of his desk. I waited for him to
acknowledge me, knowing that speaking out of
turn in this movement was never rewarded.

At least twenty minutes flew by. I wasn't sure what
he was doing or what I was supposed to be waiting
for. I kept giving cues to remind him I was

113

waiting, such as clearing my throat or tapping my foot. He continued typing away. I tried looking over at his laptop, at one point but he angled it away from me.

One hour. I started to question if I had done anything to upset him. I had been spending so much time with Liam but I thought that'd upset Fetch the most, if anyone were to get mopey over it. This was ridiculous. I was clearly bored and annoyed, doing nothing to hide that expression from him. Still, there was silence; even with my constant fidgeting. I was doing anything to get his attention but actually speak.

One and a half hours. I licked my lips. What was he doing on his laptop anyway? He seemed so engulfed by the screen like it held the secrets of the universe. I had come too far to disturb him now. If this was a game, I wanted to win.

Two hours. Two fucking hours I had sat in this chair with my mouth shut. Why was he punishing me? Maybe this was payback for sleeping in... Maybe I was supposed to get up myself and seek out my new teacher... Maybe he was *that* type of person. I felt myself dozing in and out of consciousness in my chair.

"Simon..."

I jumped, unaccustomed to the sound of his voice or giving me any sort of acknowledgment. I gulped, recollecting myself and leaning in, giving him my undivided attention.

"As a surgeon you undergo hours upon hours of surgery. I once spent nineteen hours repairing a man's brain after he had been attacked with rocks. If I hadn't of given it my all he could have lost his vision or complete function of his brain or even dead," Nicholas explained.

"You're training me to be a surgeon by making me wait two hours to talk to you?" I asked, not buying it.

"In a way. You've been assigned to me for the next month. I had no idea what exactly I was supposed to teach you but then I figured out. You're going to be my new intern, my assistant. I'm going to teach you how to handle worse case scenarios and how to assist me in practice," Nicholas carried on, "In the Moths we act like heroes but we fall like everybody else. I want to train you so if anything happens, you'll have the tools to save somebody's life. Are we clear?"
I remembered dressing up as a doctor as a kid, pretending to save my sisters' lives with a plastic stethoscope and tree branch as a scalpel. I wasn't sure if I was cut out to be a *real* doctor, those girls always died on me.

"Simon, the first step is patience. You've been patient in receiving orders, so I'm going to give them to you now. Today, I want you to knit a sweater."

I burst into laughter, thinking he was hilarious. Eventually, I stopped laughing when I realised he hadn't joined me and I realised, maybe, there was no joke.

"A sweater, you say?" I readdressed the issue, pretending my outburst didn't happen at all.

"Fetch has the materials for you. I want it done by tomorrow morning when I go to wake you, no sleep in this time. You can give it to whom you wish after as long as I see the final result first," he elaborated.

"Right. Okay."

"Off you go," he insisted, shooing me away.

I rose from my seat and left his office. Those were the weirdest orders I've ever received in my life and I was part of what they call *the mafia* for a whole lot of it. I wandered down the corridor, a frown still perched on my face as I tried to comprehend this. I was going to make a sweater for somebody and somehow it was going to help my training to be Nicholas' little understudy. It's not like I wanted to be a doctor to begin with but I guess orders were orders and if I wanted to stay in this movement I'd have to oblige.

When I entered the rumpus room, I noticed it was steaming with life. Everybody was in there except Nicholas, even Phoenix and he rarely was in there at all. I froze in the hallway to watch him. He was sitting on the bench, his legs dangling above the floor, eating a bowl of cereal. He was in mid-conversation with Fetch and I didn't want to interrupt them. Instead I found myself crossing the room to Liam who was polishing his gun.

"Liam," I hissed, throwing myself in the chair beside him and staring.

"What's up?" He asked, not evening looking up from his gun.

I snatched it away and glared at him which resulted in him groaning and succumbing to eye contact. I needed his full attention to relay this strange piece of gossip.

"I have to make a sweater."

Liam snorted and then covered his mouth at his sudden noise, but then he just kept chuckling anyway. I hit him and he laughed harder.

"A sweater?"

His laughter did not ease my paranoia.

"A goddamned sweater," I grumbled, "Did Nicholas ever make you knit a sweater?"

"No, why would he?"

"When you were assigned to him when you first joined?" I scowled.

"I was never assigned to anyone, love," he stated and shrugged.

He took back his gun and I leant back in my seat, his sentence making me wonder. He was never assigned to anyone? Was Fetch? Was Nicholas? Or was I the only one running around doing errands for everyone else? Before I could dissipate solely into my thoughts, Fetch had wandered over and gotten my attention.

"Here's your materials, Grandma Simon," they winked and dumped it on the table.
I groaned, looking at the wool, the pamphlet and the two knitting needles. I was in way over my head.

"I don't even know how to knit," I muttered, flipping through the pamphlet.

"Look I have more exciting things to do than watch you knit sweaters and talk about your back medication and how your hip replacement went and how your grandchildren are growing up oh so fast. So while you knit, Grandma Simon, I'm going to go shoot some things," Liam smirked and I hit him again.

"I swear to god if that becomes my nickname around here..." I grumbled, ultimately stressed about the knitting.
Liam left me all alone at the table and I had no other excuses to avoid the knitting. So the process began. It was the most frustrating experience of my life. I spent hours just trying to figure out how and where to start but even then I was lost. I was close to giving up.
It was time for my bath and I wasn't going to miss it because I couldn't knit a sweater. I hated the whole only washing three times a week thing, it made those days in between seem extra grimy. So I had run a nice hot and steamy bath and hopped in

and picked my equipment right back up. I leant over the bath to carry out my orders but I was failing miserably.

The door swung open and I almost dropped my needles. I had forgotten to check the roster this morning to see who was washing me and I worried it would be Nicholas and he'd be disappointed.

It was worse than Nicholas though. It was Phoenix. I rolled my eyes after he sauntered in and paused his footsteps. He stood, staring at me, judging me with that playful, confused smile on his face. He crossed his arms, continuing to watch my pathetic knitting.

"What are you doing?" He finally bellowed and I sighed.

"Thanks to you, I've been assigned to Nicholas and my first mission was to knit a fucking sweater and I can't-"

"Oh I know that, he told me already," he grinned, walking over and kneeling down besides the tub, "I meant what are you doing, you're making a wreck of it. Did you not read the pamphlet?"

"I read the pamphlet. I read it a hundred times. Fuck off!" I spat, even he couldn't tame the beast. He wasn't afraid of my agitated state. Instead of backing off, he snatched my equipment off me and took over. I didn't bother fighting for it. I leant back in the tub and eyed him off as he started undoing my tragic work.

"First of all you need to cast on and know how to knit-stitch and purl," he murmured, looping the yarn around the two needles as if it were the easiest thing he's ever done, "Here, take this and I'll guide your hands."

I took the needles from his hands and into my own. He stood up and walked around behind me. I sat up and he knelt back down, his arms stretching out over my wet shoulders and his hands grabbing onto mine. He didn't seem to mind getting his shirt damp and I definitely didn't mind him holding me like that.

"Now you need to open the loop," he whispered, guiding my hands just as he promised. His face was right beside mine, his mouth so close to my ear. I'd say it was romantic if we were turning clay on a potters wheel and I was Demi Moore and he was Patrick Swayze but no, we were knitting. He was teaching me to knit as I lingered naked in his bathtub. I couldn't decipher if this was romance or insanity.

"See! You've got that hang of it!" He exclaimed after a couple of minutes.

I grinned, happy as my hands manoeuvred the wool and a shape started to form. I wouldn't be a failure after all.

"Now put it down and let me wash you," he chuckled, moving over to the side of me.

He took it from my hands for a second time and placed it on the floor, picking up his washing materials and smiling. I gave in.

After my bath, he ended up having to dry me as I was too involved in the knitting process to do it myself. He guided me to my bedroom, the towel wrapped around my waist. When we got to my room, I plonked myself down on my bed, not taking my eyes off my work. He watched me for a couple of minutes at the doorway, probably sniggering to himself as to how I was too preoccupied to even dress myself. He was about leave when I finally spoke up and looked at him.

"Stay," I breathed and I wasn't sure if he even heard me.

He did though and he did stay.

Phoenix closed the door and sat on the armchair beside my bed. For hours he watched me but eventually he fell asleep. His arms were folded, his mouth parted and his head drooped to the side. He looked cute as he slept. The power-hungry, justice-thirsty man of the political rebellion seemed to disappear from him and he became just a boy. He was just a boy in dire need of rest. I felt blessed that he had stayed despite there not being a word spoken between us.

I stayed awake for most of the night to complete my sweater but my eyes couldn't hold out past four a.m and I ended up passed out still wrapped in my towel. Nicholas opened the door that morning and the sound startled me. I yawned, sitting up and keeping the towel over my waist. I blinked rapidly, getting my vision straight. I looked up at the doctor who had a frown fixed upon his dark face and his arms folded.

"You did it," he said, bobbing his head to my hands.
I looked down and sure enough, there was a sweater. It was complete. I had even stayed awake long enough to bind off like the pamphlet told me to. I grinned, feeling accomplished as I held it up so he could get more of a look. It was an ugly, yellow thing but I was proud of it.

"It took me all night," I yawned, happy over my victory.

"Looks like you had company," Nicholas mentioned and we both looked over to Phoenix who was still that cute resting boy.

"He gave me a few tips, I wanted him to see me finish it."

"Doesn't look like he lasted," Nicholas chortled to himself, "Should I wake him?"

"No!" I protested and then realised I came off too strong, "I mean, he looks peaceful and he probably deserves a sleep in."
Nicholas paused for a minute, looking between us with a face I couldn't read. Maybe he thought we had slept together... Then again he seemed to know more about Phoenix than I did, so maybe he knew

this was innocent. Maybe he was thinking we should've.

"How about you quickly get dressed and I'll move him to the bed? Then we'll let him get some sleep for a while whilst you begin your real training," Nicholas suggested.

We did that. We left Phoenix asleep in my bed with the covers up under his chin and his arms tucked in by his side. The curtains were drawn shut to make an artificial night that would go easy on his eyes. I hoped when he woke up he wouldn't be mad at us letting him sleep. If anger was his reaction, I hoped that it was disappear when he saw the present I left for him at his feet. A present for his presence; a sweet, handmade sweater.

xvii. confession

"I'm freaking out, Liam."
I was unable to stop tapping my foot against the wooden floor. Liam and I sat together at the table of the rumpus room. My eyes kept darting around instead of keeping focused on the open textbook before me. I couldn't even hold my pen steady as it hovered above the notepad carelessly. I kept trying to find excuses, ways to avoid my two upcoming examinations. It was like I was back in high-school.

"You'll ace it, Simon. Stop doubting yourself... You always doubt yourself," Liam grumbled, flipping through a magazine.

"For good reason," I muttered, my glare landing on him.

"You've spent how long with Dr. Kite now? Two months. Two whole months. Two months and you haven't watched a single episode of *Grey's Anatomy* to aid you and you're smarter than Cristina Yang, I'm telling you."

"Shut-up" I growled, rolling my eyes at his nonsense.
It had been two months. A long and slow two months with Nicholas Kite. The second I went into his care, the friendship between us deteriorated and a strict professional one picked up. He was so stern, so intense. He genuinely wanted to pass on everything he knew and model me to be the perfect

doctor. Well the perfect doctor under these unordinary and imperfect circumstances. I was to be used to the best of my capabilities. Everyday he pushed me to my limit but every morning after, I was ready to get right back where I left off and let him push me even harder. I never had an interest in undergoing medical practice but I was glad to be forced into it. All this time protesting murder and death and now I could prevent it. Now I had the potential to save a life… If that life didn't need any complex surgery and only some basic first aid.

"I can't fail," I breathed, "This is life and death stuff, Liam."
Liam closed his magazine and sighed. He looked straight into my eyes and I could sense unwanted advice was coming.

"Everything here is life and death stuff. That's what this movement is about. Life and Death," Liam objected, "And if you fail, you'll try again. We won't kick you out for a mistake."

"Okay."
I felt no need to argue with him, especially since he was right. He returned to his magazine and I returned to my textbook. I took dot-points down on my notepad, trying to memorise enough of the scribblings for my test. I knew the practical was first but I wouldn't be able to look at my notes before the theory exam anyway.

I wish Liam had let me practice on him though. It wasn't like I was going to cut him open, it was all First Aid roleplaying. He refused on account that he never liked doctors and that I'd do fine without a dummy. I remembered tackling him this morning and pinning him down on my bed, face to face and out of breath. I had yelled at him, begging to let me practice but then my knees toppled in and he rolled me over. He had quite literally swept me off my feet and suddenly I was the one pinned down, his hands tight on my wrists. He had chuckled and so had I. It was somewhat erotic the way he ducked his head down close to mine to whisper a harsh 'no' and then get up, storm out of the room and leave me breathless on the mattress. It was somewhat a problem that I wished it was Phoenix, instead, who had pinned me to the bed in such a manner.

I had to stop thinking about it. I had to stop thinking about my flirtatious friendship with Liam and I certainly had to stop thinking about Phoenix altogether. I had forgiven Phoenix for killing Daddy but I couldn't forgive myself if I were to fall for Daddy's killer. Hopefully it was just lust. It was the whole top-of-the-food-chain-power-deranged-cheeky-and-mysterious charm of him. It was also the fact he was rarely ever around and when he was he teased with no remorse.

"Simon."

I snapped out of my daydreaming and shot my head in the direction of the voice. It was Nicholas.

"It's time for your test," he alerted me and I nodded.

I packed up my stuff and asked Liam to look after it while I was gone, he lazily accepted.

"You'll ace it," Liam muttered without looking up and I smiled.

I followed Nicholas to his office door but as his hand rested on the doorknob he turned to me and smirked.

"Might I say, your choice of who to assist you with your physical assessment did not surprise me -"

"Wait, I didn't choose anyone?" I interrupted, confused.

"Shall we?" The doctor completely ignored me, obviously not wanting to get involved.

He opened the door and we entered his office. I wasn't surprised to find Phoenix turning around with a plastered smile and his perfect hair falling about his face. I hadn't seen him for three whole weeks, almost a month. I hadn't seen him since dinner three weeks ago and even then he was distant. He didn't look across the table at me like he always did, not even once and he left before everybody was finished. Yet there he was, all angelic and enthused. There he was ready to help me in my test and wearing the sweater I knitted him. I can't believe he was actually wearing it.

What a smug son of a bitch. This lust thing was never going to go away.

"Phoenix, if you'd lay down on the mat I've put out... I'd like Simon to get started straight away," Nicholas insisted.

"It'd be a pleasure," Phoenix said but he was still staring at me as he spoke.
Phoenix got onto the floor and laid down on his back on the mat. I took a deep breath, unsure if I could do this; at least, unsure if I could do it on Phoenix.

"Now Simon, I'll let you practice on the candidate before I test you. If you'd excuse me for a moment," Nicholas smiled and left the room.
Phoenix and I were alone. Usually we were only ever alone in the tub room and yet somehow, this felt even more intimate.

"Surprise," Phoenix grinned as I walked over to him.
I scoffed, getting down on my knees beside him. I didn't want to talk or get distracted by his flirtations. I wanted to pass this test.

"I'm wearing your sweater," he continued to be smug.

"I would've deemed that a nice and friendly gesture two months ago when I made it but it's long past the expiry date," I grumbled, unable to bite my tongue.

"At least I'm wearing it. If you had given it to Liam he would've buried it in the forest somewhere," Phoenix shrugged, as if he were offended.

"You don't know that," I scowled.
I was still kneeling next to him. Nothing was happening but this conversation. I was wasting valuable practice time on a stupid tiff.

"I know Liam more than you do," he blurted, not looking me in the eye.

"What is that supposed to mean?"
He shook his head and chose to ignore me. I couldn't believe he was about to start an unnecessary fight. I suppressed it. This wasn't about the sweater or Phoenix or Liam, this was about my test. This was about becoming Nicholas' medical assistant. I had to practice, no more excuses.

"DRSABCD" I said aloud, "Danger, Response, Send for help, Airway, Breathing, CPR, Defibrillation."

"Somebody's done his homework," Phoenix grinned. "So, Doctor Simon, are you going to give me mouth-to-mouth?"
He wasn't there to help me, to see to it that orders are met. He was there to mock me, try and rile me up. Remind himself that I thought he was irresistible, give himself some selfish ego boost.

"Can you stop?"

Phoenix stared at me absolutely bewildered. I wasn't having any more of it.

"Stop showing up to save the day and flirting with me and teasing me and being charming... Stop doing things for me and stop giving me special privileges... Stop being perfect because I can't handle it."

Not quite the way it sounded in my head. I didn't mean to praise him. Phoenix licked his lips but said nothing. Instead he laid completely still and looked up to the ceiling with glossy eyes, ready for me to treat him. At least the speech worked.

"I'm going to put you in the recovery position to start off with," I explained, returning to the matter at hand.

I rolled him to his side with his hand supporting his head, his other arm bent in front of him for stability, his head tilted back for a clear airway and the top leg bent to prop up the body and to prevent it rolling forward.

"Perfect! Now if you could sit up, I'd like to workshop some fake injuries," I demanded rather than asked.

Phoenix rolled onto his back and sat up slightly with his elbows propping up his body. He stared at me as I raised one of his knees. I was going to pretend he had an infected cut when he interrupted me before I could even begin to diagnose.

"It's because you have a crush on Liam, don't you?" Phoenix sheepishly murmured, as if he was afraid of the answer.

"Excuse me?"

"I hope he's told you he has a girlfriend and I hope he doesn't break your heart because of that," Phoenix added.

"I know he has a girlfriend," I dropped his leg and crossed my arms.

"Then why keep up the act? I saw you two on your bed today and-"

"You didn't say anything," I said, arms still crossed, nothing to hide.
Liam and I were friends. This was a preposterous accusation from, a very clearly, self-conscious man.

"Yeah," Phoenix huffed, "I just expected better from both of you, in all honesty. I'd be okay with this if it wasn't hurting somebody else, if it wasn't going to hurt Amy. I'd be okay with this if-"

"If you weren't completely, utterly and entirely jealous? The only person it's hurting is you because you have some crazed fantasy running through your mind that I'm a broken boy you can restore with your dumb acts of affection and stupid temptations and knitting techniques. I'm not with Liam nor do I have a crush on him. That's ridiculous. We're just friends. What you saw in my bedroom was just best friends fooling around. Yeah maybe he did get a little close and maybe it was a little rough and maybe even semi-erotic but I don't want that with Liam. Fuck, I was thinking about you when he was pinning me down to the bed and how much I wanted it to be your hands and your body weight and your breath on my face. God, I can't stop picturing it which is crazy because I've only known you for three months and you're the man who killed Daddy and I can't handle this. I can't handle you," I confessed, "I can't even handle myself."

I froze, staring into Phoenix's glistening eyes. A dumb confession to a boy who was nowhere close to being a priest.

xviii. bad habits

I had a split second to toss over the possible
outcomes of my idiotic confession and to ponder
on how Phoenix would react.

Option One, he'd just get up and walk out of the
room. Option Two, he'd yell at me and tell me
how stupid I sounded. Option Three, he'd kick me
out of the Moths for acting like a melodramatic,
horny teenager.

Then there was option four. As I said I only had a
split second before he reacted and I barely got
around to option four. Option four seemed so
unlikely, so insane. A fleeting thought to fuel my
imagination. Even if I had time, I wouldn't have
wanted to linger on it, it would've driven my hopes
up too much. Logically, Phoenix went with option
four.

Phoenix lunged forward, he hastily grabbed hold
of my thighs to hold me still and attacked my lips
with his own. I was stunned. His grasp was so
strong and his lips were so hungry. His lips crashed
against mine like impatient white-wash meeting
the shore for the first time. I was breathless, I was
bewildered, I was... I was turned on. I reciprocated
the kiss, tangling our lips together in a fury as he
released my thighs. My hands gripped onto the
back of his pale neck as I slid my tongue into his
mouth. He opened up wider, allowing it roam and

133

play with his own. He tasted of marshmallows and heaven. Phoenix broke the kiss and I panted heavily. My hot breaths stroked his face as he gulped hard. I couldn't open my eyes, I didn't want to as I feared it would end this perfect moment. Soon he grabbed hold of my hips and pushed me down onto the mat, flat on my back. I was still panting, my breaths only heavier from being pushed around and I couldn't help but open my eyes. He crawled over me and grabbed my wrists to pin me down. I bit my lip, staring into his wide green eyes as he smirked. He was enjoying this, teasing me, having power over me. This was what I was begging for and I couldn't get enough of it. He ducked his head back down to resume our kissing. I tried to lift my arms up to wrap around him and pull him down but he ensured they wouldn't come off the mat. I wanted to feel him, more of him. I began to buck my hips up, trying to collide into his. I continued to squirm until he finally got it. He broke our kiss again but this time to laugh and shake his head. He started to grind down on me, his tight jeans scraping against my slacks. He stared at me as he did so, picking up pace with each look. I looked up at him, moaning slightly and clenching my hands into fists. He moaned too, he moaned even louder and in a more agitated manner.

His tongue was down my throat before I knew it and one of his hands let go of my wrist. His hand crept down between our bodies as we kissed, stopping at his belt buckle. He started to undo it with such haste that he was fumbling. He couldn't keep his hand still and so I decided to take over. I broke the kiss which made him stare and I took a double glance down to his jeans and he got the hint. He stopped pinning me down and held himself up by having his hands on the floor besides my head. His biceps nearly made me drool. With my free hands I began to undo his belt properly this time, kissing him during the process. I yanked off the slippery, black character and chucked it aside. We chuckled as I undid the button and fly of his pants, relieving some tension and allowing his red underwear to poke out. Cheekily, I gently bit on his bottom lip and pulled it down. I let my hand slide down his pants but over the fabric of his underwear. He was rock hard and leaking through the material. He yelped as I continued to rub it and even muttered my name which drove me wild. Phoenix detached our lips and centred on my neck. He started to nibble against it before biting and sucking and branding me. I whimpered, it felt so good.

"So Simon, Nicholas wanted me to- oh…" The dream was short-lived as the door swung open and somebody stepped inside. Our heads shot to the Irish-tinged voice and I couldn't breathe.

135

Phoenix tore himself off my body, my hand sliding out of his pants as he did so. He stood up and ran a hand through his knotty long hair, grinning at the psychologist. How embarrassing.

"It's okay, Cillian. I was just teaching Simon about my anatomy," Phoenix winked.

Phoenix quickly fixed up his jeans and I heavily exhaled, hitting my head back against the floor and wanting to groan. He couldn't have made it anymore awkward.

"Uh... Right... Well, Nicholas is coming back as we speak, he just wanted me to be here to observe," Cillian explained but he couldn't stop flitting his eyes about as if he was the one embarrassed.

Why did it have to be Cillian? I never saw or spoke to Cillian. He was supposed to be Liam's best friend but they rarely hung out since I came along. I felt like this was another reason for him to dislike me. Stole best friend, check. Stole cult leader, check. Now I really wanted to disappear.

When Nicholas came back, Cillian had stayed quiet and kept to himself in the corner. I was thankful he didn't go blabbering to Nicholas about us wasting my valuable practice time with foreplay. Instead he took notes as I carried out my practical exam, trying to focus on anything but the man I was practicing on.

I think I did well, even with Phoenix's smirk distracting me whenever I had to touch him. It didn't help that we both had raging hard-ons that luckily nobody picked up on - or at least, they chose to ignore.

Phoenix and Cillian had left before my theory test. I was left with some peace as Nicholas browsed his computer. I managed to complete it quickly. I guess I was in a hurry. I really wanted to attend to my un-finished business with Phoenix. I wasn't even sure if he'd want to, there was a possibility it was a spur of the moment thing for him. It didn't stop me from trying.

When I got out of the office, he wasn't waiting for me at the door like I had daydreamed. I tried my bedroom but it was empty. I sauntered down to the rumpus room, it was lively but there wasn't a curl in sight. I walked towards the porch, ignoring the familiar faces. I even ignored Fetch, who smiled wide and their eyes lit up upon seeing me but diminished quickly when I barely returned their glance. I was a bad friend. I was a bad person in general. Who makes out with the murderer of their father figure? It was so wrong but I couldn't stop my body from chasing him down. I craved to have the sensation of his touch again as it had erased itself from me during the test. I needed more.

I stumbled out onto the porch, that delicious breeze moving straight into my lungs. Phoenix wasn't there but Liam was. He saw me and grinned, standing up from his rocking chair immediately. He approached me and gave me a huge pat on the back, staring at me with his brows raised in anticipation.

"So how'd you go?" He eagerly asked.

"I made out with Phoenix."

It wasn't my soul intention to blurt it out like that. I originally wanted to take it slow. I wanted to sit him down, hold his hand, politely tell him I kissed Phoenix and that I didn't know where to go from there. I wanted him to not be upset and to help me through it as a friend. I didn't want to rub it in his face when there was the possibility that he did like me in the way I liked Phoenix.

Liam's face turned sour. I narrowed my eyes on him as his eyes flickered with rage in a way I thought would only come from a charging bull. He went to open his face but it turned back into the angriest scowl I've ever seen. He crossed his arms and shuffled his weight to one side. Phoenix was right. Liam and I were more than friends without my knowledge. It seemed Liam was attracted to me and that made it even more complicated. I didn't want this lust for Phoenix to break my friendship with Liam. I needed Liam. I needed him in my life and by my side especially here, especially in this place but if I had to choose…

"I'm sorry," I bit the bullet and apologised.

"What did you do?" Liam gulped, "What exactly happened?"

"Maybe we should sit down," I hesitantly suggested, rubbing the back of my neck and staring at my feet.

"No. Tell me everything, right here, right now." Oh god, why was he so mad? If he was jealous, he had plenty of opportunities to kiss me. Surely he'd missed his chance by now.

"He volunteered to be my test dummy and we had some alone time to practice before the doctor marked me and well... I had a big rant about how he had to stop being perfect and that I craved his touch and one thing lead to another and suddenly he was on top of me with his tongue down my throat and my hand down his pants. Cillian walked in and..."

Liam started hysterically laughing and I flinched. It was such a knee-jerk reaction and I was so surprised, so shocked. I gulped hard, a little terrified of this giggling boy who had tears in the corners of his eyes like this was the greatest joke he'd ever heard. Only a second ago he was the embodiment of fury.

He recollected himself, wiping his eyes and stifling out the laughter. He stared at me for a minute before he grabbed me and pulled me in for a bear hug. He pat my back and squeezed tightly. I hesitantly hugged him back, the embrace was so sudden and I was very lost.

"Thank-you, thank-you, thank-you!" He repeated, chuckling again.

"Alright?"

"Seriously, thank-you" Liam reinstated. He pulled away and gripped the sides of my shoulders. He thanked me again with a genuine smile which I replied with a look of confusion. I felt I was missing the joke.

"I can't believe this, I'm going to talk to Cillian right now," Liam exclaimed before racing inside and abandoning me on the porch.

Or maybe he didn't have a crush on me... Maybe he was insane. I think we were all a little insane that day.

xix. a debate

Both tests were aced but I had no-one but my
mentor to share the victory with. A week had gone
by, Liam was still acting strange and Phoenix was
nowhere to be found. Nicholas decided to host a
celebratory dinner and insisted on cooking my
favourite meals. Sure enough, Phoenix was there;
the first time I had seen him since the incident.
Liam sat down next to me whilst Phoenix had
assumed his position at the head of the table. That
chair was usually empty upon his constant
absence, nobody dare take it over. He didn't look at
me, not once. It made me lose my appetite. I
slowly picked at my meal whilst Liam whooped
his down beside me. I leant on my hand and
prodded the salad with my fork like it'd poison me.
Liam carried on, chatting away, nudging me to
make sure I was listening to his conversation. I
would nod or 'mmhmm' even when I wasn't paying
attention. I was glad he was putting in effort for
our friendship again but he wasn't my main
concern.
I kept making glances up to Phoenix, thinking
maybe this time I'd be greeted with those meadow
eyes and maybe he would project a hidden smile.
He was too busy talking to Maria the whole time,
only pausing the conversation to take bites of his
meal. At least he could swallow it. I didn't want to
be the boy who wallowed over somebody who

couldn't bother to look at them or kiss them again. Time to suppress my lust and move on. I was going to be the best goddamn member of the Moths with or without him. With newfound motivation, I quickly finished my meal in a couple of hungry mouthfuls and Liam looked at me stunned.

"Are you okay?"

"I'm more than okay, I'm fantastic," I exaggerated, still staring straight ahead at Phoenix. I was going to keep staring until he felt it and *had* to look at me. I was so determined. I was going to take back my dominance. Unfortunately, Nicholas interrupted my goal.

"In honour of our newest member acing his exams by nearly one hundred percent, I didn't want to let his actions go unrewarded," Nicholas announced and they all started clapping, other than Phoenix and the couple, "The reason you are still seated is because I made dessert"
Everyone gasped. I wasn't sure why. This was new to me, I hadn't had dessert here once in the months I'd been settled. Fetch began to bring out the chocolate creme-brûlée's and placed them on the table in front of each of us. Before they could even finish their job, Tara had a fit.

"This bullshit! Complete and utter bullshit," Tara stood up and screeched, "We don't get dessert for our birthdays or anniversaries but he gets it for a test?!"

"Tara..." Maria whispered, tugging on her hand to sit back down.

This was definitely unexpected. I found myself sinking into my chair, not wanting to be seen at all. I had no idea what was happening other than that I was in the middle of the drama without meaning to be.

I watched as Tara ignored Maria's non-verbal plea. She was crying now.

"I can't take this anymore. He doesn't deserve this special treatment. I see him everyday and it only reminds me of all I lost. Now he's parading around like he's everybody's friend, like he's everybody's favourite. He's hurting people, he's stealing pieces of us, can nobody else see it? Not only is he bringing up my past, he's taken Liam from Cillian completely. Don't you remember when they were inseparable? They used to sit together and stay up late at night to talk and go hiking and do games together. Now Liam is off with Simon whilst Cillian lays awake at night wishing things were different," Tara exclaimed, the tears travelling down her reddened face.

"That's not true!" Liam roared, standing up from his seat and angrily pointing at her like his big, brute, sausage finger would shut her up, "Cillian and I are still friends, Tara. We're all adults here, you can't talk for him. You're fine, aren't you, Cillian?"

Cillian froze as Liam stared at him, slightly gaping.

"Tell her..." Liam begged.
Cillian gulped and flitted his eyes to his lap, unable to speak up. This wasn't good. I was watching the desperate interaction, Liam begging and Cillian wishing he could disappear, like me. I was part ghost and terrified someone would see the human version of me any second.

"Cillian, please," Liam stammered.

"Yeah, I'm fine" Cillian lied, we all knew he was lying.
Liam slowly sat back down, he knew Cillian had lied too. I hoped Tara's outburst was justified, dessert being the reason seemed over-the-top and bratty.

"Not to mention he's completely destroyed Fetch. Fetch adored him, they looked up to him and befriended him. All through his rest week, Fetch was there only to be mistreated for the next couple of months. He ignores Fetch constantly when all they wanted was to be cared about," Tara continued.
I took a glance at Fetch who looked away from me. I had really fucked up and Tara was on a personal mission to ruin my life as a Moth. She was on a vendetta that I was certain I wasn't entirely to blame for.

144

"Simon is a monster. He worked for a monster and became the same monster. He's selfish. He's not even an official member from what I've heard. He's just testing us out, using us. I thought Phoenix might actually realise that at some point. No, he's too busy trying to get into Simon's pants to replace the one that got away. He never even loved you, Phoenix -"

"Tara!" Maria hissed, interrupting her.
My attention was on Phoenix now and a billion thoughts about what Tara could've meant by her comment. Unrequited love was a painful phenomena I was lucky to never had encountered. In fact, hearing Phoenix had suffered through it made his behaviour make a lot more sense to me.

"It's true! The way Phoenix looks at Simon like he's a lion about to pounce..." Tara muttered.

"This isn't about Simon. Apologise to Phoenix about your earlier comment," Maria insisted, still tugging on Tara's sleeve.

"No. Aren't you all sick of walking on eggshells around this topic? He needs to get over it, they weren't even dating."
The spotlight was finally off me but I felt sympathy for the man it was cast to.

"I'm right here," Phoenix finally stepped in, "And so is Mr. Sullivan."
The whole room went silent. I wanted to be sick. No longer a ghost but a body all could see, the members kept darting their eyes between Phoenix

and I. I was glad he was sticking up for me, an act of affection I hadn't witnessed before.

"We don't discuss your private life at the table so how dare you try to undermine me by discussing mine. Simon is not a monster. I do not allow monsters into my movement. You, right now, are acting like one, though. I will not allow it. I insist Simon goes into your's and Maria's care for the next couple of weeks so you can fix the damage you have done. Make up and teach him how to be better since you have such a problem with what he's like now. As for who is friends with who, stay out of it. We don't yell at you about getting married to the woman who groomed you," Phoenix lashed out.

Everybody was scared of Phoenix now. Eyes were no longer on us but in people's laps or off somewhere in the distance. Maria had let go of Tara's sleeve, extremely uncomfortable. Phoenix got up out of his seat and strode to the other end of the table. He tapped my shoulder and I looked at him, a little afraid myself.

"C'mon ,Simon, let's go fuck. Not because we're sad about our pasts but because as fully grown, consenting adults we are capable of making our own decisions and handling the consequences of our actions ourselves," Phoenix loudly said to me, eyeing the couple off as he did so.

146

I didn't know what else to do. So I stood up from my chair, nodding. I muttered a quick thanks to Nicholas before leaving the room with Phoenix, who took my hand in his as we did so. We walked to my bedroom and he locked the door and my heartbeat sped up as he released my hand.

"So, uh..." I croaked, not sure how to start this.

"We're not actually fucking," Phoenix snapped, pacing around the room.

"Oh."

Couldn't say I wasn't disappointed. Him defending me only made me want to have sex with him more than I already did. Guess now wasn't the time.

"So they know?" I spoke up, not being able to take his anxiety for much longer.

"Know what?" He frowned at me, stopping in his tracks.

"About the other day... Before the exam…"

"No," Phoenix shook his head, "That never happened."

"Oh."

Fine, it never happened. There were plenty of other people I could sleep with. I could move on easily. I had to stop caring about these tedious waste of time matters. I didn't get hung up on Temper, why get hung up on Phoenix? I thought all these things to ignore how much my heart was hurting. Phoenix began pacing again, muttering under his breath things I couldn't quite catch. As I observed him, I watched the way his hair fell. I'd die to get

147

inside his head and decode his mind. He was beautiful but he was out of reach.

"I can't leave again. I have to stay. I have to stay and make sure Tara doesn't kill you during practice," Phoenix's muttering got loud enough to unscramble.

I widened my eyes, trying to pay attention but his jittering was distracting. The threat of death from a teenage girl wasn't even the scariest thing to me right now. It was the way he was acting, the way he thought of leaving again and the way he wouldn't look me in the eye.

"She's a good person and she deserves to be here. She just... She can't quite grasp the concept that we don't just save the majority. We save everyone and I mean *everyone*," Phoenix elaborated.

"Phoenix, you don't have to explain."

I didn't want him to explain. I wanted him to calm down. I actually wanted him to kiss me.

"I do! I do because she has big mouth which buries her big heart and that's why you can't see her for who she really is."

Phoenix came to a halt and stared at me. I braced, preparing for more heartbreaking. He walked over to me and grabbed both of my hands.

"Trust me," he breathed.

"I trust you," I whispered, staring at our entwined fingers.

"I hope you mean that," he smirked.
His tone and demeanour completely changing. I looked into his cheeky eyes before he let go of my hands and walked out the door, abandoning me with my rapid heartbeat.
I had to trust him. I had to believe he was a good guy; whatever that meant.

xx. unexpected visitor

"Wake up."

I was used to those orders but not the way they were delivered. Ice cold water hit my face at full force. A full bucket drenched my head and the pillow behind it. I sat up in shock, goosebumps covering my entire body. I spluttered, trying to allow myself to breathe again as my soaked hair fell into my eyes. I stared at Tara with glossy eyes as she watched the droplets run down my neck. It looked like she was smirking but I most certainly wasn't. Tara had the incriminating bucket in her hand, making no effort to hide it. I tried to collect myself, reminding myself she wasn't a bad person and that I was doing this for Phoenix.

Why was I doing anything for him? He didn't do a single thing for me, why should I reward him? He couldn't even kiss me again let alone acknowledge that he'd kissed me before. Despite logical dispute, I was still going to follow Tara all day for Phoenix anyway. A small part of me knowing that a kiss, despite the lack of promise of it, was enough to get me through the day.

"C'mon, sunshine," Tara smiled, holding out a hand.

I gulped, gazing over her. She seemed almost... Nice? I worried it was a trick and she was going to splash me again but the bucket was empty and her smile seemed genuine. Her sincerity was scarier than her anger. Nonetheless, I took her hand and she hoisted me up. She was strong, very strong.

"You can stay in what you're wearing," she muttered, releasing me and heading to the door, leaving the bucket on the floor.

I was only wearing grey slacks, nothing else. I prayed it wouldn't be cold, dug my hands into my pockets and ambled over to her.

"We're going to the shed today," Tara stated, hand on the doorknob, "I'm the only person with access. No-one else has been in there. Not even Phoenix."

Not even Phoenix. I followed her out of the room, surprised she wanted to take me to somewhere so secretive and restricted. I was unsure if I should've felt special or if it was time to start fearing for my life.

We got to the rumpus room, Phoenix and Liam were the only others up. As we walked into view, Phoenix took a quick glance at me in the middle of his conversation with Liam. He had to look back at me, stunned. I tried to be subtle, knowing he was checking me out. With no top on, my chiseled chest and abs were glistening with water. He gulped hard, gazing at my body as if he wished to lunge for it, bite down on it, suck it, make me tremble. He bit his lip but was unable to look away. Good. He deserved to be tortured. That's when I couldn't help but grin and look to the ground.

"We're going to the shed," Tara casually said, sliding open the glass door to the east.
It took a few cogs to turn in Liam's head to fully register Tara's words. At first he gave us a simple nod, still rambling to Phoenix. It wasn't until we were halfway out the door he made an outcry.

"What?!"

"The shed... Simon and I..." Tara simplified.
Liam and Tara seemed to be in a bit of a stand-off that even western cowboys would be impressed by. It finally distracted Phoenix from my body, feeling the need to step in before someone got hurt.

"Don't play stupid, Tara," Phoenix spoke up, glaring at her, "Simon isn't allowed in there."
Tara was visibly uncomfortable; arms folded, eyes darting to the ground. In that moment, I realised how young she was. She was only a teenager, her brain was still developing and her hormones were out of control. I hated confrontations with authority at her age, I hated them now. I gulped down, feeling bad for her for the first time since I met her.

"You assigned me to her, Phoenix. Tara is in charge," I stepped in, defending the girl who hated me.
Phoenix looked me in the eyes, he saw something there that I couldn't see. He heaved a sigh, uncrossing his arms and running a hand through

his hair. He looked at Tara, who had sheepishly lifted her head to see his reaction to my defence.

"Fine. Carry on," Phoenix surrendered.

"This is crazy," Liam shook his head.

"Let it go," Phoenix breathed, placing a hand on his shoulder.

Liam violently shook Phoenix's arm off but didn't storm away, trying to return to his conversation. Without another word from us, Tara and I slipped out the door wanting to avoid anymore conflict.

"I'm sorry."

Tara felt the need to apologise. I didn't respond as we scrambled into the forest, the wind particularly harsh on my bare skin. I wish she had let me get dressed properly.

"The shed has to be destroyed if anyone were to ever find our location. The less people who know about it and where it is, the better. So I understand their concern."

We continued through the forest and then I saw it. It looked so basic. It was like something I had in my backyard when I was little, something we used to keep tools and the lawnmower in. It wasn't scary or daunting, in fact it looked run-down and rustic. I frowned at the sight, almost disappointed to not see a fire-breathing dragon or a 'do not enter' sign.

"Just wait," she mumbled in response to my facial expression.

She took a key out from around her neck and soon we were stepping inside.

I would've been deceived by the eye into thinking
it was like a tool shed,, if it wasn't for the smell.
As soon as the door was open the aroma of
burning flesh hit me as hard as the cold water did
this morning. Besides flesh, there was also blood
and rotting and death wafting in and out. It left the
taste of metal in my mouth.

"You get used to it," she muttered, as I
scrunched up my nose and gagged.
I swallowed back my vomit, standing up but still
staggering. I took smaller breaths, trying not to
consume too much of the stench. I decided to
distract myself. I grabbed hold of the nearest, and
apparently dirty bench, and stared around, trying to
take in the view.
The floors were blood-stained which was no
surprise at all. As well as old, dried blood there
were scratches etched into the cement. There were
workbenches around all four walls of the room,
each for different purposes. The one I was leaning
against had an array of documents, photographs
and micro-film. If I looked closer, I could make-
out falsified travel papers and reports on names I
didn't know. On the wall above my head was a
detailed map of Northern America with coloured
pins stuck in certain places. Beside me was a wall
of photographs, faces I didn't recognise but the
wall next to that held photos of everyone I did
know; Liam, Phoenix, Fetch and so on. The bench
furtherest from me had a vast array of weaponry,

mostly guns and automatic weapons but there were also traditional samurai swords and Indian archery sets. Tara appeared to be a collector with the purpose not entirely known to me.

Instead of investigating, I dawdled over to the bench that held all the guns. Tara stalked me, curious as to my feelings of this place. I felt the guns beneath my fingertips, their handles, their hammers, their barrels but I didn't dare to reach for their triggers. The guns reminded me of a room we had at Daddy's house, all the Soldiers reported there to fix their guns or obtain new ones. I made out with Sparrow there once. The door locked, nobody around, nobody looking but the guns. It was his favourite place on earth. My favourite place was his arms.

"This isn't so scary," I cleared my throat.

I had pondered too far to distract myself but now I'd give anything to smell the horrid scent rather than think about Sparrow.

"Back room is for who we're tracking and any upcoming Game plans."

I hadn't noticed the door on the far back wall, it blended well with the grooves of the metal shed. I didn't particularly want to explore that area at all.

"What's with the documents?" I asked, my eyes flitting around, still swallowing all the new information.

"Research, completed Games, escape plans, related materials… This one here," she said, sneaking past

155

me and pointing to one, "is an email between Daddy and a soldier of his regarding the assassination of my parents if they were to refuse entering me into his service."

I gulped, I didn't want to read it but I pretended to look enthused. After her sincerity all morning, I didn't want to fall back into the hole of being the man who worked for her parents' killer.

"What about all the writing? All the cursive and post-it notes?" I enquired.

"Opinions and thoughts of mine and the gang. For instance, this bright pink post-it with the hella fancy writing hanging off the bottom of the email says 'I am the fury which rips the flesh from injustice' and it's me quoting the Dark Goddess of Wiccan Culture, Hecate," Tara explained, "Best work I've done actually. My handwriting usually sucks."

"Why weren't you the one to kill Daddy?" I asked, my mouth going dry as I choked out his name.

"No way was Phoenix going to let me steal the spotlight. Plus if Daddy saw me he would've gone running. I didn't mind."

"I thought assassins liked slitting necks," I scoffed.

She didn't find it funny.

"I don't like killing. I just have to. I've always had to," she solemnly justified, the mood definitely dropping.

I took a deep breath and so did she. I was about to apologise when I heard a muffled cry from the other side of the door. Our heads shot to it, we were both alarmed by the sudden noise. She was flustered, her cheeks red and I could tell she knew what it was. As for I, it was the not knowing which filled me most with fear.

I rushed to the door without even thinking, abandoning the thoughts of Sparrow and the terror of Tara's threats behind me. I opened it, stumbling in to come face to face with something I wasn't prepared for. Tara had chased me and slammed into my back when I had halted without warning in the doorway. She pushed me aside as I stood staring.

"Chop Suey?! Oh this is just perfect…"

"You two know each-other then?" Tara raised an eyebrow and crossed her arms.

There he was. His feet firmly on the tainted tiles, tied together with the harshest of fraying rope. His knees were apart as he sat in his wooden prison. His hands were pulled back and cuffed behind the head of the chair, his white shirt was stained with blood and vomit and probably tears. He stank. I couldn't imagine how long he had been tied up for. I couldn't imagine how he excreted his wastes, if he was even allowed to. I was gagging again, this was where that smell was coming from. He smelt like death. As for the burning flesh, it wasn't him

157

but there was a running fire place against the wall and it scared me to think of what Tara was turning to ash. Or rather *who* Tara was turning to ash.

"It's a terrible codename," he spat, "Try screaming it while you're fucking. It sounds stupid."

"You've slept with this guy?" Tara found this amusing.

It was then I wished Temper's foul, drying and shrivelled excuse of lips were gagged. I suppose Tara had a reason for allowing him to talk, she wouldn't have just let him say what he wanted when he wanted unless there was a reason.

"Yes," I breathed, still so shocked.

"Well maybe you can clear something up for me," Tara mumbled.

She strolled over to the bound Temper and stepped behind his back. She took something off of the bench behind her and slithered her arm around his neck. She raised what looked like a serrated knife to his throat and looked at me with a grin. Temper seemed un-phased as if he was used to this sort of behaviour from her. It appeared I was the one freaking out, as sweat ran down from my brow and into my eyes.

"Henry Lackerman, codename Temper, aged twenty five. I was unable to retrieve all his files as they appeared to be deleted before I could catch them. I was under the impression he recently joined the mafia after being fired from his job as a banker after dealing with some illicit affairs. Daddy had offered a role in his family to him out of guilt. Temper tells me that it was all a charade, a big fat lie and that he's really an undercover cop and really, he's on our side. He wanted Daddy to go down. So tell me, Simon, you're smart. You would've been able to tell. Is he telling the truth? Because I don't like liars very much," Tara elaborated, tightening her grip on the blade and it slightly cut into Temper's skin.

I watched the blood drizzle down his unshaven neck, the blade still sitting on the wound it had made. It put me in an almost hypnotic state, thinking back to the night of Daddy's murder. I realised while he was dying, Tara was kidnapping the only guy we had who knew nothing about us. Temper had terrible luck.

"Yeah, he's a cop. Why do you have him anyway?" I frowned, shooting a glare over to Tara. I was unsure why she needed someone from the family when the Moths had already taken me. The information she needed was unclear to me.

Tara ignored me and put the knife back on the bench. She walked to the other side of this more confined room to a pin-board with a proud display of photographs, maps and scribbled on paper. There were strings that had been tied to the pins, looking like an adult version of connect-the-dots. I assumed it was a tracking system. She wrote something down on a sticky note and put it next to what looked like a beat-up picture of Temper. She then sighed and turned around, looking to the floor.

"So you're an undercover cop?"

"That's what I've been trying to tell you," Temper sarcastically replied.

He was clearly pissed off, he had to have been held here for months. So much pain and torture for her to turn around and believe him now. At least he wasn't dead.

"That means you underwent a series of brutal training procedures to get to a position where you could infiltrate the mafia. That means you studied them for months. That means you know their systems and how they worked. That means you've seen their files. That means you learnt about everybody before you went undercover ..."

"I still don't know who he is, Tara!" Temper screeched and it made me jump.

He sure had the guts to scream at his captor. I wasn't sure if had been underestimating him the whole time or if he was past breaking point.

"But you do, you must!" She screamed right back, storming over to him.

I stepped back as she grabbed his shoulders from behind and tipped the seat back so he was on an angle, trying to reinstate her power over him.

"I had never heard of him before, I'm telling you," Temper's temper grew as he spoke, "He wasn't one of the people I studied. I never saw

160

him. In that whole week not once did I see him. He probably left before I got there!"

"You can't just leave the mafia," Tara scoffed, her doubts resurfacing.

She shoved his chair back and it thudded as it hit the floor. He banged his head against the tiles which resulted in him yelping. He clenched his eyes out of pain but Tara just rolled hers. She lifted him back up and checked for bleeding but he was fine.

"Who are you looking for?" I asked, unable to stand the suspense.

"The soldier who helped murder my parents," Tara hissed.

She was trembling with rage. She couldn't even look me in the eyes. She was like our version of *Batman*.

"I know all the soldiers, past and present. Just ask me. Let him go."

I was growing tired watching his pathetic pleading and although I didn't know him well, I felt the torment was exaggerated and unnecessary. Her parents died years ago, it was time to move on.

"You wouldn't know him. The other soldiers told me never to speak his name in front of you."

"Sparrow?" I breathed and both sets of eyes shot to me.

"Yeah, Sparrow," Temper frowned, staring at me as if he had gotten a new jigsaw piece to this puzzle.

"Sparrow," Tara repeated, walking over to me. Shit. I was in trouble. I was in big trouble. She stared at me with her intense brown eyes. Her dilated pupils could consume a soul; my soul.

"Tell me what you know."

"He was Daddy's favourite soldier and I was Daddy's favourite person, that was our only connection. We saw each-other a lot in Daddy's office but we barely talked to each-other," I lied, they didn't need to know the whole truth, "We got assigned to a couple of cases together, there were a couple of moments but then I got assigned overseas for three months and when I came back he had gone. Daddy told me he gave Sparrow permission to leave but I knew he was lying. Like you said, you don't just leave."

"Moments?"

"Did you fuck him like you fucked me?" Temper grumbled.
I should've played it cool. I should've laughed him off. I didn't. I froze.

"Even if he did, it doesn't matter," Tara rolled her eyes and I graciously exhaled away all my fears, "As long as he didn't fall in love with him." The fears came back. Tara watched me, trying to find a sign of weakness. I stood my ground. Sparrow was no-one to me now, it would be unfair to trial me on my past mistakes. I think she knew

162

that. Tara looked between the two of us and then left the room, leaving me all alone with Temper.

"Are you the reason Phoenix isn't allowed in here?" I asked, curiosity eating away.

"Tara's not meant to be seeking revenge."

"So you know Phoenix?"

"No. I listen to Tara and Maria's conversations. The walls are paper thin," he admitted and I nodded, "Have you screwed Phoenix yet?"

"No," I laughed at his inappropriate comment.

"Do you want to?"

I disregarded him, looking to my feet and shaking my head. It made sense Maria was the only other person allowed in the shed; Tara and Maria were practically the same person. I found the courage to look at him again, examining his bruised and beaten face. Guilt became me.

"I'm sorry about all of this," I sighed, changing the topic.

"I would've arrested you if none of it happened, so don't worry about it," he chuckled and so did I, "You enjoying the Moths?"

I shrugged. I didn't want to tell him I loved it. I didn't want to tell him I hated it. I didn't actually know what I wanted to tell him. I didn't actually know what to tell myself.

"So Sparrow?" He raised an eyebrow.

He had the piece of the puzzle but he didn't know where to put it.

"Let's not talk. The walls are paper thin," I glumly smiled and he nodded.

Tara came back. She had slammed open the door as if she was in a rage. It took a second for both of us to realise she was holding a gun in her hand and she was ready to fire. I stepped back, standing next to Temper who was pissing in his chair. His reaction clued me into the fact this wasn't a standard tactic for Tara, this was real.

I raised my hands, trying to make peace. I wasn't meant to be a threat to her. She pulled back the hammer and menacingly stared between us. She kept fumbling the gun around, as if she hadn't decided whose chest to place a bullet into. I was sweating and Temper was crying. I had forgotten about the stench.

The trigger was pulled. She had shot. I thought for a second I had seen the blinding white light but when I opened my eyes, I felt no pain. I looked at Temper, a bullet lodged right into his left eye. I could smell the burning flesh as the chair fell back and hit the ground with a thud. Tara didn't need to check for bleeding, it was saturating his curly hair and the tiles as his dead body laid strewn against the broken chair. His hands were unbound but there was no escaping.

I was still breathing.

"I don't like killing," she blubbered, tears in her eyes, "I just have to."

xxi. inner darkness

Temper meant nothing to me and yet, I couldn't
help but cry. I wasn't crying, I was bawling. I had
ran out of that shed, fell to my knees on the
overgrown grass and cursed at the sky. He wasn't
Daddy or one of my sisters, he was no-one. I got
so caught up in little moments - the breath before a
kiss, going too high on a swing set, a hug goodbye,
opening a present, watching the sunset. I had a
little moment with Temper, a reunion of sorts and
then he was shot. He was gone forever, no
redemption, no conclusion to our story.
I spent the rest of the day in my room, trying to
avoid everyone and everything. Surprisingly, I was
given peace. Nobody disrupted me as I stayed
buried beneath blankets either scribbling in my
journal or staring at the ceiling. I hadn't even
thought of eating but when I checked the time it
was quarter to ten at night and I had missed both
lunch and dinner. I decided I had to do something.
I couldn't act crippled when it wasn't my life that
was taken away from me. I had to confront Tara, I
couldn't keep moping. So I got up out of bed, still
wearing slacks, a stern pout and nothing else. I
marched out of my room and down the corridor,
knocking on Tara and Maria's door. I didn't even
know what I was going to say just that I had to say
something. The reply wasn't fast enough for my

liking so I slowly twisted the doorknob and crept in.

Maria wasn't there which surprised me. What surprised me more was Tara weeping. Her crystal eyes had swelled with tears that trickled down her freckled cheeks. She looked up at me and grumbled. She wiped her eyes and glumly smiled. I didn't have time to part my mouth before she interrupted.

"Most importantly, child, I am you. I am part of you, and I am within you. Seek me within and without, and you will be strong. Know me. Venture into the dark so that you may awaken to Balance, Illumination, and Wholeness. Take my Love with you everywhere and find the Power within to be who you wish," Tara recited with a croaky throat, unable to look me in the eye, "It's the ending of the Charge of the Dark Goddess part two, in Wiccan culture. It's the same passage as the flesh and fury one from the post-it note you saw."

I was still at the door, knob in hand. I didn't want to go in but I didn't want to leave either. Her speech ruined any plan I had at confrontation but I still wanted to talk to her about the events that had occurred. I shifted my weight, not wanting to start the conversation. She took note and started it for us.

"There's darkness in all of us and that's okay. It means we can fall asleep in darkness and wake up to the light, you know?" Tara went on, "I hang onto her not because she's evil but because she's relatable and her scriptures always say just the right thing to soothe me. I hang onto her and my Wiccan religion and culture because it's all I have other than Maria."

My initial intention was to tear her down, make her feel guilty for what she did but she appeared to be doing it all on her own. I didn't have to say anything.

"I hate myself, Simon. I hate myself so much." Tara burst into heavy tears. She buried her head in her hands, shaking it. I felt her. Being a teenager sucked but being a teenager with a body count must've been devastating. I didn't want to make her feel bad anymore.

My change of heart had me manoeuvring to her bed. I slotted in beside her, my legs around her body as I pulled her into my chest. She sobbed so hard even my heart was breaking. I gently shushed her, patting her hair and closing my eyes as I felt her convulse against me. She reminded me of my sisters. I had the urge to protect her and even justify her monstrosities. My feelings for her changed so quickly and unexplainably but I wasn't in the mood to argue with my heart.

"I don't want to but when you show up and you hate me like I hate myself, the hatred just bubbles and boils and spills."

"I don't hate you. I never hated you," I attempted to soothe her.

167

"Shut up," she blubbered, "Let me speak."
Bold of her. I rubbed the side of her arm, signalling that she should continue.

"I care about the people I kill because the people I kill are a part of my life the second I end theirs. They're with me forever."

"Okay," I breathed.

"He wasn't necessary anymore, a waste of resources that we couldn't afford. Hearing you two laugh sent me spiralling because I can't see him as human... I can't see him as someone with relationships. Otherwise I'd be another walking corpse in this movement."
She looked deep into my eyes. She was so young and vulnerable. She didn't belong here.

"I was going to kill you," she admitted, "I don't like you. You don't like me. You're the closest thing Daddy had to a child even more so than his actual child... but that's also why I didn't."
It made no sense to me. I stopped rubbing her arm, my hands dropping to my sides. She looked straight ahead so I couldn't see her face. We both were grieving, what we were grieving wasn't quite clear.

"There's a reason assassins only get the name and location of their targets. Maybe a sentence or two on reasoning or even a history if it's an important case, if we're lucky. I'm in too deep with you now... I know Fetch idolises you. I know Liam absolutely adores you, I know he'd defend you even if it meant losing everybody else. I know Nicholas thinks you're the greatest attribute to our team and I know he wants you to be a doctor if you ever got out of this mess. I know Maria thinks you're cute and that I should give you a chance because I gave her a chance... I know what Phoenix thinks of you. I know the look in his eyes whenever you're mentioned or whenever he sees you. I know he smiles wider than I've ever seen him when you're around. I know you miss Daddy everyday even more than your real family. Now I know about Sparrow. I know that you loved him and that he broke your heart," Tara exclaimed, "My head is exploding with these facts about you. There's no way I could kill you when I know so much about you. I'm too invested in your life to take it away. The Moths are my family and my family are too invested in you for you to die. It'd be like killing a piece of them. It'd be like killing a piece of myself."

Tara's assassination skills were wasted with this group, she was no murderer. She was a damaged child with no parents to guide her from those who found it so easy to manipulate her. She had no sense of self, all she had was hive mind and a wrongful dedication to the movement. Maria was keeping her as a pet. If she had any sense of humanity, she would've left Tara to lead a normal life a long time ago.

169

"So I'm sorry about Temper and believe me when I say I'm sorry about Daddy. Phoenix did to you what Daddy did to me. Daddy killed my parents and was going to force me into his care, Phoenix basically killed yours and forced you into his. I've thought of nothing but Daddy's death since and I'm sure you wanted to murder Phoenix too. I want to say thank you for not doing that. I know it's hypocritical but like I said, the Moths are my family and that includes Phoenix. So thank you for wanting to fuck him rather than wanting to kill him."

We both chuckled and I shook my head to dismiss her, a smile still plastered on my face. For selfish reasons, I was glad to be with her now. I did hope, one day, she could leave this deranged way of living and bloom into the woman both Phoenix and Maria prevent her from being.

"Trust me, I want to kill him," I joked, she didn't need to know my thoughts.

Her tears had dried and I was thankful for that. I couldn't stand when people cried even though people had to constantly watch me break down.

"Tara, you're not a bad person," I insisted.

"And you're not a monster," she replied, "Does this mean we're friends now?"

"I think so," I smiled.

"Curse you. They warned me of your compassion but I thought I was too much of a bitch to fall for it. Fine, we can be friends. Now get out! Maria is gone for the night so I finally have the bed all to myself. Do you know how much of a hog she is?!" Tara babbled.

She playfully pushed me off her mattress and I laughed to myself as I wandered out of her room. From friends to enemies, it was something I was mastering with those in the group. One by one, I was gaining a following.

I shut the door behind me and dawdled down the corridor, not paying attention. Due to my horrible observational skills I had to run into something, no, someone. Phoenix fucking Jackson. It was always Phoenix. Although disgusted by the way he was keeping a young girl hostage, I couldn't help but fall back into the school boy crush routine. I guess I'd forgive him for anything at this stage.

"I heard crying and yelling and I thought..." Phoenix began to speak but couldn't blurt out the rest of his words.

"You thought she was trying to kill me?" Phoenix shrugged, "Is everything okay? Are you guys okay?"

It was then I broke out into a grin, wanting to give him a taste of his own medicine. I grabbed the side of his arms to hold him still and he looked at my grip then into my eyes in alarm.

"You'll just have to trust me," I winked.

"I trust you."

"I hope you mean that," I cackled.

I released his arms and then crept passed him. I strolled down the hall with all the confidence in the world and I could feel his hungry eyes on my back. It was good.

I was good.

xxii. under the skin

This was not lust…

"Is fada an bóthar nach bhfuil aon chasadh ann."

"I don't speak-"

"It's a long road that has no turning."

"Is there a problem?"

"I just told you."

One month had passed again. The months seemed to roll on by like tumbleweed in a cowboy's nightmare. Tara and Maria taught me what they thought was best for me. I spent a lot more time in the shed than was probably necessary. I liked it there, though. I wasn't a sadist but it was quite tranquil after you got passed the smell. Plus, it was easy to keep track of everything, all their documents were there to file through. My indifference to Maria wasn't noticeable to the two, so we kept a civil training schedule. I learnt a lot about recognising weapons, the makes and models of guns and some basic technique to sneaking and staying undetected.

It was a good month but it was time to move on. Tara always welcomed me to join her in the shed for lunches just like Liam always invited me out hunting or to his secluded bonfires. I had friends now but I craved more. I wanted friends but more than that, I wanted to increase my knowledge when Phoenix thought there was nothing left for me to learn. I decided he was wrong. I didn't want to go on alone in this movement, I still thirsted for guidance so I sought it out myself against Phoenix's will.

"I don't think I can give you what you're looking for, Simon."

"Cillian, I'm yours. You can't do anything about it. I need this."

Cillian sat up slightly. He stared at me as he slowly took off his big, black glasses that enhanced his terrifyingly stern eyes. They reduced back to normality and I held my breath as he parted his mouth. He held his hands together as they rested on his desk and I bit my tongue. He remained silent.

"It's not a delay to stop and sharpen the scythe," I retorted, using his Irish proverbs against him. I shuffled over to his door, planning on slamming it in rage as I exited his office. It was starting to feel like a waste of time. If he wasn't going to teach me any new tricks, I could always consult Sarah for technology training.

"Simon," he spoke up.

I had opened the door but stopped to look back at him with my eyebrows raised.

"Your first job is to socialise. Stand closer to the people you don't usually stand close to and stand further away from the people you usually don't stand far away from. See what they do. Pay attention to their feet. Also stare at someone for longer than you deem appropriate. It's a basic task, so you'll be able to handle it. Tell me what you notice at the end of the day," Cillian added and I sighed in relief.

The human mind always fascinated me. All we were were a concoction chemicals and electro-magnetic pulses. I wanted to learn all about it. I wanted to know what could make someone sad and how the same thing could make someone else happy. Humans were so complicated and it was a mystery I wanted to slowly unravel. I was excited to be undergoing even the most basic of tests for Cillian. I knew he could quench my lust for knowledge.

In the rumpus room, I saw Phoenix and Liam deep in conversation; like always. It was perfect. I could stand away from Liam and see if he finds my distance uncomfortable. I could give him only glances and not maintain eye contact. As for Phoenix... I wasn't sure what to do with him. I didn't really ever stand close to him nor far away. He was always at a reasonable distance, just like his lips and state of mind. I decided I was going to stand close. I was going to be so close, we might as well be conjoined twins. I wanted to feel his heat and I wanted to be smug. I wanted to see his reaction and I wanted to know if he'd move away. I ambled over, hands behind my back. I stood next to my target, not too close at first but still beside him and in front of Liam. This was where I could really utilise my talents; brain games and mind tricks.

"So I was telling this kid... Oh hey, Simon," Liam interrupted himself, smiling at me. Phoenix took a sideways glance at me before returning his attention to Liam. I barely looked up at Liam, nodding in response and keeping a distance.

"Uh where was I?" Liam grumbled, my presence making him lose track of his words.

"You were telling me about the kid..." Phoenix cleared his throat, trying to steer their conversation on the right path.

I looked at their feet as Liam's story droned on. Liam's were quite open, pointing at both myself and Phoenix whereas Phoenix's were closed off, directly aimed at Liam. He didn't want me there. Well, I wasn't going to let him get away with that. As they conversed and I pretended to listen, I shuffled closer. Every couple of seconds, I'd subtly move an inch, until suddenly our arms were brushing and I was biting my lip. Phoenix looked at me, a finger grazing his chin, his arm was held by his other arm which crossed against his lanky chest. I looked back at him, maintaining eye contact. I stared right into his glistening pupils and I tried not get lost in them. This was a social experiment, a psychological encounter. I couldn't get transfixed, not even for science. I was waiting for him to look away but he never did. It was if he was drawn to my eyes. He looked so bewildered at first as to why I was staring but now he was too caught up to even question it. He was enjoying the inappropriate nature of the eye contact when he was meant to be talking to Liam.

"And that's when the banana came in," Liam started laughing which startled both of us. Phoenix snapped out of our gaze, returning his own to Liam with a small smile. I found it hard to believe Liam hadn't noticed our moment.

"Ah yes of course," Phoenix nodded. Phoenix's smile had become smug. He wasn't smiling to protect Liam's feelings now, he was smiling because of me. I had flicked a switch inside him. Phoenix moved closer to me as Liam continued with such enthusiasm. I gulped, this wasn't part of the plan. He dropped his arms and I felt his fingers tease my own, playing amongst them. I lost my breath when Phoenix looked at me again with such cheekiness in his eyes, I was going to pass out. I couldn't handle it.

"Sorry, chaps but I have to go talk to Sarah," I lied.

I wanted to continue with my experiment but if I stayed with Phoenix, I'd be too distracted. As I was leaving I thought I'd be sly by going around Phoenix and brushing my fingers against his lower back. I wanted to feel the dimples at the bottom of his spine and I wanted to conclude my segment on him. Phoenix snapped his head to me as I came back into his view, his grin even wider and I winked.

I carried on with my socialisation research as Cillian instructed. I tested it on a couple of people and most of the outcomes had resulted in subtle responses. I had missed lunch and I was getting hungry. So I had sauntered over to the kitchen which extended off of the rumpus room. I was getting a snack, standing on my tippy-toes to reach the top cabinet when I felt him. His hands had groped my hips and his head popped over my shoulder, our cheeks brushing together as we looked at the food. I swallowed hard, biting my lip and closing my eyes. I was enjoying his heat and his touch and his scent and, well, his everything.

"I have a bone to pick with you," Phoenix whispered and I shivered.

I flattened out my feet, losing my height and the touch of his cheek. Nonetheless, he didn't let go of my hips, instead he spun me around to face him and pushed me back into the bench.

"Yeah?" I breathed, appreciating his dominance.

"Yeah. What was that stunt you pulled earlier while I was talking to Liam?" Phoenix asked with a grin.

He liked it. He wasn't expecting it but he liked it and that's why he was so close now. I smirked and hopped up on the bench, sitting but still facing him. He moved closer, not willing to part our touch. His hands still gripped my hips and so he pulled me into his torso and my legs wrapped around his body. I wanted to melt.

"You can spank me if you want," I teased, burning with desire.

He grinned and shook his head at my flirting. He removed his hands from my waist and grabbed onto my hands. He guided them upwards and around his neck, then he travelled back down to hold my torso still. I obliged to his silent demand and left my arms draped around his pretty white neck.

"I just might," he whispered and licked his lips.

"Mmhmm," I moaned, staring at his wet lips. I didn't realise how close our faces were until his started moving even closer. He tilted his head and I subconsciously tilted mine. Our lips pressed together and I swooned. We continued to kiss until I got bored and started to explore his skin. I kissed his jawline and he grunted, I had found a sweet-spot. I decided to play on it, kissing it, biting it, sucking it and polishing it with a few flicks of the tongue. He was moaning the whole time which evoked me to give him more. I carried on down his neck, delightfully gifting him with colourful bruises to tattoo his skin. I felt powerful giving them to him. Although hickeys were obnoxious high-school signs, it felt good branding a man who was not to be branded. I was marking him as my own when he was nobody's. His fingers found my chin and he lifted my head back up so he could look into my eyes. His look was stern, he knew what I was doing and my motivation for doing so. I think he wanted me to stop, so I settled for plunging my lips back on his and sliding my tongue down his throat instead of across his neck. Phoenix wasn't prepared for that. His hands found my cheeks as we made out under the sunlight coming in through the kitchen window. It lasted for a couple of minutes before he pulled away with a sigh. He solemnly shook his head and I knew this was over.

"This never happened, right?" I grumbled.

"Yeah."

"Maybe I need to spank *you*," I angrily muttered.

He smiled at me before opening the kitchen door and rolling out. I had forgotten all about my snack. Instead of replenishing my hunger, in my rage, I rushed out of the kitchen and out of the rumpus room and down the corridor. I got to Cillian's office and slammed open the door without knocking. I needed answers, I needed them now.

"Simon?" Cillian whimpered, taking off his glasses and looking up at me.

He noticed my reddened cheeks and my posture and his curiosity dissipated into concern.

"Tell me why he does it?" I growled.

I wasn't angry at Cillian but it was coming across that way. I was mostly angry at myself and at Phoenix and at circumstances. I couldn't read him,

I couldn't understand his signals or his facial expression. Did he want me or didn't he?

"I'm going to assume you're talking about Phoenix because that's all you talk about," Cillian calmly replied.

"Excuse me?" I spat.

"You tell your best friends over and over-"

"Who do you think are my best-friends?" I questioned.

I never talked to Cillian, not out of malice but we were clashing personalities who found it better to stay apart. I was surprised he had some idea in his head of who my best-friends were, if I had any at all.

"Liam and Tara."

"Tara's not my best-friend" I scoffed, still full of unjustified anger.

"Yes she is. Simon, don't lie to me. Don't lie to yourself. I know you were on her service but you talk to her like a sister and you look at her with admiration. You're the only one who goes to the shed with her anymore, not even Maria can stand it," Cillian refuted, shaking his head.

"I don't see why it's just a bunch of photos and a bit of blood... Hey, don't distract me. We're talking about Phoenix," I snapped, my anger revisiting.

"Take a seat," Cillian sighed, gesturing to the other side of the desk.

181

I hesitantly obliged although I didn't feel comfortable. I was angry and hurt and Cillian was really the last person I wanted to talk to. However, my feet had lead me back to him.

"What did he do?" Cillian continued, putting his paperwork aside.

"We kissed and then he basically told me to stop."

"I don't see why you're angry, I thought you were a respectful man."

"I am and I know when enough is enough and I listen to consent and I stop when somebody tells me no and I'm always on my best behaviour but..." I whined.

"But?" He raised an eyebrow.

"But I've been sitting in agony pretending I didn't feel his touch that day of the exam. I have to pretend that the lust in his eyes never existed and that he didn't pin me down to the floor like he'd go crazy if I escaped. I have to pretend that I don't know what his lips tasted like or how his weight felt on mine. I have to pretend that I've never had my hands down that stupid boy's pants when all I want to do is jump back into them. He asked me to pretend that it never happened but if you... Cillian, if you hadn't had walked in we would've kept going and we would've ended up fucking."

"You're blaming me for the ruptured nature of yours and Phoenix's relationship?"

"No. I did for a while but you're not entirely to blame. Maybe he wouldn't have asked me to pretend if it didn't happen, if you didn't walk in but nonetheless it's not your fault. It's the idea of you, of somebody, of a close friend, finding out. We could've fucked and he would've been fine if somebody like you didn't know. Though what doesn't make sense to me is you could've told everyone."

"I didn't," he mentioned, not defensively but informatively.

"I know but you could've. Why should I pretend if everybody knows already? It doesn't make sense to me. So I need you to tell me. I need you to tell me why I have to pretend and I need you to tell me why he asked me to stop today and I need you to tell me why he's like this? You're a psychologist and one of his oldest friends?! Surely you know. Surely there's something from his past which is limiting his moves here in the present," I babbled on.

"Simon, you need meds not a psychologist," he bluntly replied.

"Maybe I do but I want to know his backstory first. Did someone screw him over? Is that why he's so closed off and mysterious? Because someone screwed me over once too and I can empathise with him-"

"Simon, stop!" Cillian shouted and I almost jumped out of my skin.

183

I wriggled back in my seat and crossed my arms, glaring at the psychologist. He was flustered, rubbing his creased forehead.

"You're getting carried away," he continued, looking to me, "Do you want me to teach you or do you want me to listen to your thoughts and delusions?"

I didn't reply. I wanted to be taught but it felt good to rattle things off of my chest at the same time. I had never seen someone before, never been diagnosed with a mental illness although it felt at least fifty of them were rampant in my brain.

"I think the way we proceed is I can teach you but you also need counselling. Once a fortnight, please see me so we can work through your problems. You clearly need it and I can't blame you, you're essentially a captive here," Cillian continued, "As for your next assignment, I can teach you about lying and reading expressions. It may help with Phoenix."

"Okay," I breathed.

I had no fight left in me. If he felt I needed someone to talk to, so be it. I would happily let him be my doctor if it meant he was also my mentor.

"Meet me in the rumpus room at six thirty and I'll give you a quick session before everyone joins us at seven, okay?"

xxiii. profiling

Eyelashes. He liked my eyelashes.

"Micro-expressions," Cillian stated, "Know what they are?"

It was now six-thirty and I was learning.

"Dr. Paul Ekman devoted his life to studying micro-expressions. They last for about a fifteenth or twentieth of a second on somebody's face. They're very brief facial expressions and only occur when somebody conceals a feeling either unconsciously or deliberately. There are seven universal micro-expressions and they are anger, disgust, fear, sadness, contempt, happiness and surprise," Cillian elaborated.

"Okay, how do I learn how to spot them?"

"The micro-expression used when somebody is lying is usually fear. Brows will be raised and drawn together, wrinkles in the forehead are in the centre between the brows but not across, the upper eyelid will be raised but the lower is tense, mouth is open and lips may be tensed or stretched and drawn back."

"And I'm meant to recognise all that in a fraction of a second?" I scoffed.

"You're excited," Cillian grinned and I frowned at him,"The happy micro-expression. The corners of your lips were drawn back and up, your cheeks were raised, crows feet embedded in the sides of your eyes and a wrinkle ran from your outer nose to your outer lip."

"I guess I'm always up for a challenge," I shrugged, suppressing a smile.

"It's important to know the happiness one, especially in the task I'm about to give you because these people are your friends and will be more smug about lying than fearful," he insisted.
I nodded, wondering whether or not I'll be able to read my friends' micro-expressions.

"Other things to note when people are lying, which will be easier, are to check if they cover their mouth or touch their nose. A person's voice is also a good indicator, they might start talking faster or slower, their pitch might change, usually higher, and they might start stuttering. Observe the level of mirroring, people naturally mirror those their interacting with as it builds rapport and a show of interest. Liars generally stop mirroring as they are trying to create another reality for their listeners. So watch their body movements, a good one to watch for is if they lean away or are fidgeting. Liars tend to avoid hand gestures and may touch vulnerable parts of their body, like their neck," he explained, he wasn't that much older than I was yet it felt like there were scores between us.

"Is that all?" I enquired, I wanted to be as smart as him.

"No. Eye movements are important. When people remember details their eyes look up to the left but when they make something up their eyes look up to the right. This is for right-handed people and the opposite is true for left-handed people. Watch for rapid blinking but don't be fooled by looking away or staring into your eyes. It doesn't indicate a lie or a truth," he concluded.

"You've had years of practice, how am I meant to live up to it?" I swallowed.
It was a sorry excuse for inadequacy, trying to compare myself to someone better. He knew I couldn't live up to his name but he expected I created my own legacy. I was so worried about messing everything up, I was trying to make him believe I wasn't great to begin with. Of course, he saw right through that. I shouldn't have wasted my breath.

"Well, consider this the start of your years of practice," Cillian smiled, winking at me.
He got up from his seat and patted my back on his way out. I was so nervous that I began to sweat. All I had to do was try, there was no real consequence here. Micro-expressions, body language, nose, mouth, mirroring, fidgeting, hand gestures, eye movements…

"Simon."
I jumped and turned around to find Cillian, Tara, Maria and Liam.

"These people will all be telling you something about themselves but one of them will be lying. Tell me who you think is lying," Cillian stated as the three lined up.
Liam.

"I once aged a deer for one week instead of two and gave the whole crew food poisoning."
Tara.

"My middle name is my mother's first name."
Maria.

"I've dated over twenty people."
I replied with no hesitation, "it was Liam."

"Why?" Cillian enquired.

"Tara wouldn't lie about anything to do with her parents. I don't know Maria very well but... Liam, I do and I know he wouldn't ruin a hunt."

"Hmm, too easy," Cillian murmured, "You're all dismissed."
They left and the next three people followed Cillian in and I licked my lips. Fetch, Nicholas and Phoenix. I stared at Phoenix, a glint of cheekiness in my eye which he reciprocated. It made it so hard to hate him.

"Do we go? I'm going to go," Fetch stammered, they were as nervous as I was.
Fetch.

"I've never been outside of the country."
Nicholas.

"I haven't seen my family since before I met Rose."

Phoenix.

"I fell in love with someone and they inspired me to start this movement."

This lot was harder. I sat thinking about what I had witnessed and the way they ere all holding themselves now.

"It has to be Phoenix," I confidently assured Cillian.

"Why?"

"First of all he was holding onto the back of his neck pretty tight and he stared at me the entire time…"

"I told you not to use eye contact as a signal," Cillian disputed.

I tried to think of another scientific explanation of why I believed he was lying but I couldn't conjure it in my mind. I couldn't recall any micro-expressions or eye movements. All I had going for me was my background of the subjects and I was going to use whatever I could.

"He's totally incapable of love."

The room was silent. Stunned.

"Simon, try not going off what you know about the subjects. Pretend they're strangers," Cillian insisted, watching me, uncomfortable.

"I can't do that. I know too much. He couldn't love anyone like that."

More silence. Phoenix's eyes were red and watery. It dawned on me that my analysis could've been incorrect. I felt so confident in my answer but it was based on nothing but rude assumptions and clouded emotions.

"Thanks for that," Phoenix choked as if his heart was caught in his throat.

He had to leave, walking down the corridor before the tears leaked from his eyes. I had never seen him in a state like that. He had passed me the knife and I had stabbed him instead of putting it aside.

"It was me," Fetch sheepishly spoke up.

"Thank you, Fetch," Cillian spoke for me, "You and Nicholas may leave now."

I never wanted to hurt him. I bit the insides of my cheeks to stop myself from crying. Cillian leant back in his chair, examining me for a moment.

"You should never let emotions get involved in your work," he blankly said, looking out at the trees through the glass doors.

I nodded, feeling stupid. That was the first rule of everything this movement has trained me in, psychology should've been no different. There was something about Phoenix that often had me ignoring it, however.

"You're exactly what he needs," Cillian finally exhaled, as if he had been holding that thought in for a while.

I looked to him as if he was insane, "What? I was brutal, horrible, I hurt him."

"You're exactly what he needs," Cillian repeated, this time nodding to himself.

The night was over and he wasn't going to
elaborate. I went to my room, instead of him
leaving me in the dark, I would actively seek it out.

xxiv. let the games begin

Eight months since I started my trial of the Moths
and I thought I'd be prepared for anything.
Throughout the time I spent with Cillian I only
heard one thing fluttering around the cabin. It was
on the tip of everyone's tongues but they seemed
to bite down when they were around me. I heard it
mentioned, several times and each time I tried to
join the conversation it was subtly changed to
another topic. I was moving in and out of groups,
following what felt like a ghost, chasing down
whoever said the word last until eventually
somebody slipped. Liam was unaware I was in
earshot when I heard what I wanted to hear; a new
'Game' was in order.
All I had to decipher was what that really meant. I
knew we wouldn't grab out Monopoly and have a
crack at it one night. I knew it was more serious
than anything a normal person would deem to call
an actual game. We weren't going to be kicking the
footy around, I imagined it was something along
the lines of what they did at the masquerade ball.
In all honesty, I was terrified to find out.
I asked Cillian one day who had shaken his head
and started talking about Sigmund Freud and the
conscious and unconscious mind instead. It was a
good lesson but my mind was elsewhere. I had an
itch with an urgency to scratch. I would've asked
Phoenix about it, if he ever stopped brooding. He

wouldn't talk to me let alone look me in the eye. He was still mad about what I said, there was no way he'd let me in on something like this.

With sunken eyes and dirty grey slacks I hadn't washed in over a week, I couldn't sleep the night after Cillian's lesson. I was so tired, even the sheep I tried to count had fallen asleep and left me awake to suffer. I decided to go to the kitchen, grab a glass of water and maybe even jump into Liam's bed. It was a habit I had picked up whenever the insomnia was really bad.

On my way to the kitchen, I noticed the rumpus room light was on and heard the harsh sound of angry whispers. I tip-toed down the hallway, getting close enough to eavesdrop without getting caught.

"I'm not going anymore."

"Why?"

"Because I won't let them," I recognised Sarah's stern voice.

I assumed it was Fetch who wasn't permitted to go, Sarah finding any way possible to keep them out of danger.

"Fetch is their own person, Sarah. They can make their own choices."

I recognised Phoenix's voice this time, he was as stern as she was. I inched further, remaining quiet but desperate to not miss a thing.

"No! It's too dangerous. We were queer counsellors in the DC. We'll instantly be recognised, you've invited practically our entire old client base. They won't be participating in this Game and I won't be either."

"Phoenix can't go in the truck by himself. You know what he's like..." Liam bluntly stated.

"What about Nicholas or Cillian?" Maria asked. I was able to make out the voices a lot clearer now. It sounded like nearly everyone in the team was there and voicing their concern. It made me more curious about the Game and my absence from it.

"They both wanted to sit out on this one and I can't force them into it. I don't want to," Phoenix disappointingly muttered.

"What about Simon?" Sarah asked.
I didn't hear anything but I imagined Phoenix shook his head. I could visualise it as clear as day, the look on his face and his complete indifference to the idea. I couldn't understand why he invited me to be part of the group when he didn't trust me to take part in our main activities. He couldn't have it both ways and I was about to show him that.

"I'll do it!"
I hurried out of the corridor and into the light where the mumblers of the night gathered around in a circle. They turned around and stared at me, partly surprised and partly alarmed.

"I'll do it," I repeated with such hope in my lungs.

None of them knew what to say. They were all still processing that I was listening to them. They couldn't comprehend I was volunteering to something I was vague on the details about, especially since Phoenix was so against it.

"I'll accompany Phoenix in the truck," I clarified in case they were confused, "If nobody else can do it then I'll happily-"

"No," Phoenix spat, shooting me down immediately.

Now the attention was all on him; us.

"Excuse me?" I hissed.

"No. I don't want you to come," he shook his head, "Why do you think you weren't invited to this meeting in the first place?"

His eyes remained on the ground, not once did he look at me. Everyone else was awkwardly staring, not willing to say anything. I wasn't going to bite my tongue like they did anymore.

"Well that's too bad because it appears you're out of options," I brutally spat back at him.

I was starting to understand what Cillian meant about Phoenix needing me and my brutality. Phoenix still looked hesitant but I could see his walls slowly breaking down.

"Dude, he's right," Liam shrugged and I shared a look of gratitude with him.

"I have been training for this. I'm ready. I'm ready for whatever you throw at me. So throw it at me, goddamnit," I growled.

195

I wasn't going to take no for an answer. I was beyond him infantilising me and treating me like deadweight. He realised I wasn't backing down this time.

"Fine," Phoenix grunted, still not looking at me but instead looking to Liam, "We'll leave tomorrow evening but Liam, you and the girls should head out now. Get a head start."
The group disbanded. They all went down the corridor either to go to bed or gather their things to take off. All that was left in the quiet, haunting rumpus room was Phoenix and I. I turned to him, hoping to catch a hint of his forest eyes but he was still looking away. He walked towards the couch, putting his hands on the head of it and clenching at the fabric. He bowed his head, as if in shame.

"You shouldn't have done that," Phoenix almost laughed.
I glared at him as he breathlessly chuckled into the stiff air. I cautiously made my way over, only stopping when he turned around with a smile. He was smiling but he wasn't happy at all. He was manic.

"I hate you so much right now," he wheezed, was he laughing or crying?
All I could do was blankly stare. He took the few extra steps to be only inches away from me and he reached out his arms and grabbed onto my shoulders. He grabbed hard.

"I can't drive alone because they think I'm suicidal," Phoenix confessed.
He really was a murderer. Nobody was safe. Not even himself.

"I can't crash the car with you in it. I would rather live a thousand hells than to see you die. So if you're coming to this Game or any other Game in the future, you have to promise me you won't die. You're not even allowed to get hurt. Okay? You can't die. You're not allowed to die, Simon Sullivan. There's no way I'd let anything happen to you especially not on my own accord. You have to keep breathing. You have to…"
I shushed him, pressing a finger to his trembling lips. He was getting carried away. He was in pain. This was the reason I wasn't invited to participate, he'd be in too much pain. Phoenix swallowed hard, tears in his eyes. I pulled away my finger and he brought our faces together. He pecked my lips like a couple that had been together thirty years would do to say goodnight and then he withdrew from my presence. He gazed over me for a little bit longer before he walked away.
This was not lust...

xxv. stoned

Vinegar. Cocaine. Sweat. Sex. Gasoline. My nose
was in over-drive whilst my vision was impaired.
Phoenix had taken the liberty of covering my eyes
with a makeshift blindfold. The black cloth still
allowed the light in but I couldn't make out any
shapes. The reason he gave it to me was to keep
the location of the cabin a secret, seeing as I
wasn't a fully-fledged member of 'The Moths' as
of yet. I wanted to explain that I was too far in to
give them up now but he didn't know me that well,
he never bothered to.
The truck ride was silent. Neither of us wanted to
make conversation and I guessed that Phoenix
wasn't a fan of radio. I listened to songs in my own
mind, wondering if he was doing that same. The
scent was making me dizzy. I almost passed out
but my overwhelming desire to resolve this riddle
was stronger. I had to figure out where we were
going and what the purpose was, even with this
disadvantage.

"We're here," Phoenix breathed, leaning over to
tell me.
It had taken maybe an hour or so to get to that
point. I still hadn't put the pieces together but I
wasn't in a hurry. Phoenix removed my blindfold
and I saw he was in his porcelain mask. Before I
could question him, he hopped out of the car and I
assumed to do the same. I got out, the scent even

198

stronger. Although the winds were cold, I could feel heat radiating onto my small body. I looked around. We were parked on top of a hill and when I looked down the crop of grass I could see a huge bonfire. It was bigger than anything I had ever seen. The red and orange flames were licking the sky, tasting the stars with every sizzle and crackle. It was screaming. The bonfire did not sit alone, it was surrounded by colourful people and they were chanting... No, they were singing. They were singing and laughing and drinking and having fun. I didn't expect this. This was not how I envisioned the Game at all.

Phoenix began making the awkward manoeuvre down the hill and I followed. The crowd got louder as we approached and the heat of the fire grew stronger. It was essentially a party, something you'd see college graduates throwing to overcompensate. As we walked through, I took note of the people. They were young and lively. Everybody I saw didn't look a day over twenty, so my theory wasn't entirely wrong. Tattoos, piercings, dyed hair, punks, goths, pastels, pigtails, lipstick, flannels… A diverse crowd. It took me a while to recognise it but they all had the same thing in common. They all had same-sex partners. We managed to get to the other side of the fire, to the boombox that was blaring old hip hop tunes. I didn't hear it when we were on the other side, these kids were almost as loud as the fire. Phoenix stopped the music and a couple of people stopped dancing and sucking face to stare. Phoenix left me standing in front of the fire as he whispered to somebody I didn't know. They had vivid green hair and the most incredible grey eyes. I couldn't decipher their gender, not that it was any of my business, I just knew I was attracted to them. They quickly disappeared over to the other side and I managed to get eye contact with Phoenix. His look was stern and mine was confused but somewhere in the middle, they both turned into wonderment. People started walking around the fire and over to us. The group grew larger as the North side was abandoned and the South piled on. People squished in as Phoenix made his way over to me, we were positioned at the front. Our backs were to the flames as we watched the youth turn their attention to us, like we were important, like we had something to say, like they had been waiting for someone to take charge.

The sound of screeching tires against pavement took over the roar of the fire and everybody's heads shot up the hill. There was a van and it wasn't stopping. It raced down the steep slope and I thought we were all goners before it stopped itself in time to pull-up right beside us. I sighed in relief, looking to see if anybody else was worried too but nobody had even flinched.

Liam jumped out of the driver's seat and Phoenix stumbled over, leaving me out the front. I had no business out the front. I tried not to obtain eye contact with anyone, watching Phoenix and Liam as they walked to the boot. I had no authority here and I didn't want anybody to think I did.

Black bags were the first things I saw as the boot opened. Black bags over the heads of the Moths' latest victims. Hands bound by ropes that were sure to leave bruises and blisters. Accompanying them were dirt-stained knees and the smell of urine. Maria and Tara had exited the car and were carefully watching the two bound men like hawks. I was starting to piece it together, the purpose of the Game being the men who Tara and Maria were now pushing towards me. I assumed they were going to pay for whatever crimes Phoenix deemed they had committed, much like Daddy had to pay for his. I felt unwell.

Liam and Phoenix took out boxes from the van. Small, pink boxes that looked like they could only fit a pebble or two. The boys began to hand them out to our audience, carefully slotted in the palms of the hands that weren't holding someone else's. The van had a whole abundance of these boxes, nobody was left out despite the large population of our party. As it was occurring, the black bags let out muffled cries. All I could think about was Daddy. Daddy used to be one of them and he was murdered, so their fates couldn't be far off.

Liam came and stood beside me, rubbing my back at the notice of my nerves. Phoenix, however,

201

stood in front of all of us, closer to the crowd; signifying he was the star. He was the one with something to say. It felt better being out of the spotlight but I was terrified for the horrors to come.

"I imagine you all received my letter."
The crowd giggled as if this were a comedy show and I had missed the joke.

"Thank you for coming, those of you who weren't scared off by our symbol anyway."
He was smiling, beaming, actually. The spotlight was where he truly belonged. He made his way to the men. They whimpered behind their material cages as they heard Phoenix's footsteps. Phoenix stood between them, turned around to face his audience and yanked off their black bags at the same time.

"Looks like we're not in Kansas anymore!" He exclaimed, throwing the bags to the ground.
I stepped forward, leaning in slightly so I could see their faces. I didn't recognise them. One was pale, skinny, bearded and maybe in his thirties. The other would've had to be fifty or so, his belly as round as a tire, his hair balding and his metal framed glasses smashed in on one eye. The younger one was crying, convulsing and sobbing as hard as he could without shame. The other appeared strong but disappointed, as if he knew this was coming.

"Glenn and Justin Martin, extended friends and family of a certain person who runs a certain religious church," Phoenix alluded.

I licked my lips and crossed my arms. I would be lying if I were to say I wasn't interested. Not recognising them made me want to hear Phoenix's speech. What had they done to lead them to this fire, this night, this man?

"Now, this particular church is known for its hatred towards the queer community. Not only that but they actively seek to protest against it and ruin our lives whenever they can," Phoenix sourly elaborated, projecting his voice to reach the very back of the crowd.

I looked at Liam, who couldn't help but return the gaze. My eyes were begging for him to explain where this was going but his eyes told me to wait. Most days I loved we could talk through our eyes, today was not one of them.

"Now the reason I present these radical hate mongers before you, some may say it's for revenge but I want to call it justice."

The young one let out a yelp of horror and Tara kicked the middle of his spine. He buckled over, his forehead against the ground as he continued to weep. The elder rolled his eyes and harshly whispered for him to 'take it like a man'. Maria jabbed his spine too and he yelped as well.

203

"Let me tell you a story. When I was a teenager, when I came out, my sister promised to take me to Pride. When we went, I was decked out in rainbows. I had painted them on my face, they were on my knee high socks and they were smeared on my shirt. My sister was proud of me. We marched together with hands held and chins high. I loved it. I had met two people who changed my life that day at the march who ended up walking alongside me and they walk alongside me now, years on. They ended up being some of my closest friends."

I reached for Liam's hand. Phoenix was pacing now, reciting his memories for the audience. I knew, too well, that his happy stories had not so happy endings.

"It was noon. The four of us had managed to sneak to the front of the march and I thought I would never be ashamed of my sexuality again. Nothing was going to ruin my day. Then I met Glenn and Justin... No, not formally. I met their harsh, rushed words and slurs as they stood metres away, spitting things and claiming things and cursing us on behalf of God. I met the flick of their wrists and the stones that flew out of their hands; the stones that met my face. Sharp, heavy stones that cut me and bruised me and hit my cheeks, my nose, my chest, my shoulders. I was being attacked by these men and I didn't even know their names.

Finally, a huge rock struck my temple and I collapsed with blood in my eyes."

He had excellent composure for someone recounting such a gruesome life event. I had the urge to go over and hold his hand instead of Liam's. All of it was news to me, I was saddened by the fact these strangers were learning something so personal he had not thought to share with me first.

"Luckily, I had an amazing doctor who took care of me. My sister and my new friends never left my side. They were worried I would lose my memory and I did, for a while. Rigorous brain training for months on end lead me to recall memories that slipped away during surgery; my sister's name, my place of birth, my pets, my sexuality and the hate crime that nearly killed me. These men, these human beings had the audacity to stone me. They tried to stone me in a public place when I was celebrating my pride. They were trying to hurt me for being who I was. And for what? God? Jesus? I believe in a world where God condemns hate and crime and loves all. Jesus would not want this. Jesus would love me no matter who I fuck," Phoenix screeched, "I couldn't let them get away with it. So I hired a lawyer. The best goddamn lawyer I could find and afford and he was good. He was so good. We made a case, we found out these horrible people's names and discovered their association with the church. We

were going to sue. We were going to put them behind bars. I didn't deserve the pain of the stones and I certainly didn't deserve the pain of having these men roam about like nothing had happened just so they could do it again to someone else."
I had forgotten about the heat of the fire and the sound of its flames. I had completely forgotten that we were surrounded by hundreds people. I was lost in Phoenix's speech and I could feel his aching from where I stood. It was overwhelming but I kept my feet on the ground. I feared the smallest movement would send me flying away with the breeze.

"Even the best lawyer could not persuade the judge or the jury. We lost the case and my pain never rested. Although these events took place years ago, I carry that pain around with me to this day. I can still see their vile faces and their pink boxes filled with their cruel stones and I remember every single harassing phrase they hissed at me. They didn't even know me but they hated me and that's what hurt me the most. I was wronged. I was robbed of my pride and now I want to rob them of theirs."
The world came back to me. We *were* surrounded by hundreds and they were *all* holding pink boxes that phoenix had passed out. It dawned on me what it was, what was happening. This was revenge, not justice. I had figured out the Game. I let go of Liam's hand.

Phoenix gave everyone a moment to swallow the information and to look inside their boxes and inspect their stones. There was a variety of different looks shared amongst themselves and with Phoenix.

"You have in your hands a stone. Either cast your stone or step aside. There is no judgement here," Phoenix explained.

"Phoenix," I whispered, shocked.
I stumbled over to him, grabbing the side of his arm. My eyes were pleading. This was wrong. The doors in his eyes slammed close and he jerked away from my grip. He walked away from the victims, Tara and Maria followed. I had no other choice but to step away too as the crowd drew closer and closer as they started digging out their weapons from their pink coffins.

"He that is without sin among you, let him first cast a stone," The younger captive screeched, tears fleeing from his red eyes.
A pitiful attempt at salvation. Bible passages were wasted on this crowd. He tried to save himself but in likeliness, dug his own grave.

"Fuck you!" A random man from the crowd cried in anger.
It was he who cast the first stone.
The others took no note either as the rocks came left right and centre to break their brittle bones. I gasped so loud my lungs could've collapsed. I couldn't see anybody walking away as the stones

were pelted at their bleeding, bruising bodies. I cringed when Maria started to help out and it broke my heart to see Liam pick up a stone. Tara laid back in the shadows, unsurprising for her not to participate. I wanted to talk to her. I wanted to see if she was close to puking as well. Instead of approaching her my eyes were greeted with something that distracted me. Phoenix had no stones in his rough palms and he wasn't even looking at the Game he had set up. His eyes were glued to the dust and dirt at his feet and his lips were dry.

Morality was twisted. If I was learning anything, it was that the world wasn't as black and white as I once thought. I could argue until I was black and blue that I was right because I had never killed anyone but the crowd could argue that they were right too. They could justify their actions by using the past actions of the men they were harming as evidence. Psychology made no sense and maybe Cillian *could* never teach it to me. All I knew is that everyone on the planet all thought they were right, nobody thought they were wrong and what a mess that made.

I watched as Justin and Glenn faded away into a mass of blood, snapped bones and discoloured skin. I watched as everybody inched closer, hoping one of their stones would hit the men and be the one that ends them. I watched as nobody in the crowd's face changed. They looked angry, pumped, thrilled, adrenalised. I watched as my own best-friend smiled when he heard the crack of a neck. I watched my own nightmare personify.

I saw Phoenix out the corner of my eye. He was leaving. He was making his way around the bonfire and back up the hill. I chased him but his steps were fast. He was at the top of the hill before I was. He climbed into the van and took off his mask. He sat at the driver's seat, staring out into space. I slowly walked over, observing him from the passenger window. He seemed so lost. He reminded me of myself.

I opened the door and hopped in, sliding into the passenger seat. I buckled in my seatbelt and looked forward into the fog and stars. I didn't want eye contact with him, it'd hurt too much. Everything I ever thought he was, everything I thought he'd never be, it was all a lie. It all came back to murder and vengeance and hate and extremities and that made me so sad. I was naive to believe his perception of 'right' was the same as mine.

He started the engine, strapping himself in and twisting the steering wheel. He got us back onto the road and then the highway. No words were spoken between us, just icy breaths. I was still so mortified. I curled up into a ball in my seat, trying to hold myself together. I closed my eyes and took deep breaths. I held onto my knees so tight as if I'd come undone if I let go. I was cold and I was scared. No wonder he didn't want me to come, I really wasn't ready.

It took an hour to get back home. It was the most uncomfortable hour of my life. I tried to go to sleep but the images of Justin and Glenn sprawled out, mangled on the grass, corroded my brain. I couldn't stop thinking of Daddy either. I couldn't stop thinking about his throat and the way Phoenix drained it. I couldn't help but picture Phoenix draining me of life as well. He was just so good at it. We pulled off the road and into the forest. The familiar height of the trees easing the tension slightly. A fair way in we found the cabin and parked right in front of it. It was the first time I had seen the front of my home. No blindfolds this time. As the car stopped, the lights turned on. I didn't move as he tore off his seatbelt and licked his lips the way he always did when he had something to say. I stared straight ahead as he twisted his body to face me. Out the corner of my eye, I could see his eyebrows raised. I suddenly understood he had nothing to say, instead he was waiting for me to speak and in classic Simon fashion, I couldn't bite my tongue.

"How could you..." I muttered, "How could you do that?"

"I think your trial is over," he bluntly said.

I see he did have something to say after all.

I turned to look at him in shock. The audacity to take me to a stoning and then force me to make a decision. In that moment, I hated him.

"Are you going to stay or are you leaving?"

I hated him. I hated him. I hated him. I hated him.

"I don't know," I choked, "I can barely breathe."

He nodded, keeping a straight face. He leant back, his back against the leather seat and one hand still gripping the wheel.

I didn't hate him.

"Phoenix, I think I lo-"

"We should have a vent circle," he interrupted me and I swallowed my words.

"Okay?" I frowned.

Before I could question him further, he got out of the car. I groaned and slammed my head back into the head of my seat. What was I going to say anyway? What would it have accomplished?

I jumped when he knocked on my window from the outside. When I glared at him, he smiled and gestured for me to hop out. I stepped out and he locked the car, the light going out and darkness consuming us. He grabbed my hand and entwined our fingers, pulling me along the cobbled path to the front door.

I knew what I was going to say. At the most inappropriate time, when my mind was filled with hate for this evil man, my mouth began to confess because my heart was aching for him.

Phoenix unlocked the cabin door and we hurried inside. He stopped me before I could retreat to my room, before I could become a puddle of tears. He hugged me.

xxvi. the bagman's eyelashes

The Oxford English Dictionary defines love as: *'A feeling or disposition of deep affection or fondness for someone, typically arising from a recognition of attractive qualities, from natural affinity, or from sympathy and manifesting itself in concern for the other's welfare and pleasure in their presence.'*

This was not lust. This was... This had to be...

I spent the whole day in my room. I wanted to stay under the covers for the rest of my life. I had never professionally been diagnosed with a mental illness but I knew I had one. Someone days were better than others but the bad days were really bad. There was something rotten inside me, eating away at my insides and gnawing at my happiness. Eventually I'd be hollow and empty. I'd be nothing inside. From the depths of my bed, I felt that wouldn't be the worst thing in the world.

Late at night, there was a knock on my door. I heard Cillian's soft accent from the other side telling me the circle had been set up. I had to get up. I had to get over it. There was still so much inside of me left.

In the rumpus room, I didn't know how to take in what I saw. The group were in a circle, sitting in dining chairs and bean bags and stools and pillows, an assortment of colourful and comfortable seats.

Candles littered the room, their scents overwhelming and their illumination bright. When I entered, everybody's head turned to me with expecting eyes.

Cillian lead me to vacant seats and we sat next to each-other, becoming part of the silent group. Much to my dismay, I was in a bean bag, I was below everyone. My eyes flitted around to the mellow faces above and around me, it appeared Liam and the girls had returned. It hurt to look at Liam but, at the same time, all I wanted was to hug him.

"We like to have vent circles every couple of months when things get hard and fear or stress take over. Unfortunately, we haven't had one in a year or so but I thought it was time, especially with Simon's inability to handle the Game last night," Phoenix explained.

I scoffed, not bothering to be subtle.

"Each person gets a chance to talk. You can say anything. Whether it be an issue bothering you now, something someone said that upset you, an event from your past, your views and opinions on something… anything. Say whatever it is you want off your chest. We'll move in a clockwise direction," Cillian elaborated, swooping in before I could make any snide remarks.

"Can I start?" Fetch asked.

Cillian nodded and gestured for them to go on. I leant back in my noisy seat and folded my arms,

214

intrigued to how this could operate without offending anyone.

"My boyfriend just got his pilot license. I'm so proud of him, it's something he's wanted for a long time. He won't stop asking me where I am now, though. He wants to be with me. I've told him my work is confidential, he knows nothing about what we do here, he's in the dark about the whole thing. The worst and best part is, he doesn't care. He's usually patient but now… We've been together three years and I've seen him once in person in that entire time. I don't think he realises it kills me too but what we do here is too important to give up on… But he's also too important to give up on. I don't know what to do."
A pause.

"After someone has taken a turn, others in the circle may offer a piece of advice, a compliment or words of comfort," Cillian added, filling in the silence,
I zoned out during the tumbling waves of compliments to boost the little one's confidence. Until it was my turn.

"Simon?"

"Oh, uh," I snapped my head up, staring at Fetch, "Look, who gives a shit about your boyfriend. What really matters is if you are happy. Your first priority should be yourself and your needs. Are you happy here? Would you be happier there? The best advice I can give you is learn to

make yourself happy because people, more often
than not. will disappoint you."
Probably wasn't the type of advice they were used
to, judging by the look on everyone's face. Fetch
didn't seem upset, however, they slunk back in
their chair with a look of genuine contemplation.

"I guess it's my turn," Liam cleared his throat,
taking control of the space.
I wondered what Liam would say. I knew
everything about him. I wondered what he'd deem
alright to share with everyone.

"I'm going to break up with Amy."
My face dropped. I certainly didn't know that.

"I don't want to talk about why or when or
anything. I just wanted to say it out loud. I needed
to say it. It makes it real. I have to go through with
it."
There was no one in the world I knew whose
problems didn't involve somebody else. We were
social creatures but we were also selfish. There
was no correct balance, we were all winging it.
The compliments began rolling in. 'I like your
eyes, I like the way you make sure we have meat
on the table, I like your hair', they were all basic
and meaningless. I'd kill myself if I ever sounded
as bland as the rest of them.

"Liam, I shouldn't have to say anything, You
know I love you," I shrugged it off.
I wanted to go back to bed. This was a waste of
time. Even if I wasn't in such a sour mood, this

wasn't my cup of tea. Liam appreciated my input despite my lack of effort and we all moved on to the next victim.

"I'm with Liam, I don't really want to talk for long but I do have something," Tara insisted, "I found missing files the day of our Debut when I kidnapped Henry... Temper... Whatever. They were about me. They were about my parents. They were about my brother. That's right, my brother. I have a brother…"

Tara relished in her praise but I knew her and I knew she was dying inside. The agonising confessions and agonising compliments went on but I zoned out again. They skipped over me when it was my turn to give feedback because, clearly, I was a waste of breath. I was ruining the event that was being held in my honour.

"Simon?"

I was startled by the call of my name. All eyes were on me when I returned to reality and it unnerved me greatly.

"It's your turn," Cillian urged.

I looked at Phoenix as he leaned forward, his chin resting on his hand and his soulful pupils looking into mine. My mouth went dry and I fidgeted in my seat. The whole night I was so against this system, this forced therapy but I found myself having a lot to say.

"I don't know what you want me to say," I admitted, "You want me to tell you that I miss my family? I have four sisters and a sickly mother who is probably worried to death. There's no doubt they heard about Daddy's death because the family were taking care of them and they probably think I'm dead too. Or do you want me to talk about how much I miss Daddy? The man everybody here hates so much even though Daddy did to me exactly what Phoenix has done to me. Daddy tore me away from my family and forced me to work for him and be part of his family, sound familiar?" Tension developed between the group. Phoenix's eyes stayed on my movements.

"How about the time I was a drug mule for three months? Three whole months of my life I spent learning how to make cocaine and heroin and subsequently sneak them across the border,. How about those three months doing Daddy's dirty work meant I lost the most important person in my life? And for what? Was he offended? Were his morals set too high? I loved him, for fuck sake, and I stuck around even when I was appalled that he murdered people, so why would he disappear because of drugs? People ask for drugs, they don't ask to be killed," I ranted, drowning in sweat, "He left and I screwed a lot of guys. I had sex everyday and I drank everyday and I regretted all I did as a mule. I couldn't tell if I wanted to wash away the taste of him or remember the colour of his eyes. I could've sworn they were purple even though that's impossible. Not like it matters. It's over now.

He's gone and I'm here. I'm here and I'm terrified because I watched two men get stoned to death last night and I'll never be the same. I am traumatised, I can almost taste their blood. It was brutal and immoral and inhumane."

Phoenix's brows furrowed into a line and I was having trouble catching my breath. He was watching me very closely. Something propelled me to keep going.

"I was a Bagman. I am a Bagman. Nothing should scare me," I emphasised, "Phoenix scared me last night and if I'm being honest, he's scared me every minute since I arrived. He's the only person I've ever been scared of."

I closed my eyes and nervously smiled, shaking my head. My voice had weakened and my heart was racing and the air felt as though it did not belong inside of me.

"But I guess that's just it," I exaggerated, trying to regain my confidence and strength in my voice, "Hopefully by the next Game, I'll be stronger. I want to be stronger for you. I want to be stronger for the Moths. I want to be stronger for you, Phoenix."

Now everybody was looking at Phoenix. I audibly sighed, bowed my head and twiddled my thumbs in my lap. I was waiting for their useless compliments. I felt I had run a marathon and their words would be more like a mouthful of salt than the water I desperately needed.

"My favourite thing about Simon is... his eyelashes," Phoenix breathed so carelessly and the whole room went silent.
Eyelashes.
He liked my eyelashes.

xxvii. phoenix's gambit

I stood underneath the heavy rainfall, the droplets becoming stowaways in my mouth. I lifted my face to the sky to let it replenish under the water. My eyes were shut and my hands were holding onto my arms. I was cold but I was not going to leave. I needed this.

"Simon."

I sighed and tilted my head to look at who called. I knew, I always knew, but nonetheless. I looked at who I found because I had found him, he had not found me. I found him in the very depths of my soul, the crevice of my weak heart, in the very lining of my tears. I found him everywhere, in everything, before I even met him.

"I couldn't find peace..." I mumbled, running a hand through my soaking hair.

I wiped the water out of my eyes so I could watch him walk over to me. I watched as the rain continued to pour and he began to dampen when he stepped out from the porch. He leant against a pole connected to the stairs, keeping a reasonable distance from me. He wasn't sure if he should touch me, considering all we had been through.

"Why'd they all disappear when you said you liked my eyelashes?" I sheepishly asked.

Phoenix didn't reply, instead he looked up at the moon with his arms crossed and his curls damp.

221

"They all began packing up and clearing out. You might as well have said cock or something. They wouldn't have freaked out as much."
He chuckled, his eyes returning to me and he yanked himself off the pole. I dropped my arms by my sides and stared at him, my eyes begging him to come over.

"Why did you have to say eyelashes?" I blubbered.

"Because I was being honest," he calmly spoke, "They say eyelashes are the most attractive feature of a human. It's my favourite feature of yours and to be honest, yours happen to be my favourite in the world."
He dawdled over, coming closer until he had his hands on my hips. He was hesitant, at first, to hold them but when I shuffled closer, he didn't think twice.

"What does it mean? It can't only mean you like my eyelashes," I asked.
Phoenix shook his head with that damned playful smile. There had to be another meaning.

"You know why they packed up, so tell me," I insisted, although a small part of me knew he wouldn't.
He wiped my dripping fringe from my eyes and left his warm hand on my cheek. He wasn't going to answer, he was never straight with me. I hated being right.

"Tell me about your past," I mumbled and changed the topic, giving up on that secret and moving to another.

"Did you just change the subject, without my help?" He cockily grinned, his hand slipping down to my neck.

I shivered and my breathing got heavier, slower.

"Yeah. Sitting in that circle, I wanted to hear your story and whatever's eating you up inside. I wanted to know about the love of your life, the one that got away. I wanted to know a lot of things and you still have the chance to tell me. Right here, right now."

"*You* are eating me up inside," he hazily replied. He ducked his head down and leant in. He kissed my cool neck and I couldn't help but let out a surprised, satisfied moan. He continued along my neck, drinking in all the raindrops that resided against my skin. The moan turned into a groan when I realised he was doing this to distract me.

"Phoenix," I breathed, my hand on his shoulder as if to push him but not pushing him at all.

"Mmhmm," he uttered with his lips travelling down to my collarbone.

"Stop kissing me and talk to me instead."

I was putting my foot down. I wouldn't let his lips coerce me any longer. Phoenix pulled back, straightening his back and trying to read me. He noticed my sudden air of accountability and smirked.

223

"That wasn't kissing. You think that was kissing? This is kissing."

He viciously grabbed both my flushed cheeks in his large hands and pulled me into his. Our lips touched and the moon exploded. My mouth on his was home. My hands dragged through his knotty, wet hair and I tugged on it as he kissed me. I latched onto him like dew drops on flowers and I never wanted to leave home. Life seemed to dissipate and my lips caught on fire every time we kissed.

I hated being drawn back to reality, so I pouted when he pulled away. He smiled at me and I removed my hands from the tangle he called curls and flung my arms around his neck. I leaned on him and with a shaky breath, I spoke again.

"Tell me about yourself."

"Maybe one day," he sighed, using his words to steer us away this time.

"Okay," I settled, his lips had successfully coerced me again.

"Are you going to stay?"

"What do you mean?"

"Well your trial is over," he shrugged, playing it cool, "Are you going to leave or will you stick it out?"

"I have to stay."

"Good," he breathed and with an air of sincerity, "I'm sorry about last night."

I actually believed him. He frightened me but that
wasn't his true intent. He wanted me to believe
they could salvage this wretched scrap heap known
as the world. He never meant to bury me under it. I
watched his curious eyes after his apology. I liked
this. There was no fear or turmoil here. It was nice
being close to him, our bodies only a chest rise
away and our eyes entwined like knotted cherry
stems.

"If you're staying, you have to get initiated
first," Phoenix softly mentioned.
Oh Christ, what would I have to do? Maybe I'd
have to sit another physical or theoretical exam.
It'd have to be multi-purpose. It'd have to include
all areas of my training from hunting to
psychology. This is what I had been working up to,
I had to prove my strengths and overcome my
weaknesses to get initiated, to be part of the crew,
to be part of the Moths. Maybe I'd have to organise
my own Game and carry it out. Maybe I'd have to
kill someone... I didn't think I could do that, at all.
Panic. I began to sweat and my eyes flitted around,
feeling nervous under this sudden declaration.
Phoenix pulled one of my arms down from his
neck and found my hand. He took my hand and
glided it in the air and placed it on his own chest.
My right hand rested flat on Phoenix's chest and
his hand stayed over mine to secure its position. I
could feel his heartbeat, I was right above his
sweetly beating heart.

225

"Repeat after me," he whispered, "I, Phoenix Jackson."

"I, Phoenix Jackson," I teased and he playfully nudged me, "Okay, fine. I, Simon Sullivan…"
The full passage went like this:

"Will dedicate my life to the Moths. I will put aside my past and endeavour in my future. I will love and treat each member with respect. They will be my siblings, my brothers and sisters. I will protect humanity and all mankind. I will deliver nothing but the truth. I will not discriminate and I will not corrupt. I will promote awareness to the public, no matter the cost. I will parade in stormy weather and thrive in sunshine. I will not let anything stop me, not even death. I am the Moths, we all are."

"I will also kiss Phoenix whenever I want even when there are people around because I want to and I know he does too," he cheekily added.

"I don't think-"

"I will crawl into his bed when I get nightmares, not Liam's, from now on," Phoenix interrupted my interruption.

"Hey, I-"

"I will deal with his mood swings and crazy ideas and random sex drives and murderous thoughts and changing attitudes because my heart is in it. I'm in it."

"I feel like this isn't what you got everybody else to say," I cockily retorted.
I took my hand off his chest and crossed my arms, my eyebrows raised at him. He wasn't playful anymore, though. He was serious and his eyes had begun to water. I regretted moving my hand away from his heart.

"Simon, I'm in it," he repeated and he grabbed my hands. He held them so tight and his eyes were screaming commitment and all I wanted was to feel his heartbeat again.

"Phoenix…"
He kissed me again and I felt his heartbeat through his lips. I had forgotten about the cold and the rain. All I remembered was him. All I felt was him. All I was, was him.
This was love.

xxviii. new plans

"Has anyone seen Phoenix?"
The documentation was scattered across the table.
Nobody was paying attention to me as maps and
blue prints were laid out. I sat down to join them,
but they all continued to ignore me; continuing to
arrange items and talking amongst themselves.

"I haven't seen him all week and I'm worried,
you know? And every time I ask, somebody
changes the-"

"Looks like we're all here," Nicholas boomed,
interrupting my panic.

"…Subject," I muttered, folding my arms.
I couldn't understand why they were being
secretive. After the night in the rain, I thought
things between Phoenix and I would be different.
At the very least, more open and honest. Yet he
had run away from me again and gotten his goons
to avoid talking about it too.

"The next Game is in two days. It's bigger than
the last one and it's all hands on deck. Everybody
needs to participate for it to work," Nicholas
continued.
He stood at the head of the table, leering over
everything and everyone as if we were his
children. People had started taking their seats,
giving him their full attention. I knew I wouldn't
be able to concentrate until I got my answer.

"Before we get into this, can somebody please tell me where Phoenix has been?" I spoke up before Nicholas could go on; I wanted to know, I needed to know.

"Oh for Pete's sake, Simon!" Fetch hissed, twisting in their chair to glare at me, "He's been at his other house all week."

"He has another house?" I frowned.

"Yeah, he left on his motorbike on Monday," Liam shrugged.

"He has a motorbike?!" I gaped.
Liam rolled his eyes and turned his attention back to Nicholas. Phoenix was living a double life and nobody was willing to fill me in until now. I couldn't believe it. Nicholas had opened his mouth to begin again but I cut in.

"Hold on a minute," I grumbled, "You wouldn't let him drive the van alone last week and now, suddenly you're all fine with him driving his motorbike by himself? For an entire week? What the fuck?!"

"Calm down, Simon," Cillian insisted, looking at me with his gentle eyes that could ease a hurricane.
I took a deep breath but still waited for somebody to answer me. They knew I was stubborn when it came to that man, somebody was bound to crack first.

"That was before he said he liked your eyelashes," Tara carelessly replied, "So we let him take off on the motorbike. He hasn't been in like over a year... He deserves the downtime."
I didn't want to argue any further. I was still unaware of the significance of eyelashes but there was no use asking again. I had enquired too many times for it to be considered okay now. I would have to accept the meaningless answer and move on.

"Banks," Nicholas felt it was safe to continue. I had to let go.

"Banks?" I questioned.

"Banks," he confirmed, "We're going to blow up the banks."

"Seems a bit dramatic," Maria scoffed and Nicholas scowled at her.

"Not all the banks," he rolled his eyes, "Just Kingdom-State Banks in Washington DC."

"Why those particular banks?" Cillian asked, straightening his glasses.

"Their cruel insurance policy is what killed my Rose," Nicholas bitterly explained.
I had heard this all before.

"She filled out a form ten years prior to her hospitalisation," Nicholas began.
He started it exactly the same way he did when he washed me for the first time. I remembered it clearly. Nicholas raised my leg from the depths of the water and placed the soapy sponge on my

230

upstanding hairs. He began to scrub my skin, watching my leg glisten as he spoke.

"Everything she wrote in it was legal and honest except one thing. She lied on the smokers section. She wasn't a smoker, she hadn't been since she was young but she failed to mention she was. It was only four months of her life she took up that filthy addiction and she was only fifteen, she gave up before her sixteenth birthday. She had a hard childhood and she didn't think bringing it up on her health insurance forms was a necessity," Nicholas continued, switching legs, "Alas Kingdom-State Banks disagreed. When Rose was hospitalised and needed treatment, she had called the bank to make sure it was all in tact. Instead of helping her, they were going to end her insurance due to a technicality. A worker discovered Rose's lie after going through her old doctor reports from when she was a teen and had told her GP she was smoking. Kingdom-State Banks refused to pay for her surgery because smoking was the leading cause of lung cancer although she hadn't touched one for decades! They were going to send her to her grave because of one mistake."

"That's cruel," I had mumbled, shifting my position in the bathtub.

"They gave her an offer. They could revive her contract, if she would fill it out again without missing any gory details. Rose mailed and paid for her new insurance and waited. Well, we waited.

231

We waited and waited until one day Rose started to code. I was crying as I watched the other doctors take over. She survived but she was weak. Not only were her lungs crumbling but her heart was in shreds as well. I called the bank, I told them that we had to do surgery that week if she was going to live any longer. You know what they said? 'Our insurance policy requires the patient to have had the insurance for at least eighty days before it can take action. We're very sorry but we only just received her information.' What a joke."
I felt so sorry for Rose. I felt so sorry for Nicholas. He dangled his wet hands over the tub, his head down as if it was taking all his energy to retell the tale. I knew what it was like to lose someone but not in the way he had. To be in love so deeply only for them to fall, I hoped never to experience it. Sparrow was enough of a heartache but there was still a chance he was alive.

"I begged the chief of surgery to do it pro-bono, I begged for him to let me pay for it myself if we couldn't do it for free. I told him how much I couldn't lose her, I admitted she was the love of my life and I couldn't see me coping without her. I needed her, I couldn't breathe without her. My confession only lead to me being fired. Patient and Doctor relationships were strictly prohibited. My heart was crushed but even more so when I came in three days later to collect my things only to find my Rose had died."

Nicholas was a reasonable man, some would even say sane but I knew better. He was the deadliest of all of us. A silent man who plotted before he would strike.

"So we're going to blow them up and expose them that way?" Liam confirmed, sitting forward in his seat.

My reminiscing made me miss a few parts of the conversation but Liam's voice snapped me back into reality.

"Exactly," Nicholas smiled right back.

"How are we going to do it, doc?" Fetch enquired.

"There are twelve Kingdom-State Bank centres in the DC, including two or three skyscrapers. We're going in pairs and we're going to hit one or two each... Sarah and Fetch, Tara and Maria, Liam and Cillian, Simon and Phoenix... I'll be by myself as I've got a better shot going solo than anyone else as I've organised the operation," Nicholas elaborated.

Nicholas made eye contact with me after announcing this. He knew I'd be happy to go with Phoenix. A small part of me believed that he deliberately paired us just to get a smile out of me. I was looking forward to this operation now. No-one was getting hurt and I got to spend the night with a vague mess of curls.

"Phoenix and Simon will take the motorbike, I'll be taking the truck and I've hired vans for the other teams. Tara has done us the curtesy of crafting the explosives. She will talk you through them now and then, I'll map out what buildings everybody is hitting, where they are placing the bombs and how each team will escape,"

Nicholas let Tara take over but I zoned out.

I should've been soaking up every word so I could repeat it back to Phoenix but I had no energy to reengage. I was useless. It was Phoenix's fault for leaving me alone. He was meant to be my eyes and ears here. I watched Tara although I drowned out her words. I missed Phoenix and I couldn't help but think about him.

xxix. the revolution

On the night of the next Game, I had fallen asleep.
It wasn't on purpose, I was just so tired. I had spent
the past few days learning the routine of that night
inside and out. I stayed up at ridiculous hours to
learn the floor plan and where X marked the spot
and what to do if someone caught us. It was
exhausting but so was the will to survive.
Everybody was leaving in their pairs and yet,
Phoenix was still nowhere in sight. I was starting
to panic. I had asked Nicholas where the he was
and when he'd come. Nicholas had rubbed my
back and smiled. He very patronisingly told me to
wait in my room and Phoenix will come when he
comes. Nicholas left shortly after and I was left in
the cabin all on my lonesome. So, I went to my
room and I sat on my bed and I watched my open
door. I didn't even realise I had fallen asleep until I
was rudely awoken by a rapping on my window
like Poe's raven at midnight.
I slowly fluttered my eyes open, gripping my
sheets up under my nose as I looked over to the
window. A silhouette, a shadow lurking outside
with their knuckles against the glass. I would've
panicked if I had not recognised the rings on his
fingers or the mop of brown hair that caught the
moonlight. I scrambled out of bed to the window,
unlocking it and pushing it up. He leant against the
sill, his head ducking under the glass so he was

halfway inside. I folded my arms and stared at him.

"Is the front door too mainstream?"
He chuckled under his breath and shook his head.

"Can you just crawl through, please?"

"Ooh I don't know it's past curfew and my parents are in the next room," I teased.
He hastily grabbed my hips and yanked me down to kiss him. I smiled as we kissed and panted when we stopped.

"How about now?" Phoenix breathed.

"I suppose for a pretty boy like you," I giggled. I made the awkward manoeuvre through the window and ended up tripping into Phoenix's arms... Not that I was complaining... He helped me to my feet and we shut the window together. He started to walk towards an opening between the trees and I followed. We halted when we came across the infamous motorbike of his and I crossed my arms and gave him a look.

"The bombs were meant to be set up hours ago, you're late," I grumbled.

"Luckily I set them up hours ago myself," Phoenix grinned, strolling over.
He threw a leg over and positioned himself at the front of the bike. He took the handle bars in his hands and then bobbed his head behind him to gesture my participation. He was always so mischievous and mysterious, I never knew if I

should take him seriously or laugh off his snide remarks.

"Then what the hell are we doing?" I groaned. I still strolled over and hopped on the bike, grabbing hold of his sides out of fear. He leant over to the other side and picked up a helmet that had been placed on the ground. Phoenix tossed the helmet to me and urged me to put it on.

"What about you?" I hissed.

"Not that important," he shrugged.

"Of course it is! Go grab one from inside if you have to, I can wait. Please."

"Simon, shut-up," he growled, "It's my only one and I want you to wear it, put it on so I can start the engine."

I didn't argue, I was too scared to. I strapped the helmet on and wrapped my arms around him like a koala bear. He started the engine and it purred and meowed and my heartbeat was rapid. We took off through the trees; a lightening bolt in the night. I couldn't help but laugh with joy, I had never done this or felt like this before. I held onto him closer and tighter. I'd never breathe normally again. Eventually we broke out of the forest and onto the highway. I was salivating from the adrenaline. After a while of twisting and turning and changing the roads we were on, we were in the city and we were in deep. I was afraid of being recognised but when you're going so fast Newton's Laws do not apply, you tend not to look the same.

We pulled up on a quiet street, under a lamppost where the light was broken and left us in the dark. I crawled off the bike as did he and we stood on the sidewalk. He faced me and helped me take off my helmet, putting it on the handlebar and letting it dangle.

"Follow me."

And I did. I followed his jutting back down two blocks and a half before we turned down a street called '*Pennsylvania Avenue*'. I wasn't paying attention as we dawdled along the cement path. It wasn't until Phoenix physically had to stop me and turn me around to face the magnificent building that I realised where we were. The White House. I swallowed my own tongue as I stared at the neoclassical structure in which that grubby President resided. He smiled at my awe and strutted to the gate, hinting I should follow. I thought he was going to attempt to climb over it or dig under it; either way he'd end up getting shot. I walked over to him as he examined a small mechanical pad at the side of the gate that was flashing with red lights. If I knew anything, red wasn't usually a good sign. He was just staring at it with one hand in his pocket. He looked scared.

"I don't know if this will work," Phoenix sighed, pulling out a small plastic card with a barcode smeared on it from his pocket, "Sarah already deactivated the alarms, she just couldn't deactivate the gate so... Here goes nothing."

Phoenix swiped the barcode against the pad and it started flashing green. Phoenix began to manually pull back the gate and it worked, it was unlocked. He yanked it open enough for us to squeeze through without anybody noticing and he shut it behind us when we were on the inside. We were trespassing. At any second a security guard could find us and kill us on sight. This was terrifying but it was also thrilling. Phoenix had to stop getting me into these predicaments.

Phoenix and I crept over to the garden wall. We stood amongst daffodils and daisies. We stood before rose vines that clung onto a flimsy net-like picket fence that climbed all the way to the roof. My sneakers dug into the soil when I saw him sink his claws into the vines, through the holes of the long fence and I realised what he was doing. We were going to climb up the thorny fence, up to the roof. I audibly sighed, I knew him too well but he ignored me as he started his venture, I would have to reciprocate. The fence was bouncing off the wall as he made his way to the top. I was quite impressed with his ability to climb without breaking the whole thing. Once he had made his way to the roof, which he scrambled onto in such a hurry, he leant over the edge to hold out a hand. I didn't hesitate to follow in his footsteps. It was a lot harder than he made it look but I was smaller than him so the flimsy structure wasn't as close to falling apart as it was for him. My hands got stuck on thorns and made them bleed and the knees of my jeans were fading but when I got so far as to grab his hand, it all felt worth it. He yanked me up and I collapsed on the roof.

The roof of the White House was not where I thought I'd end up that night. It felt like it had happened in a blur, one moment I was asleep and the next we were here. I was lying down on the roof of the White House, I couldn't get over it. I was living. I couldn't help but burst into laughter at the ridiculousness of circumstance. Phoenix laid down beside me, laughing with me as we observed the sky. We were watching the flicker of the stars on the rooftop of the White House. I'd never tire of saying it. It had to be the most magical and insane moment of my life and it was all thanks to him.

"We can't see the explosions from here," I breathed after we had settled down, "They'll be going off any minutes now but there's not one for miles from here."

"You're not meant to," he sweetly replied, "You're meant to imagine it. You're meant to feel it."

I laid still, eyes glued to the balls of light in the navy sky. I tried to imagine the explosions, the destruction of the banks. I imagined skyscrapers imploding, crumbling in on themselves until they became nothing but ashes in the wind. I imagined the sound, the ear-shattering pitch of the bomb as it

240

went off. I imagined what the bankers would say when they woke up for work the next morning. I closed my eyes and drew a deep breath. I smiled, something shaking my bones. It all made sense now. It all felt right.

"I can smell it," I said.

"What? Money burning?"

"No," I smiled wider, "the revolution."

He took my hand and held it tight. His exhale was shaky like mine. The moment meant as much to him as it did to me.

"Phoenix, you make me feel like Sparrow never existed."

Phoenix brought my hand to his lips. He gently kissed the back of it before returning out entwined hands to our sides. I could still feel his cold lips even after he had pulled away, his touch forever cemented on my skin. He made me want to be a better person.

Riding home, I felt my wings outstretch and brush against the wind. My arms around his waist was the only reason I wasn't going to start flying. I wished we could've stayed on that roof forever. I wished we could've cuddled until we starved. It was too perfect but perfect had to end some time. When we got back to the cabin my wings folded in as the engine died and our feet touched the ground to hold the bike up. I tore off my helmet and he twisted his body to face me for a second. In that second, he smiled and I knew I was sold. For the rest of my life, he was going to give me wings and I would be sold. We hopped off the motorcycle and I hung the helmet off the handlebar again. He took my hand as we wandered through the dark to the front door. Before he could open it, I stopped him and he turned back to see what my issue was.

"My favourite colour is red and I'm always cranky when I wake up. The song that means the most to me is *Heroes* by Bowie. I've kissed so many people I've lost count. I've never killed anyone and you know that now. I don't have a big secret, at least I don't think I do. My saddest memory is Sparrow leaving and my happiest is now laying on the roof of the White House whilst holding your hand. I prefer inside than outside, bath than a shower. Yes, I have issues with identity... My whole life and everything I know about myself has been torn away from me twice now, how couldn't I? Yes, I hate myself and yes, I'm capable of hate. Everything makes me cry and I fight for you and my family. I fight for Daddy, for the life that you took away from him. Also I'm not sure if I've ever been truly in love but I'd like to think so..."

I exploded with information, something I had been holding in since he snapped at me the first time he washed me in the bath. I had so much to say, so little time.

"Phoenix, I want you to know me. I want you to know the real me not the person you read off a file," I added.

He paused for a second and then laughed. He was still smiling so widely, so brightly, when he took my face in the palm of his hand.

"My full name is Phoenix Nathan Jackson. I was born in Cheshire back in England although we moved to the States when I was young. My favourite colour is orange. I haven't killed as many people as you think I have, definitely less than ten and I've only had two people who have kissed me in my lifetime. My sister's name is Jen and I fight for her. I fight for her and my mother and everything I left behind after the stoning at Pride. It changed me and I like to think for the better. I've met so many wonderful people because of what it spurred inside me, I wouldn't have the Moths without it. The man who abandoned me, that I loved, who everybody is always gossiping about, was my lawyer on the case. That's all I'm going to say for now. One day you'll get the whole thing but this is just a taste. I don't want to be the man that killed Daddy to you, anymore than you don't want to be a document I stole to me."

I was finally getting somewhere with him. I nodded and he opened the door and we strode inside. I felt liberated, I felt cleansed, I felt new. We made our way to the rumpus room where everybody was still awake and waiting for us. We were gone for so long the probability of them only just waking up made more sense than them waiting up for us. The group were all sitting down, huddled around a television screen that was playing old re-runs of sitcoms. They looked dreadful, cuddled together with droopy eyes and cracked lips. They were awake this early for a reason, though, they were waiting for something. There was only a single couch available for us to join in, so Phoenix threw himself on it and got comfortable and pat his legs to gesture I was welcome. I curled up on his lap, holding onto his shirt as I rested my head against his chest. I drifted off to sleep quite easily, unable to hold on for whatever they were expecting. I dreamt of the White House, of the roof and of his kiss.

I only got an hour nap before I felt the sun on my face. Phoenix rubbed my back as the rest started to screech with delight. My head shot up, my eyes wide open and I looked over to the ecstatic group. I glanced over to the television which everybody was drawn to. It was seven in the morning and there was a News report flashing before my eyes. The news explained how all Kingdom-State Banks in the DC area had been blown up as a terrorist act by known criminal association, the Moths. The reporters theorised that the attack was targeted at the President, reason being that investigators discovered the Moths' tag on one of the back wall's of the White-House. The President made no comment. Reporters went on to say that luckily nobody was injured or killed in these attacks. We did it. We won.

I started to laugh with joy as did everybody else. I jumped up and down and yanked Phoenix up. I took his hands in mine as we laughed and swayed together. He spun me around, as if we were dancing and I felt so at peace. I stared at the others. I watched Maria and Tara kiss, Fetch and Sarah laugh together, Liam and Cillian passionately embrace. I watched Nicholas, still sitting on his chair with heavy tears rolling down his face. He had avenged his Rose.

We weren't terrorists. These people, my friends; we weren't terrorists. We were the embodiment of justice. We may have put a lot of people out of jobs but we had also enlightened them to the corruption they had been blind to. We were the Moths and we would never surrender and what we were feeling now was why.

xxx. his body

Things were settling down after the Game. We were all riding out our highs. Everything was falling back into normal routine and it'd stay that way until the next Game. People were keeping to themselves; Liam was hunting and collecting food for us, Tara crawled back into her shed everyday or into bed with Maria, Nicholas would stay on his laptop all day until he had to prepare us dinner, Fetch played their video games and Sarah did whatever Sarah usually did, I wasn't exactly sure about her. Cillian and I hung out a lot as everybody else was busy, we'd watch movies or just talk and it was nice. Phoenix went away a lot but came back every night and slept in my bed. It was innocent. We never did anything. He slept with his arms around my body like I was his favourite teddy bear. It was nice.

I checked the bathing roster to see who I was washing and I found something that made me smirk. I was washing Phoenix. Phoenix was always the washer not the *'washee'*. Whenever it was his turn to take a nice steamy bath, he washed himself and got it over with. Nobody was allowed to see him until he was out and squeaky clean. I grinned wide when I read the schedule. He put me on there for a reason and I prayed to the God I didn't believe in that this meant I would finally get laid.

246

I waited for him at the bathroom door. I leant against it with my arms crossed and my foot propped up. I was so excited, I had to stop myself from drooling. When he stumbled down that corridor with those tiger eyes, I almost tripped on the air. I walked a couple of steps to meet him.

"Not here," he shook his head.
Did he know my fantasies? Is that what he was referring to?

"In the lake," Phoenix added and he bobbed his head toward the rumpus room, "I want you to wash me in the lake."
I followed him into the rumpus room and out the large glass doors. We trod on the fresh crop of green grass and wandered into the forest. I marched behind his back, further and further into the woods where the birds stopped singing and the flowers stopped growing. Eventually we hit the small clearing that sat at the bank of the small river.
He moved out further, kicking off his shoes to feel the soil sludge between his toes. I licked my lips as he tore his shirt off and the sun bounced off his back, as if it was embedded with diamonds. I watched his glittery exposed chest as he continued to undress. He dropped his pants and I tried to remain breathing when he took the fabric of his boxers between two slim fingers and slowly began pulling them down his lanky legs.

I watched Phoenix, naked in the meadow as he strode toward the lake and slowly emerged himself in the glimmering, cool water. When the water was up this chest, he ducked under the surface to wet his hair. He turned around to face me, pushing his hair from his face and smiling at me. He beckoned for me to join him and I was *certain* I was getting laid today.

I hastily tore off my clothes, my caramel skin bathing in sunlight and Phoenix's stare. I made my way to the lake and I couldn't stop smiling. I put a foot in, the water cold but refreshing. I continued until I got to Phoenix's depth and he grabbed my hips from below and pulled me into his body. I chuckled as my legs wrapped around his waist and my arms flung around his heavenly neck. I pushed our lips together and rested my forehead against his, water dripping into our eyes.

"Thank you for existing," he breathed.

"I wouldn't be here without Daddy, you ought ta thank him. Oh wait," I cruelly teased.

He scoffed and broke our bodies away, floating aimlessly against the stream.

"Don't forget Daddy also forced you into becoming a drug mule," he grumbled and I rolled my eyes.

"Sounds crazy but I loved the butterfly feeling when I successfully finished each trip without being caught," I explained.

I had never talked to anyone about it before. It was refreshing to finally open up about it.

"Where'd you even go?" He asked, floating back to me.

Phoenix swum behind me, his hands wrapping around my shoulders as I leant back into his body. It felt so peaceful.

"Thailand and then Bali," I confirmed.

"You're fucking with me," he said with disbelief, "After all that commotion about the Bali Nine from Australia? How did you do it?"

"I was one of the lucky ones," I shrugged, "I was so successful because the people before me weren't. I'm glad I never got caught like them."

"Well I'm glad you didn't or else I wouldn't be able to do this," he muttered, pecking at my neck with his soft, wet lips and I couldn't help but smile again.

His kisses were everything I've ever wanted and yet, an uneasy feeling was nagging at me. I was being pulled away from what I had been chasing.

"Their punishment is inhumane," I added, my mind still stuck on Thailand.

"You don't deserve it and nobody else does. Does nobody believe in rehabilitation anymore? The Bali Nine had ten years to their name. People change a lot over ten years, people change a lot in just ten days. It was cruel and unfair not to offer them another appeal. If I believe in one thing, it's that everybody deserves a second chance. We're all capable of changing and rehabilitation," Phoenix elaborated.

I lost my smile, frowning in confusion instead. The feeling was staying and more prominent now.

"Hold on," I mumbled.

I spun around in his arms and he reciprocated my frown upon seeing it. I ran a hand through my hair and looked at the naked, enigmatic boy.

"Then why do you kill everybody that annoys you?"

He slowly edged away from me, as if he'd been shot and he was clearing space for the pooling of thick, red blood. No blood tainted the water, only malicious stares. I had called him out on his hypocrisy and he wasn't used to anybody doing that. He was genuinely stifled, scrambling for a response.

"The people I kill, they're the initiators. They're the ones who don't grant the second chances to those who deserve it. They implicate the lives of millions without remorse. Take Justin, for example, him and his dad single-handedly changed my life when they cast their stones and they didn't think twice. They took their prejudice out on me without thinking. People like that, they don't deserve a second chance. They're selfish, they're the real killers, not me or the people who missed out on rehabilitation," Phoenix defensively argued.

"Well then so am I? The drugs I delivered and exported from Thailand and Bali not only complicated but implicated the lives of their consumers. Drugs are harmful, Phoenix, just as harmful as people throwing stones, the people who take away the rights of the LGBT, dodgy insurance policies that kill, the murder of people of colour, the mafia, misogynists, whatever.. So, why don't you kill me? I'm an initiator. I didn't give second chances to the people I sold drugs to and I probably ruined all their lives. I'm as bad as the rest of them. Kill me."

Phoenix went silent at my speech, his face twisting in horror. He knew I was right. I was a mafia child and a drug mule. By his philosophy, I should've been on the Moth's hit list, not on their team. I was evil to anybody with common sense but not to Phoenix. Phoenix couldn't kill me even if he wanted to, even if he agreed with me.

"I don't want to talk about this anymore." Phoenix hurried out of the water, accidentally splashing me as he passed. He grabbed his clothes and began to pull them onto his drenched body, only resulting in getting them soaked as well. He tried combing his knotty hair with his fingers but it ended tragically and he grew frustrated. In his agitation he turned back towards the lake and shot a glare at me. He parted his cranky lips as if to speak but said nothing. He looked as if he was a

251

rugged pirate staring at his sinking ship. I was unsalvageable.

I thought maybe I could speak up, protest his anxious getaway and demand he hop back into the water. Yet, when I parted my lips to speak as he did, I found myself doing the same thing. My words got caught in my throat and disintegrated. Phoenix was being melodramatic, he was being surly and he wasn't worth the breath. Phoenix couldn't keep making exceptions for me off the slim chance that he was in love with me. I was an enemy but this whole time he treated me a friend. I wasn't sure I could handle it anymore. The least he could do was stop pretending and accept my past but also recognise my future as a hero not a villain. Phoenix swallowed it all down and hurried away. He left through the forest and I watched his shadow disappear until it was composed of rustling leaves.

Totally *not* getting laid.

xxxi. eight months

Dear Journal,
That sounds tragically cliche and as much as
I wish I could return to the unorthodox
scribblings or astronomical doodles inside the
margins, I must emit my emotions somehow
and since I sound smarter on paper than I do
when I speak, I must project it on these pages.
Phoenix hasn't been home for a week. Well
when I say home I mean this imprisonment
they call a cabin that I hold dear to my heart.
He hasn't been heard of since the mishap at the
lake and I worry his disappearance is linked to
my foul temper.

- Simon

~

Journal,
Two weeks on the clock. My silver tongue has
cursed my rotting heart.

- Simon

~

Journal,
The credit goes to Phoenix Nathan Jackson for
the encapsulation of my heart and soul but he
is not using his achievement wisely. Instead
he's run off because I said something that hurt
his stupid feelings and quite frankly, it feels
like he's holding a grudge. Grow up, Jackson
and come back home. It's been one month and

you're wasting valuable time that could be spent on future Games or fucking me, just so you can prolong a temper tantrum.
We need you here not on the pages of my journal.

- Simon

~

Dear Journal,

My fingers are covered in paint that smudge against the pages. Splotches of purples, blacks and reds inking up my skin because instead of having sex, my recreation is art. I paint such dreadful things at the back of my journal. Images of death and blood and sorrow taking up pages that I could write on about such things. If I had half of Phoenix's guts, I'd seek him out. I'd find out where he's been hiding and confront him. He probably took off on his motorcycle to that secret house of his... Cillian told me specifically to be brutal to Phoenix and so I was. I was brutal when I told him he might as well slaughter me like he slaughters everybody else but clearly he couldn't take it and that frustrated me. What a baby and I just let him walk away? Maybe I'm the baby. Anyway my plan is to confront him and tell him he's being a baby. A murderer acting like a baby. The thought makes me laugh. Maybe I'll paint that next.

- Simon

~
Love is an illusion, the feelings impossible to prove.
~

Journal,

Liam took me out for a drive today. It felt nice to break free from the forest for a little while, even if I wasn't allowed to exit the confines of the car. He had to go grocery shopping, so I stayed buckled in the passenger seat as he took thirty minutes to get in and out and load the truck. As I sat, sat and waited, a little girl wandered into the car park. She appeared lost and yet, naively happy. As she weaved in and out of the cars in her blue dress with a doll in her hand, she managed to maintain a smile. Sometimes she would skip or sit down to take a break and talk to her doll. Her rosy cheeks and pigtails let me assume she was no more than five. I looked hastily for the parents every two minutes. How could they let this beautiful, oblivious girl walk the streets alone? She was clearly clueless of what life was like and needed to return to their embrace. I wanted to exit the vehicle and help her but I was under strict instructions. When Liam returned and got into the passenger seat, I told him about the girl and went to point her out but she was gone. She was gone. Phoenix is gone. My eyelashes can't fix this now.

255

- Simon

~

Journal,
I've lost count of the days and every inch of me
is aching. Everybody I talk to can see the
misery in my eyes and the carelessness in my
actions. Liam is gentle about it, trying to
nurture me like a child. Tara is mean, she
thinks I need to get the fuck over it. I was
something before him so I can be something
after him as well. She reckons he'll be back
anyway, he's not going to abandon The Moths
just because his crush said something stupid.
Tara is right, he'll be back and I should
toughen up but I hate this waiting and the not
knowing. I hate that he has such a power over
me. I hate that I miss him and that I miss
kissing him and holding him and him, him,
him.
Him.
Just take me back to lying on the rooftop of the
White-House.

- Simon

~

Journal,
I hung out with Maria today. I never do that
but she insisted. We watched Stanley
Kubrick's Clockwork Orange and as much as
Phoenix's moral compass and murdering
enrages me at least he wasn't Alex. She could

tell I was thinking about Jackson, there's just some things you can't fake. She says that he'll be back in time and will welcome me with open arms. I told her I'm not all about that and that I miss my family and Daddy too, to make it seem like I wasn't so desperate.

She told me that she misses her ex boss who died and left her all that money, the one who was like a father to her. I don't know why I never talked to her before, our situations are so alike. Her slaver become her father figure as Daddy was to me and we both missed them tragically. At least now I have someone to mourn to about that but I'm still mourning Phoenix.

- Simon

~

Journal,

To think I was finally getting somewhere with Phoenix and he goes and pulls a stunt like this? I opened up to him and he opened up to me and we were finally happy. If my comment is the reason he left then his mental stability seriously concerns me.

Why do none of his friends know where he is? It has been so crazily long I'm beginning to doubt he even existed.

Don't be distracted, Sullivan.

- Simon

~

Dear Journal,

I had no idea that the first Game was a little over my one year anniversary of being their prisoner and soon, in two months, it'll be two years. Is it crazy that all I want is for Phoenix to come back and celebrate it with me?

- Simon

~

Journal,

The President has one more year left of presidency. He can't run again as this is his second time in office. I worry that Phoenix is going to let it slide. I worry that all his hard work will just diminish if he lets the President run his course until the next sack of crap comes along and messes things up more. I seriously wonder whether Phoenix will ever come back, for me, for The Moths, for justice. Whatever happened to fighting against this white, cishet, racist, homophobic, xenophobic rich old man? There has to be another Game, there has to...

- Simon

~

Journal,

Absence is meant to make the heart grow fonder and it has for me. I'm not sure whether the leader of our democracy feels the same about me. I crave laughter and I crave contact. I crave everything he has to offer. I can't handle weeping myself to sleep in Liam's bed anymore or spending the day in the shed even when Tara isn't there just to get away from everyone. I can't handle not having orders or someone to guide me, I hate not having a task to carry out. Sometimes I watch Liam hunt or Tara document files or play video games with Fetch or whatever to distract me from this undeniable pain of having him be gone for so long.

I've become absent-minded in Phoenix's overwhelming absence and I don't want to fade away. Daddy would kill me if he found I was dating another Sparrow. Phoenix was so much like Sparrow now.

I'm getting bruises from pinching myself so hard but I'm not waking up.

- Simon

~

Journal,

This group love me and that's all that should matter, right? These wonderful, gorgeous, self-righteous people want to make me happy and I feel as though I don't give back enough. To celebrate my two years, they're arranging a dance - like a high school prom. This would be something I'd find beautiful if I was under any other circumstance than I was now. I hope in two days I can pull off the happy thing,

even if it's a lie. I want to dance away my
heartbreak. I want to relax and be at rest.
It is unlikely I'll ever be at rest from this pain.

- Simon

~

Phoenix, I'm sorry about the journal entries
and needing you.

~

xxxii. lithium

"I need to learn to be faithless."
I mindlessly rolled the rubber end of the pink
balloon between my fingers as I stared through the
glass door in front of me. I watched the
harmonious sway of the forest and I wished I were
a tree. Everything would be so simple as a tree.

"If I was faithless, I wouldn't be so upset all the
time," I added.

"I think you're getting faithless confused with
heartless," Fetch muttered, "Pass me that balloon."
I sighed, holding it up high for them to grab. They
stood on the highest rung of the step ladder,
stringing up balloons for my dance tonight. They
took the sightly deflated balloon from my hands
and tied it with the others. I grabbed another one
from the packet and began blowing into it.

"Faithless people don't care about the hearts
they break or who breaks theirs. They just don't
allow theirs to get broken, full stop," I spoke
between breaths.
I tied the end off and passed it to Fetch. This
boring, monotonous routine only sparking my
sadness. Fetch wasn't letting me indulge in these
feelings, however.

"That's not true. I'm assuming when you mean
faithless you mean people who cheat or who are
home-wreckers or people who constantly have one
night stands."

261

"No because I used to have one night stands, it didn't mean I was faithless. I was in mourning because the person I was faithful to abandoned me…"

"Simon, whatever the case, they're still human and they still have feelings. They're not robots, I'm sure their hearts break sometimes," Fetch protested, sick of my whining.

"Maybe I need to start sleeping with people again or drink myself into a coma. That's how I handled it last time and then Phoenix came along and put me in the same situation. Fuck, I need sex," I bitterly scoffed.

"Shoving your dick into someone isn't going to help... Neither is wishing to be faithless. That's stupid. So shut the hell up and help me out. The other decorations are in that box over there," Fetch demanded.

They pointed to the heavy box that sat besides the television. I groaned but did as they wished. Before I could get to it in time, Liam had raced inside and beat me to it. I punched his arm when he took the box in his hands and lifted it up. He chuckled and I rolled my eyes. We stumbled back to Fetch as they were hopping off the ladder. I threw myself back in my chair as Fetch took the decorations and repositioned the ladder so they could reach above the glass doors. Liam stood beside them as they hurried to the top step and started handing them the paper lanterns and decorative stickers and tinsel and whatever it was they wanted to light the place up with. This whole charade was stupid. Liam looked nice, though and it gave me dirty thoughts.

"Where have you been?" I asked Liam.

"Just Phoenix's other house," he shrugged; oh so casually.

"Oh, here we go," Fetch groaned, seeing my reaction without even looking at me.

"Simon, before you say anything, calm down," Liam laughed at my shock and shook his head, "He wasn't there nor was his motorbike but the bread in his cupboard was fresh and it smelt like coconut in the hut instead of the usual horrid scent the moisture brings and his bed sheets were unmade and warm. I'm assuming that's where he's been camping out but he must've been out when I stopped by."

I was so *angry*. I had never felt such rage in my life before. It almost felt like betrayal. I had trusted Liam, he was my friend and yet he had been lying to me this whole time. My fists automatically clenched and my throat was burning. It was like I was choking on acid.

"You knew where the house was… this whole time, you knew…"

"Simon, if he had wanted you there he would've taken you."

Liam was terrible at defusing any tension. I knew he probably meant no harm but my heart was

263

screaming, telling me he hid this from me with malicious intent. I wanted to fight, to punch him square in the face. I could feel my fists trembling, ready to pounce.

"Or he would've assumed you'd tell me and take me," I rebutted.

"Simon, leave it alone. I love you but Phoenix left for a reason and he left you in the dark, all of us in the dark, for a reason. Let it go and start getting excited about tonight."

"Will Phoenix be there?" I shakily questioned, "Tonight, will he be there for the dance?"

"Probably not," Fetch croaked.
Liam was silent, guilt-ridden. He couldn't bring himself to answer the question. Instead, he wandered over to me and reached out his hand. I eyed it off with pouty lips and a sinking heart before I decided to take it. He hauled me onto my feet and pulled my body into his for a hug. He kept me close to his chest and buried his head into my shoulder. He clenched hard onto the fabric of my t-shirt. I was worried if he let go, I'd fall apart. I hugged him back, letting out an exasperated exhale, hoping it'd ease the weight I kept inside. He stepped back and placed a hand on one of my shoulders. I swallowed hard, ready for the pep talk.

"I know it hurts but he'll be back. Even if he comes back and wants nothing to do with you, there are people here who want *everything* to do with you. We want to be the cause of your happiness, not your pain. Look at Fetch go, they are working so hard to prep this dance for you. All the people who dance with you tonight are celebrating your presence here and they're going to smile at you and compliment you and reminisce with you because they love you and appreciate you. We all do. Forget about Phoenix, even if it's just for one night and focus on us. No, even better... Focus on yourself," Liam passionately spoke, trying to ease the burden he had accidentally given me.

The anger had finally subsided. It wasn't replaced with ease or happiness but emptiness. Liam could give me all the motivational speeches in the world but until Phoenix was in my arms again, I'd never be at peace. I'd have to pretend for the night.

"Hey, what are you doing after the dance tonight?" I asked.

"Not sure, why?"

"Don't fall for it!" Fetch exclaimed, "He'll just persuade you into having sex with him so he can stop wishing away his faith!"

"You speak from experience, Fetch?" Liam chuckled and I did too.

"Shut up," they rolled their eyes and jumped off the ladder, "For that you have to help me vacuum and move the furniture."

"Whatever you say, kiddo," Liam grinned, "Simon run now before they take you too."

"Guess the sex is off," I teased.

"Please, there's no chance in hell I'm missing getting a piece of that," he joked and I was smiling again.

He told me once that he was bisexual and in the state I was in, I was sure I could get that joke to become a reality. That being said, I wasn't sure if our friendship was one that could handle sex. It was definitely something I had thought about. He was tall, built, attractive and brooding, some of my favourite elements to a man. I felt guilty thinking about it, even with Phoenix out of the picture. Maybe I could control that guilt in future but for now, friendship was all I needed from Liam.

I hurried outside and started heading for the shed, still pondering the pros and cons of having sex with my best-friend. I saw Tara disappear out that way earlier and I could've used her company. She was a friend I definitely wouldn't be tempted to have sex with. So I followed the shrubby path with an aura I hoped was cleansing.

The shed came into my sights and I wasted no time scurrying to the metallic door. I went to to open it but it was locked. It was never locked when either Tara or I were inside and I swore Tara was there. So I knocked and I waited for a response. When I received nothing, I knocked again with a furrowed brow but still nobody answered the door. I went to get the spare key from under the mat but I heard the sliding of chains and the door creak open. I stopped and looked to the door. It was open just a

266

crack with Tara's face peering through but her body hidden behind the metal. Her cheeks were vividly coloured and her hair askew, her eyes wide and glossy when she stared at me.

"What's the go?"
She rushed her words, an air of secrecy shrouding her.

"I wanted to hang out."

"Ah, Simon, it's not the best time," she puffed as if she was out of breath.

"Okay?" I frowned. "What's going on?"

"Uh... Well..." She quickly glanced back behind her before returning her attention to me, "I'd tell you but I'm not sure Maria would appreciate it."

"Maria? Oh god, I'm so sorry," I blushed, looking to my feet.
So much talk about sex and missing sex, I forgot people actually had it. I was somewhat jealous. It must be nice being married.

"It's okay, just a misunderstanding. Come back later?"

"Well later the dance will be on so... forget it. Have fun, I'll see you then."

"Yeah, bye," Tara panted before slamming the door in my face.
I sighed and turned to depart, feeling foolish for embarrassing myself like that. As I started walking down the hill, I saw something shiny out the corner of my eye. I halted and slowly turn to face it. My heart wasn't sure whether to elevate or sink.

A sleek motorbike with a helmet dangling off the handle bars. Either Maria was cooler than I thought she was or... Or Tara was a liar.

My steps became more cautious as I continued through the forest and back to the cabin. My head was racing with insane and painful thoughts, the image of the bike burnt into my brain. As the cabin came back into view and I could see everything clearly in the rumpus room through the glass, it was only then the latter was confirmed. Maria waved at me through the window and I waved back.

He was back and I wasn't faithless.

xxxiii. Simon and Phoenix

I watched the movie '*Big Fish*' for the first time
when I was twelve. Tim Burton was one of my
favourite directors, telling stories so unique and
bizarre that they were captivating. My favourite
part of that movie was when Edward Bloom meets
his future wife and promptly says - 'They say
when you meet the love of your life time stops and
that's true' and then everything stands still.
Everybody was frozen in time except young
Edward as his eyes transfixed on this marvel of a
woman across the room. Edward moved towards
her, pushing past the statue-like humans, walking
through a hoola-hoop, brushing popcorn out of the
air to get to this beautiful woman. It didn't last long
until time sped up to return to its natural order and
the woman disappeared but Edward's heart
remained set on her. The reason I was thinking of
that movie was *not* because I met the love of my
life at the dance. The paper lanterns and fairy
lights that hung above our heads illuminated the
room a pale pink colour, although setting a
romantic tone, did not make me fall in love. The
fruit punch could've made me see someone in a
different light, but it didn't. Not to mention the
way everybody looked so happy as they danced
amongst each-other and chatted and laughed,
dressed in their nicest most formal attire. I could've
laid eyes on someone and instantly had known.

Considering there were people here I had never
met before that Liam assured me were on our side,
that they were members of The Moths from
different bases. Two years in the movement and I
had no idea we had other bases. So it was more
than possible to fall for one. I could forget about
Sparrow and Phoenix and let myself fall.

Yet I recalled '*Big Fish*' because when the dance
was over and I was helping Fetch clean up, I
noticed somebody I had *already* met and time
stood still. Fetch stayed hunched over picking up
empty paper cups with a clump of used streamers
in their spare hand, Liam stood still at the opening
of the hallway and Phoenix... Phoenix posed on the
porch, back to me with fingers tracing his lips and
not a curl had bounced. I manoeuvred through
frozen time to clamber out onto the porch and
stand behind him. I took deep breaths. I knew it
was his motorcycle, I knew he was back.

I stayed still as if the silence had taken me too,
beside a wooden table with a boombox proudly
sitting on it. I saw this as an opportunity and found
a track I liked. When the music started to play so
did everything else.

Time brought itself back up to speed and I found
Phoenix turning around to see why *The Smashing
Pumpkins* had began to sing to him. When time
stopped for me, it wasn't the first time I had seen
the love of my life. The reason it stopped was
because I was seeing the love of my life as the love

of my life for the first time and that was close
enough. Almost a year apart and I had finally
accepted it, that this crazy, selfish man was who I
wanted to spend the rest of my life chasing.

"You missed the dance so I thought I'd bring the
dance to you," I lovingly whispered.
His face lightened as I walked over to him. I
melted into his body and we became one.
Colliding, I draped my arms around his neck as he
squeezed my waist with tender hands. He gazed
over my features; double, triple, quadruple times,
checking every inch of my face like he was scared
he'd forget even just a pore if he were to look
away. He had missed me too.
My breaths were shaky as we started to sway to the
rhythm. I was dancing with Phoenix Jackson. The
world was okay again.

"I think I've missed more than just the dance,"
he solemnly replied, guilt twanged his voice.

"I know," I whispered.

"I'm sorry," he whispered back.
I said nothing more as I rested my head against his
chest. I felt overwhelmed to hear his beautiful
heartbeat again. He was safe and alive and he was
with me. He was with me, after all this time. I
never wanted to let go in fear that he'd vanish
again. I didn't even want to speak in case I'd scare
him away.

"I've been thinking about what I want," he
mentioned.

271

Phoenix took one of his hands from my hips and raised it so he could stroke my matted hair. I bit my lip to stop myself from crying, closing my eyes and gulping hard. I loved his touch and the sound of his voice.

"And what do you want?" I sheepishly asked. He didn't reply. We continued to dance under the light of moon and faint glow from inside. I could have lived like this, if only he could've too. I rose my head from his chest and looked up at him. I liked to see his pale face up close, with his sunken cheeks and chubby nose and pink lips and wondrous green eyes that stared right into mine. He smiled when he realised my gaze was wistful.

"You know I'm not gay…"
His laugh cut me off and I couldn't help but grin when I heard that sound. I wanted to drink it up from the air. I had made him laugh with a dumb joke and it was the greatest thing I had accomplished in months.

"Defiant and naive until the end, aren't you?" Phoenix continued to laugh.

"Shut up!" I giggled, "I was going to say that even though I'm not gay... Well... I was just letting you know that…"

"Spit it out," he cockily insisted, hand still playing with my hair.

"You could kiss me again... if you wanted to." His smile dissipated and I feared he was next. Instead of vanishing, he brought his trembling hands up to my cheeks and our eyes connected and I thought, maybe, he'd stick it out this time around. Phoenix leant in close, his hot breath heating my awaiting face. Our lips clashed together and I could feel his heartbeat pulsating through them as we kissed. Electrifying. Magnetic. The kiss was everything. It was everything to me.

Suddenly I wasn't standing on a creaky porch in the middle of the woods somewhere in Washington but I was floating amongst the stars. No, I was soaring through them as they fell away like melted butter whenever I went to touch them. Twirling. Spinning. Although there was no atmosphere and I could barely breathe so high above the Earth, I knew that I'd be okay. We'd be okay. My hands crawled up his neck and into his knotty hair. I tugged at it and rocked my body into his as my tongue longingly slid across his and down his throat. His hands returned to my hips, drawing me closer, although there was no space left to conquer. I was taken away from the Galaxy and brought back to Earth as Shakespeare writing his very first sonnet. Oh, how the words sprawled across the parchment as if they were going on a sunny evening stroll. Then I was Oscar Wilde, another highly admired writer and poet but I wasn't him when writing his killer plays, no, I felt I was him when he first kissed Master Alfred Douglas. Oh, how the gates of a world he never knew existed flung open and how he belonged there so very

273

much. He loved that boy no matter how much he took from him or how many times he went away. Phoenix soon lifted me from the floor and I couldn't help but haul my thighs up until my legs were wrapped around his waist. He turned us around and walked towards the wall until my back was pressed against it. Our lips didn't once part although the buttons of the grey vest I wore over my white dress shirt did. He leant a hand against the wall beside my head for support, as the other one held me up. Although, I was doing a good job at clinging to him like a monkey.

From the universe to magnificent writers to a ruler of the sea. I became a pirate, the captain of my own ship. Not just any pirate but Sir Francis Drake, a pirate doing Queen Elizabeth the First's biddings. I was coming face to face with the Spanish Armada, sending them crumbling with each blow in my radiant knighthood. I was the sea dog, the Spanish enemy, the king of the sea. Phoenix broke the kiss but kept me against the wall. We both were panting, eyes shut with our foreheads touching like the way we used to do it. The kiss was everything but so was I.

"Are you ready for the next Game?" He questioned.

I tried to regain my breath but I couldn't muster up enough energy to reply. I let him assume my heavy breathing was a 'yes'.

"We're going to kidnap the President."

I was Simon Sullivan; scared and confused.

xxxiv. just

He only just came back and I felt I was losing him
again. My head was pounding with the worst
headache I had ever experienced. I rubbed my
temples, wondering if there was a painkiller for
migraines and heartbreak.

"Fake IDs, passports, birth certificates, driver's
licenses, you name it and I've collected it,"
Phoenix grinned.
The Moths sat on the edge of their seats as they
listened intently to Phoenix's maniacal whims. I
gulped hard, my elbows against the table as my
head remained in my hands. With my eyes shut, all
I could focus on was my pain and wish that it'd go
away. I didn't even care about the Game at all.

"Tara is bringing them down from the shed as
we speak. I was with her yesterday, mapping this
all out."

"What exactly is the plan?" Nicholas howled, he
was also skeptical.
The group were agitated. Phoenix had only been
back a day and he was unloading such a heavy
burden on us. It didn't help that he was being so
vague about his extravagant ideas.

"I met up with a girl named Nicola while I was
away and she works in very close contact with the
President. Now, I've known her for years and she's
quite charming and upon seeing me she foolishly

exclaimed she'd do anything for me if only I'd stay a little longer…"

Great. This magical Nicola was the reason for my despair. I slumped back in my chair, watching the leader. I imagined him fucking this image of Nicola that I had conjured in my mind. I felt ill, unsure whether my headache was causing my nausea or if it was my imagination.

"Nicola helped me the first time we tried to kidnap the President. In our soiled youths, we had ruined the capture but I believe it's due to naivety, lack of members and our irrational impulsivity. If we had waited, mapped it all out before we jumped in right away... If we had formed a relationship, if we had done it from the inside out then maybe... Maybe we would've gotten away with it," Phoenix explained, the passion in his eyes the size of the moon.

"So what did Nicola do for you?" Liam huffed.

"One night while we were clubbing we shared a couple of martinis over the bar. She may have had one too many and started blubbering facts I really shouldn't know. You see, she's the President's secretary, she had been promoted since last I saw her. She told me she was taking a six month holiday soon and the President was looking for a qualified stand in and that it was up to her to hire one. He said he wouldn't trust anybody but the one in the position now. She also told me because of the Kingdom-State Banks scare the President's personal assistant was fleeing the state. He simply packed his bags and buggered off, leaving this beautiful window open for anyone to grab. Now the President simply cannot survive without having a shadow, somebody to take his calls and give him snacks. So, he's in serious need of a PA and a secretary. Luckily for him, two have just become available," Phoenix cockily elaborated, the thrill in his tone something of a five year old boy at an amusement park.

"Lucky for him," Liam muttered under his breath and I couldn't tell if he was mocking him or he was genuinely in awe.

"So who's going to be the secretary and who's going to be the body-man?" Maria enquired.

"Did you just say 'Bagman'?" I snapped my head at her.

"She said body-man, actually which is the term they use for personal assistant," Phoenix replied, "Funnily though, you still responded."

"Oh great, no, of course," Cillian snarled and folded his arms. "Of course it's him."

"What did I do now?" I scowled.

"He's not the body-man yet," Phoenix responded to Cillian, completely ignoring me.

"Not only am I a trained psychologist and the most qualified person for the job but you have emotionally manipulated Simon to the point of instability. He is not fit to be participating in any Games right now. You abandoned him for no good reason. You can't expect to come back, play the loving boyfriend and for him to jump into your next dangerous mission because he will and thats torturous! He loves you so much that he is willing to do anything for you right now if it means you won't leave him again. How do you not see how toxic this is?" Cillian hissed, harshly defending me, unconcerned about any consequences.

This room was always falling silent. Phoenix was shocked at Cillian's uproar, finally realising that our relationship dynamics and us, as individuals, had all changed since he last saw us. We now had the courage to stand up to him, well, most of us did. Cillian was glaring at him with such stern eyes, Phoenix appeared not to have anything to say back.

The glass door behind us slid open. We all turned to watch Tara walk in with mass yellow envelopes in her little hands. She had no idea of the argument she had walked in on. As Tara started laying out things on the table, Cillian hastily got up and left the room. Tara didn't question it, arranging the documents for everyone to have a look at.

"I've secured the secretary job, considering Nicola was in charge of the hiring for that I didn't even have to meet the President. Although, Nicola has arranged an interview for Mr. Atlas with the President himself, in regards of the PA job," Phoenix got back into the groove of his announcement.

I reached for the envelope closest to me, looking over the driver's license in particular. There was my face, startled like it was a mugshot in the corner of the page. I looked over the information, sure enough my alias was David Atlas and I was the one who had to impress the President.

"Phoenix, he knows me. If not my face, my voice... This isn't going to work," I groaned.
I threw the license back on the table and I rubbed my throbbing temples again. Everything was so loud and confusing. I didn't want to be in that room, at that table. All I could think about was Cillian.

"Simon, that was two years ago! He would've forgotten you by now. Do you know how much happened that night? You mean nothing to him."
His words rippled through me like a bullet, leaving me bleeding and gasping for air. It was hard not to read into that statement. What a fucking asshole.

"Thanks for clearing that up," I swallowed hard.
I rose from my chair, every step I took chipped in to making my headache just that little bit worse. I was happy, though, to get away from that room.

"Simon, what are you doing? We're not done," Phoenix hastily called out for me.
I stopped at the opening of the hallway and turned around. I had a blank expression on my face, although on the inside, my blood was blistering and boiling.

"If you were gone for two years, would I have stopped meaning something to you?" I calmly asked.

"What? I-"

"Am I so easily forgettable? You seemed to forget all about me in just shy of a year. I thought you came back for me, Phoenix. You only came back for more bullshit you call justice," I roared, unable to keep my cool, "So play your little 'Game' Phoenix but I refuse to be involved. How dare you ask me for this favour when you did nothing favourable for me in months."

Phoenix's heart shattered in a way that could only be displayed on his face and the way it dropped. I didn't want to feel sympathy for him after all he did to me, so I hurried down the corridor before I could feel a thing. I locked myself in my room. I started scrummaging through my things in hopes I'd find aspirin or paracetamol or a narcotic of sorts. Anything to wash a way this terrible pulsation that scraped along my skull. I felt my brain would burst. I needed sleep.

There was a knock on my door.

"Go away, Phoenix," I shouted but flinched at my own loudness.

"It's Liam," The knocker uttered.

I stumbled to the door and unlocked it. I walked over to my bed and crashed on it. Liam opened the door and closed it behind him, sighing when seeing me in such a state. I wanted to cry.

"I know you're going to go through with it anyway," he said.

He made his way over to me and threw himself down on the bed. I grumbled because I knew I would too. He reached into his pocket and pulled out a packet of aspirin and I almost cried with gratefulness. Cillian was right. I was a dumb boy with abandonment issues. I'd do it for Phoenix, if it meant he'd stay.

"I'm going to give you a pep talk anyway because I'm great at those," Liam teased and I rolled my eyes.

I quickly scoffed down the pills and rested my head upon my pillow. He played with my hair, trying to soothe my pain until the medication kicked in.

"I saw you kissing on the porch last night," Liam mentioned.

"I was caught in the moment."

Liam grabbed my legs and pulled off my shoes and socks. He started to rub my feet to loosen my tension. I closed my eyes, relaxing.

"Simon, you love him. We all know it. He loves you, we've all known that since the eyelash thing... Now he's asking you to take part in the biggest Game of Moth history. He wants you to right his past wrongs. He wants to deliver history with you. He doesn't hand his work over like that lightly," Liam explained, "He didn't forget you these past few months. I'm sure he thought about you every night but it killed him. That kiss was all the thoughts that broke his bones brought to reality. Phoenix is my friend and I know he wouldn't have left without a good reason. Now he's come back and he's pumped for this Game and he wants you to be too. I know you're upset but you'll regret it if you don't hold his hand through this."

"I know," I murmured as he continued to massage my feet, "But I'm afraid and lonely."

"You'll never have to feel lonely again as long as me or Phoenix or Tara are here," he smiled.

"Appreciated... So when's my interview?" I asked.

"Next week. I'll tell Phoenix you're still in this. We'll go over the Game plan over the week, okay?"

"Okay."

"I'll let you rest."

"Okay," I repeated, feeling sleepy.

Liam put down my feet and headed for the door. As he opened it, I called his name and he stared at me with curiosity.

"Tell Phoenix to come here."

When he left and Phoenix returned in his place, all I could do was start crying. Phoenix crawled into my bed and slid in beside me, wrapping me up in his embrace as I weeped. He brought the blankets over our bodies and without a word, I fell asleep in his arms with his lips playing softly on my neck.

Words are pointless. Arguments are pointless.
Anything is pointless when you could do this
instead.

xxxv. David Atlas

It would be a solstice day. I couldn't tell if it was winter or summer but nonetheless, this would be either the longest or shortest day of my life, metaphorically speaking.

I tried to keep my breathing under control as I sat in my navy blue suit, the tie was done up so tight around my neck I thought I'd choke. I tapped my fingers against the armrest, foot tapping on the marble floor. I kept looking around the high-ceiling room, sweat dripping down my brow.

"Calm down," Phoenix murmured, patting my jotting knee.

As if what he was demanding was that easy. My documents were shaking in my hands, I wasn't coming back from this. Either the President would kill me or I'd kill myself; I couldn't wait to find out.

"You've got a persuasive charm. People meet you for the first time and they instantly like you. I know I did," Phoenix grinned.

I glared at him, "This isn't the first time I've met him. Do we need to go over this again?"

"Make him believe it is. Just steer away from Simon Sullivan, the on-call Mafia boy and lean more towards the sweet Mr. Atlas, the missionary who's suddenly sparked an interest in politics and aiding the President, yeah?" Phoenix insisted, "Probably shouldn't mention the Moths either."

"I'll see what I can do," I, David Atlas, assured him.

I had to think the part, not just act it. I was going undercover for at least six months, method was the only way to be convincing. I had to become this humble, religious man who lived and preached the good life. A man even the President would respect. The cream-coloured door opened and a woman stepped out. She had a clipboard in her hand and a pen behind her ear which was almost bombarded with her fraying light brown waves of hair. She smiled at us, her eyes matching her hair. She had to be who I thought she was. Only a fool would turn her away if she requested to stay a little longer. It didn't mean I'd forgive Phoenix though…

"David Atlas," she called, very professional. Phoenix and I stood up and he walked me over to the woman.

"David, this is Nicola," Phoenix formally introduced me to her.

"It's good to finally meet you," Nicola beamed, "Vince talks about you all the time."

She outstretched one of her olive-skinned arms and I politely shook her hand. Vince was Phoenix's alias. Vincent Dakota, the new Presidential secretary with a background I couldn't even remember. It all felt so unnecessary, I felt no need to retain that useless knowledge in my memory. I had a job to do, that's all I needed to remember.

"We're quite close," I replied, jealousy getting the best of me.

"I bet! Unfortunately, though, he isn't allowed to come with you for your interview. This is where we leave him," Nicola explained, her perky tone infuriating.

I turned to Phoenix and he could see I was uncomfortable. He stroked my hair and smiled, devoting his attention to me.

"I'll be waiting here and when you're done we'll take off on the bike, yeah?" Phoenix assured me.

I nodded and he gave me a quick kiss on the cheek before taking root in one of the waiting chairs again. Nicola bobbed her head towards the hallway and so I followed her through the daunting door.

I was so nervous as she shut the door behind us and we started walking down the hallway towards the President's office. What if he saw through my charade? What if he did recognise me even after two years? What if I mess up somehow and ruin Phoenix's entire plan?

"Simon, are you sure you want to do this?" Nicola asked, all the happiness in her tone was gone.

"What?"

I was startled, why was she using my real name? And why would she ask such a thing?

"I trust Phoenix more than anyone in the world but I wouldn't trust him on this. I'm worried about you."

"You don't even know me!" I snapped.

I wasn't even angry that she was trying to befriend me, I was being defensive of Phoenix. They were supposed to be friends, he had just spent the last year with her and she had the gall to backstab him now. It was a betrayal all over again. It wasn't even mine but I was angry nonetheless. All that time he could've been with me, he had wasted on someone he couldn't even trust.

"I know that you're in love with him," she shrugged, "I know that you think doing this for him means everything, but Simon, your life means more. If you get caught it's game over and I don't think Phoenix will protect you."

"I think we should stop talking about this now," I hissed.

We had reached the glimmering double doors of the President's office and had come to a halt. She restrained herself from sighing, shaking it off and forcing back a smile. She was glowing again when she held out her hand for another handshake and I took her up on the offer, despite my unease around her.

"Good luck, Mr. Atlas," she said, "Until we meet again."

"Until we meet again," I repeated, hoping we never would.

Nicola opened up the doors and we proceeded inside.

"Sir, this is David Atlas for the interview," Nicola addressed the President.

There he was. The man who was making me sweat like a pig in this formal attire. He was hunched over his mahogany desk, his blazer strewn across the back of his chair and his hands resting on his temples. He was pouring over something as the sun poured over him through the window. It shone on him like he was God when, really, as he looked up, he looked nothing more than a common man. He immediately stood up and gestured for me to take a seat on the other side of his desk. I obliged and as I sunk into the hard wooden chair, I could hear the click of the closing the door. Nicola had left us alone. He sat back down but returned to his papers, like he had to finish up. I looked around the room, soaking in sights I had only seen in photographs. The yellow curtains were horrid as were the designs of the couches in the middle. The flowers on all the tables were all dying in their dusty vases and I even noticed one of the paintings on the wall was placed upside down. The only thing in the room the President seemed to care about enough to look after, was the American flag behind him.

I cleared my throat but not out of anxiety, out of demand. I wasn't nervous or paranoid anymore. When I looked at this feeble old man, I didn't see power but fear. He was terrified. I didn't bow to the terrified. I would not buckle for someone as weak as him. His office was in shambles, a good indicator that he was too. So, I demanded the attention, I was going to prove to him that he needed *me* and not the other way around.

"Mr. Atlas, are you an impatient man?"

"Yes," I bluntly answered.

That made him look at me again. He pushed his papers aside and put his hands together on the desk. It had certainly gotten his attention, time to make sure I didn't lose it.

"I apologise for testing your patience," he replied.

"I accept the apology."

I passed him my documents and he looked over them. As he inspected my resume and qualifications, I tried to watch for any clues in his movements as to who he was. His reactions meant everything.

"Not many have the guts to stand up to the President."

"If I can stand up to you it means I can stand up to anyone, including those who stand in your path. I'm perfect for the job," I pitched myself to him. The President moaned in contemplation, putting the papers down and leaning back in his chair. He watched me intently, probably trying to get a good judge of character as I was for him.

"It isn't good to be impatient in this job though."

"I'll make it so," I insisted, "Besides this job requires someone to be fast on their feet. An impatient person is always quick to act."

The President thought about this, narrowing his eyes on me, "I've seen you before. I've heard your voice. I swear…"

"I was Daddy's nephew," I confirmed his suspicions.

Phoenix would kill me but I knew what I was doing. I was taking the direct approach. I was going to be direct and blunt and brutal. If it worked on him, it could work on the President. Honesty wins a heart over, at least that was the theory I was risking my life over.

"How could I forget?" He nodded, recognition flickering over his face.

"It's exactly why you need me."

He started to laugh and shake his head like I was being ridiculous, "If I hire you and somebody finds out you were from Daddy's family, my career would be ruined."

"Luckily you only have one year left," I crudely stated.

"I suppose," he shrugged, "Nonetheless, a year is a year."

"I want to help you."

The President burrowed his brows, leaning forward, elbows on the desk, still unsure how to read me or the situation. I continued to look him in the eye, unafraid.

"Why? Why does somebody from the mafia want to help me?"

I stood up, re-adjusting my blazer and walking over to the bookshelf. His eyes followed me, I could feel them. It was a pleasant surprise to see that amongst political biographies and priceless ornaments, on the shelf was a worn-in copy of 'The Godfather' by Mario Puzo. I picked it up, flipping through the pages and smiling to myself.

"I have been out of a job since Daddy died. I have been trying to find somewhere my skills can be put to use but it's all below me. I am worth more. I can do more than what they're delivering. You may not be the mafia but you're the second best thing," I lied, not looking up from the book.

"Flattering."

I snapped the book shut and turned to him, throwing it on the desk before him. He looked concerned by my outburst but didn't alert the guards. I walked back over to the desk, standing over him, looking down on him, making him small.

"Shut up and let me talk," I snarled, "I am smart and I do what I'm told and I'm quick on my feet and that's what you need. We all know politicians lie, there's nobody who understands that more than me. I lied to get here, to get this interview. I'm not David Atlas, I'm not a goddamn missionary. I'm far from it but I'll be him if you want me to... If the

292

public, your voters, want me to. I followed Daddy around day and night and not once did I question him. That's what you need. You need someone who will follow you and feed you and lug around your brief case and accompany you on flights. You're pretty much hiring me to be your best friend and your mother and your body guard and your chauffeur and your travel assistant... You want me to be everyone in one and not to question you along the way unless you ask to be questioned. That's what David Atlas has to offer, so let me be David Atlas for you."

The President wormed around in his seat, looking away from my stare. I decided it would be better to sit back down, let him take control of the room again. He settled after that.

"So you're saying that because you're used to being fucked over by the scum of the planet, it makes you perfect for the job?" He frowned, "And even though that fact should make me *not* want to tell you any secrets or trust you with anything, that it's that exact fact that allows me to trust you?"

"Basically."

A beat. He reorganised himself and took a moment to think. Eventually, he chuckled and I smiled with him.

"Ha, I like you, Atlas."

"I haven't even told you about my work with the Moths and how I'm in love with your biggest threat," I cheekily added, testing the waters to see how much I could get away with.

The President started to heartily laugh, rising from his chair and I followed his lead. The interview was over. He wandered around the desk and we shook hands. He guided me to the door, his face red with laughter.

"Have you read the book?" I asked, gesturing to the table.

"It's my favourite," The President smiled. With a firm pat on the back and another handshake, I figured I had done just fine. He opened the door, the golden doorknob shining in the sun's reflection. I stepped out into the hallway and shared a final look with him.

"Nicola will call you in the next week or so to let you know if you got the job," The President informed me.

I knew I had the job already.

"I look forward to it, sir."

He shut the door and the solstice day was over.

xxxvi. white lies

Paranoid. Exhausted. I was sitting crossed legged on my bed, my pen dotting the blank page of my journal. There was no way to convey my thoughts onto the page. Nothing made sense enough to put into words.

My inability to write was hastily interrupted when Liam burst into my room. He had slammed the door so loud, I jumped out of my skin. His eyes were wide, the bags under them red and scratchy. He was trembling with what I could only imagine was fear. I was immediately thrown into a panic by the sight of him alone.

"Something's happened," Liam screeched, clueing me in on his wild state.

I swiftly got up in a matter of seconds. I was waiting for my thudding heart to burst out of my chest the same way Liam had burst into the room.

"Is Phoenix okay?" I slurred my words, he was the first person I thought about, he was the only person I thought about.

He didn't respond but began running out of my room and down the hall, no choice but to chase him. I almost tripped over my feet a few times before he stopped and I almost crashed into him. He put his hand on the knob of the door in front of us. It was the dining room and I knew Phoenix had gone in there earlier. I wanted sob, I was so scared. I hated being scared.

"Simon..." Liam mumbled as he opened the door, "Surprise!"

There was a roar that repeated Liam's exclamation from inside the dining room and I jumped out of my skin for the second time in two minutes. The whole group were siting down at the dining table with Phoenix at the head of it; all dressed in their finest attire and all raising champagne glasses in a celebration. The table decorated with a golden linen table cloth, brightly lit candles, bundles of flowers in vases at each end and fine china at every seat. They were going all out and it took me a minute to realise that they were doing it for me. I smiled, trying to calm down from the shock. Liam pulled me in for a hug, laughing at my reaction to the surprise dinner.

"You did it, man," Liam said as he pulled back.

"Did what?"

"Simon, I got a call from Nicola," Phoenix added, putting down his glass, "the President, he didn't hesitate to make sure you got the position. I thought we could do something nice to celebrate. You start next week."

I cracked a grin, it was all going to pan out the way Phoenix wanted it to. I had genuinely impressed him *and* the President. A sense of accomplishment embraced me.

"Dinner will be ready in a minute, if you'd excuse Fetch and I, we'll go dish it out," Nicholas informed us.

I nodded and they left the room to prepare my special dinner. Liam guided me to our seats and I was slightly annoyed that I was at the opposite end to Phoenix. There was an advantage to this position. I was directly in his line of vision and we could gaze gooey-eyed at each-other all we wanted. The horribly romantic thoughts I had were sickening but I couldn't help it. He plagued every inch of my mind.

"So, how was it?" Tara asked.

"What did you say?" Maria followed up.

"Did you stick to the script?" Cillian enquired.

"Did you remember the part about the dog? Did he laugh?" Liam also added.

I was being bombarded with questions that I wasn't quite sure how to answer. I had exposed our movement to secure the job but I wasn't sure that's what they wanted to hear. I also knew lying to them wouldn't put me in the greatest position either.

"I talked to him about the Moths and the mafia," I honestly replied, hoping for the best, "I forgot about the dog entirely."

They all started laughing and I did too. I guess they thought I was joking, might as well keep it that way. If it came back to bite me, at least they couldn't say I didn't try to tell them.

Nicholas and Fetch arrived with our food on a service trolley. They started plating people up, a bountiful display of vegetarian meals. We went through entrees, main meals and even dessert. I couldn't believe I was being rewarded for this. When all was gobbled up and talked about, the group began to disband. I insisted I helped with the clean up but Fetch and Nicholas just as equally insisted I leave them be.

As I was heading back to my room, someone grabbed my hand and spun me around. I fell into their body and as I looked up, I didn't have time to react before they plunged their lips on mine. We kissed and I melted, the usual routine.

"Congratulations, Atlas," Phoenix teased, giving me another kiss.

Our hands entwined and we played with them as we kissed and talked like this was normal. Nothing about it was normal. Regardless of the situation on the whole, he never kissed me in the hallway where anyone could walk in and see. He was serious about us now and I prayed it would stay this way.

"I didn't doubt myself for a second," I arrogantly stated.

"I didn't doubt you either."

Another kiss.

"I've been meaning to ask you something," I mentioned, still playing with his hands like they were made just for me.

He raised his eyebrows, waiting for me to continue. It didn't take much for me to intrigue him. I was the only one on the team he couldn't read the thoughts of. At the end of the day, he barely knew me. I was always full of surprises to him.

"Nicola said something weird before I went in for my interview..." I bit my lip.

"What did she say?"

"Not to trust you, well not about this anyway. Something about you wouldn't protect me or whatnot..." I stammered, afraid of his response. Phoenix laughed in an almost cynical way, shaking his head in disbelief. I wasn't sure if I had made the right choice in telling him. After all, he chose Nicola over me for the past year. What's to say he wouldn't pick her over me now?

"No fucking way," he deprecated, still in shock.

"I don't believe her but I don't know… She did spend a lot of time with you while I was out of the picture and I think she'd know you better than anyone."

"Simon, I've known Liam and Cillian for years and *they* barely know me. The measure of time I spend with someone doesn't measure how much they know me. You know me. You've seen me. You've held me. You know me," Phoenix persuaded, holding my hands again.

"Okay."

"You can trust me... Well, now you can."
I dropped his playful hands, gulping down hard. Part of me didn't want to know what that meant. I was starting to be swayed by what Nicola had told

me, bitterly swallowing it down like unwanted medication.

"Could I not trust you before?" I asked, stopping myself from throwing up.

"In all honesty, no," he shook his head, "But you can now, I've changed my mind and I'm going to fix things as soon as I can because we're bulletproof. You and me. I'll protect you at all costs."

"Okay..." I hesitantly replied, unsure how to handle this.

"I've got you... I've got you," he began to whisper, repeating it over and over.
He engulfed me in his body, kissing my forehead and stroking my hair. Somehow this man could make me feel safe and scared at the exact same time. I wasn't sure who to trust anymore but I was sure I loved Phoenix even if I didn't trust him.
I got on my tippy-toes to kiss him again, hoping it'd distract me from his riddled words. He grabbed my warm cheeks and took control. Our lips colliding in a manner that reminded me of our first kiss. It was hot and seductive and tasted like the raspberry frozen yoghurt that was served with dinner. I rested my hands on his chest and let myself succumb to his touch. He moved his hands down, his arms locked together against the small of my back and I pressed against him. I wanted him, my jeans were tightening and I knew his were too. We continued to kiss and somewhere along the

way, he lifted me off my feet and spun me around. I giggled so much my cheeks started to hurt. He put me down, giving me a quick peck to conclude our little moment.

"I really, really, really want to have sex with you," I bluntly said.

Despite the overwhelming, intrusive thoughts of trust issues, I was drawn in by the way he was looking at me. I felt like he was a predator, watching every move of his prey. His bright green eyes were glued to me, his hair falling about his face in perfect curls and his muscles were subtly flexing in his arms. I could tell he wanted to have sex with me too. He was waiting to pounce. I was waiting to be ripped apart.

"Of course you do," he chuckled.

"I think I deserve it. You know... As a present for winning over the President."

"Mhmm," he nodded, salivating too.

His ducked his head and his lips started to trace along my neck. It was such a weakness for me. I was already moaning, harder than a rock, what more did he want from me?

"I want you," I breathed as he kissed my neck.

Phoenix pulled away, returning his eyes to mine. His expression was calculated, it looked as though he was delving deep into the depths of my blue eyes but still in a world of his own. I tried to remain steady and not get swept away by his eye contact or the fact he was so close. It was my turn to try and read his thoughts, wondering if I'd get what I'd want today or if I'd have to wait a little longer.

"I can't have sex with you, Simon," he bluntly replied.

His head swooped back down so his lips could caress the other side of my neck and I moaned again. He grabbed hold of my hips to keep me still. I would have to endure his torment longer.

However, his hand contradicted his words. I felt it brush against my jeans until his palm was pushing against the outline of my cock.

"But I can suck you off," he shrugged, acting innocent.

"Excuse me?" I disbelievingly scoffed.

"C'mon, don't tell me you never thought about my lips around your big, throbbing-"

"I think it's best we get out of the hallway now," I insisted, overcome with lust.

I gave him a kiss before I dragged him into the closet. We were laughing and we were excited and we were turned on and he was taking off my clothes and I was running my hands through his hair; we were what we were.

xxxvii. give and take

*He dropped to his knees before me and I pressed
my back against the cupboard wall. His hands
fumbled to make contact with the fly of my jeans
and I tilted my head back, ready to burst. His
hands playing with my jeans only made me harder
beneath his fingertips. I bit my lip as he dragged
my pants down slowly, as if to torture me further,
his hands gliding up my legs on the way back up.
He took the lining of my briefs between his teeth
and started yanking them down too.*

*"Fuck," I groaned, grabbing onto the nearest
shelf so I had something to hold onto.*
*His sweaty palms were on my thighs again, his
head aligned with my pulsating cock and he
smiled. He looked up at me and I looked down at
him.*

I stood behind the President, lost with the fairies
that circled around my head. The thought of
Phoenix was driving me insane. All I could think
about was what happened last week in that dark,
cold cupboard. I could practically still hear his hot,
rapid breaths and I kept looking behind me to see
if he was there. He wasn't there, though I wished
he had been.

From bagman to body-man. It was a massive first
day on the scene for me. The President was hosting
a secret meeting with the Prime Minister of
England. Apparently it was a matter of urgency

and national security. The Prime Minister was flown into the country in the middle of the night as not to alert the public. The President foolishly trusted me enough to be by his side through the secret meeting. I couldn't decide if he was incredibly stupid or he thought the Prime Minister was. Nevertheless, I had to concentrate and figure out what was so urgent to bring them together like that. However, I was barely there.

"What are you grinning about?"
I couldn't help but grin back at him as I asked. He squeezed my thighs and licked his lips and already, I felt my eyes roll back inside my head.

"Tell me you want to fuck my pretty little mouth."
My grin was replaced with a smirk and my hands reached for his hair. I started playing with it, curling strands around my tanned fingers and leaving a pregnant pause so I could watch him drool for his meal.

"I want to fuck your pretty little mouth," I whispered.

"This is hysterical, sir," The Prime Minister cackled which brought me back into reality.
I shuffled closer to the back of the vivid, red couch the President was lounging on. Directly in front of him, behind the coffee table that held sweets for them to share, sat the Prime Minister of England who was engaged in a conversation with him. For

the moment it seemed causal and I didn't think I had missed anything.

"This isn't hysterical," The President refuted, "It's all under control."

"I doubt it," The Prime Minister scoffed, reaching for a biscuit.

They nibbled on their cookies and I restrained from groaning. I could've been doing a thousand better things or one better person…

Phoenix nodded, opening his mouth a little wider and coming a little closer and so my grip on his hair became a little tighter and my breaths got a littler louder and my movements became a little stiffer.

Phoenix's tongue quickly flicked over the tip of my cock and I shivered. This was what I wanted. He was what I wanted. He gave it a good couple of licks before placing his lips around it and he ever so slowly started moving towards the base. His tongue glided along the underside of my shaft, curling around here and there. It wasn't long until I could feel the inside of his fleshy throat and I found it promising that he was slightly choking.

"Atlas, get us some tea, will you?" The President more so demanded rather than asked.

I gave a slight nod of the head before leaving the office to go to the coffee cart which was outside in the hallway. I politely asked the runner to fix up a teapot and tray and as they did their job, I did mine. I was, after all, serving the President. It said nothing in the job requirements about daydreaming.

Phoenix removed his mouth from my cock and I pouted at him. His smug expression didn't change, he knew what he was doing. Phoenix moved back in and placed a delicate kiss on the tip of my cock. I stared at him as he started to place a multitude of tiny little kisses along my rigid shaft and I found myself blushing. His tongue started to polish the places his lips had been. I was in heaven as he brought his lips back around the tip and started to suck, his tongue working wonders again.

I panted, my cock soon covered in a thick sheen of his warm saliva. My hands were still roaming his curls, following his head as he bobbed along to a silent rhythm. I clenched hard, almost forcing his head to do my hand's bidding. I wanted to watch his hair frazzle and his large pink lips engulf my dick all day but I couldn't help but fling my head back in pleasure.

"Your tea tray, sir," The clerk smiled. She pushed out a small grey tray on wheels and handed it over. I took the trolley with the tacky American flag teapot filled with steaming herbal tea, and the clinking teacups, and wheeled it back into the office. I lugged it around the lounges, bringing it to a stop at the coffee table.

"You are so fake! How do I know you're not really a spy? Spying on me like Britain always does..." The President growled.

306

I listened in. I tried to be subtle about it. It sounded like a heated argument and could be good information to report back to the group. I took the teapot in my hands and started pouring the contents into teacups, distributing them amongst the two leaders.

"We're just looking out for you..."

"Ahh! I won't have it!" The President spat. He angrily reached for his teacup and woofed the whole thing down. I found myself pouring him another round already.

"Atlas," he addressed me, "What do you think? Is he a spy?"

I frowned, unsure whether he was being serious or not. I looked over to the Prime Minister who was rolling his eyes and muttering something under his breath. I sighed and returned to the President with a smile.

"Be careful, his bowtie is really a camera," I jokingly referenced, clearing the empty sweets plates and putting them onto the trolley.

"Ah, a true Garfunkel," The President smiled.

"Sir, please," The Prime Minister pleaded, knowing things were getting off topic.

One of Phoenix's hands grabbed onto the base of my cock and started accompanying him on his journey to get me screaming his name. He started to pump, his wrist twisting and keeping in time with the bobs of his head. His lips would meet with

307

his hand every couple of seconds, working
symbiotically.
I could feel everything. I could feel his wet, round
lips grazing against my skin. I could feel his
curious tongue trying to brush against every inch
and get it damp. I could feel his heated breaths
each time he was brought back to my trembling
pink tip. I could feel the softness of his hand
against the firmness of my cock. I could feel the air
around us, I could feel the light that crept in under
the door, I could even feel the hair falling in his
eyes.
I used to get a lot of people to suck my dick but not
like this. This wasn't the same. Phoenix wasn't just
one of those guys. Phoenix was Phoenix and that
thought alone was sending me uncontrollably
moaning, incapable of shutting up.

"Simon, please excuse us," The President
insisted although his eyes didn't come off the
Prime Minister.

"Sir?"

He wasn't as stupid as I was lead to believe. The
moment was taking a more serious turn and he was
sending the newbie away. Finally, a smart decision
on his part. I was annoyed. I didn't want to leave
his side but I couldn't argue with him on my first
day and especially about this, it'd be too
suspicious.

"Take an hour lunch break. Wait at the door
until we're done. Thank you, off now."

I had no choice. I sombrely exited the office, so confused as to what was happening. My daydreaming cost me valuable information I could've given to the Moths. I had no idea what that conversation was about and I'd never know.

"Phoenix... Oh... Ah... Oh god, yes!"

I squirmed, banging my head hard against the wood and panting like a wild dog. I pulled his hair and started rocking slightly. He noticed my agitation and he reached for my hips. As my cock still occupied his mouth, his nails dug into my flesh and I squealed. He was clawing at my sides as I started to thrust into his mouth. There was no politeness to this anymore. I wanted to cum and I wanted him to take it.

I continued to yank his hair and he continued to scratch my hips and I continued to thrust but a little more vigorously this time. It felt so good to fuck Phoenix's mouth. The man in power had no power over me, not here, not while he was on his knees. My orgasm was abrupt but appreciated. I moaned so loud I thought it would echo throughout the whole forest. Phoenix's name kept rolling off my tongue as my juices oozed onto his. He eased off my twitching cock, the cum dribbling out of his mouth and down his chin. He swallowed down what he got and wiped away the rest. Phoenix licked his lips and stared at me as the sweat travelled down my brow. I was so exhausted, unable to even breathe properly.

"You get to kiss me now."
So I did.

I waited anxiously outside the double doors, my palms were sweaty and I could barley concentrate. I swore I could hear birds but there was no windows in the room I was in, maybe they were circling my head. It had only been a couple of minutes and I was supposed to be eating or sitting somewhere in the sun or just doing anything away from this office. Yet I couldn't help but feel I was letting the team down by not being in there, by not knowing what was going on.

"Hey."

I jumped when I felt someone poke my side and step in front of me. I calmed down when I saw it was 'Vince' the secretary.

"Lunch break?" He raised an eyebrow.

"Yeah" I breathed, still on the verge of a panic attack.

"Wanna feel each-other up in the bathroom?"

"Always," I smiled, needing no convincing.

I followed him down the hallway, excited to relieve my tension and get a new experience to daydream about. Phoenix was a bad influence on me.

xxxviii. reviewed footage

"Did you ever find out what your meeting was about the other week?"
The meeting was a fortnight ago and I hand't really thought about it since. I was too preoccupied with Phoenix's and I's time aligned lunch breaks everyday and how he would always whisk me off to the bathroom to have his way with me.

"I'm ninety nine percent sure it was about the Moths," I grumbled, "I still can't believe he kicked me out... Maybe I'm not cut out for this."

"Pfftch."

"Excuse me?"

"Simon, come with me."
Phoenix grabbed my arm and began dragging me down the corridor.

"Oh, I'm not sure, Phoenix… I don't think I could possibly receive another hand-job, it needs to recover from yesterday."

"Shut up," Phoenix laughed, pinching me harder for being cheeky.
I groaned as our steps fastened, like he was in some big hurry. We turned down a hallway I had never been down before. It was narrow and dark; no windows, no sunlight. I was squinting, it was ridiculously dark and when Phoenix pulled me up I started to feel around for something, anything. My fingertips brushed against paint that was peeling

311

away. As I continued to trace it, a splinter embedded itself into my finger.

"Ouch," I groaned, bringing it to my lips. Phoenix moved his hand down my arm and locked our hands together so he could guide me and I could avoid anymore splinters. His spare arm reached out and I heard the creak of an old door. Phoenix shut the door behind us, resulting in another groan from the rustic door. We pushed on and the pattering of our feet was loud against what imagined were tiles. It was still so dark, even in this new room and so I continued to be paranoid about hazards. The room gave me chills, there was something ominous about it. There was something wrong about it. I was almost scared to be wandering through it, even with Phoenix's hand in mine. Phoenix stopped and let go of my hand. No, this was much worse.

"Phoenix," I rasped, trying to find him again. He hadn't gone far, he was bending over to do something. My fingers grazed his back and I sighed in relief. I was such a coward. There came a buzzing, then a loud inhuman wheeze. The incomprehensible noises ended in crescendo with a loud, other-dimensional screech. I jumped and shut my eyes. I was never scared of anything but now everything Phoenix did scared me. There was light pressing against my closed eyelids which excited me. Why is light always associated with safety? Turning on the lights never stopped any murderer before. Nonetheless, I opened my eyes; feeling safe.

I was greeted with an ancient computer. The odd green and black screen welcoming to me as was the hum of the struggling monitor at our feet. The screen flashed with pixelated numbers, it appeared to be a loading screen. Once loaded, it shifted to a blue screen with bad graphics. The home screen hosted a bunch of folders labelled with a strange combinations of letters and numbers. I stared at Phoenix in confusion. He was grinning.

"Sit down."

I tried not to question it. Since the computer light was so bright, I could make out the desk it was propped up on and the wheelie chair in front of it. It looked brand new, refurbished, the computer seemed way outdated to accompany such a chair. I sat down on its cushioned pads, getting comfortable.

"Now click on the file labelled S, the number two and C," Phoenix instructed, standing behind me.

My hand found the inanimate mouse and clicked on the certain folder. A bunch of thumbnails flashed on the screen. They were all videos and they were all dated. These specific ones in this folder were all from the past two weeks. The thumbnail all showed the same thing; The Oval Office.

313

"I still think you're cut out for this. Find the one with the meeting and tell the group back at home what you find out. We can add bits and pieces to Tara's pin-board if it's really juicy."

"This place looks so... And this PC, it's so…?"

"It's a disguise. Only a fool would believe this computer held anything of value," Phoenix shrugged, "Anyway I gotta head off. Important secretary business to uphold. Make sure you shut it down when you're done and close the door."

"Wait," I impatiently mumbled.
He raised an eyebrow, leaning in closer in expectation. I grabbed his cheeks and pulled him down further for a kiss. Our lips clashed and it took him a couple of seconds to overcome the surprise and succumb to the moment. He smiled as we kissed and I found nothing better than that. When we were done he softly pecked my forehead and then dissipated into the darkness. I was all alone in this creepy place but at least I had one thing. I had flickering hope.
I returned to the computer, trying to look for the date the meeting was on. My hope was being haunted by my overthinking, however. As my eyes were glued to the screen, scrolling through timestamps, my mind was racing with invasive thoughts on Phoenix's trustworthiness. How did he know about this computer? I tried arguing with myself that he was the President's secretary, it was probably part of his duties here. I came back with a

rebuttal for myself, that although that might be true, how did he know the exact folder of the meeting? Had he seen the video already? If he had, why was he making me watch it and not relaying information to the movement already? All my justifications were undermined by more questions. I found the date and I eagerly pressed play, pushing Phoenix from my mind. Luckily the speakers weren't as dodgy as the piece of junk it was playing off. I watched the video, elbows on the desk and hands to my lips.

"I appreciate your visit but I do not appreciate this unnecessary concern. This meeting was to be about your economical debt not the Moths," The President shook his head.

"That was the plan but all has shifted now. Those banks exploding weren't nothing, it's textbook terrorism! You and the rest of America were given a huge scare. They graffitied your sacred building, the one we sit in now and nobody knows how they got in unless you had a man on the inside. Sir, if you'll allow me to call you sir, you could have a rat on your hands and you have the audacity to tell me this is not hysterical and accuse me of being a spy? If this was happening to England, there wouldn't be anything I wouldn't do to stop it. I would take every precaution to destroy the Moths and ensure this never happens again for the rest of history," The Prime Minister angrily insisted.

"You may call me sir and I will call you sir out of the same respect. So, sir, I don't have a rat on my hands. I know perfectly well whom of the Moths broke into my humble abode and decorated my building. Not taking every precaution is not hysterical. The Moths are not a problem and never will be. Banks are just banks, there are others and those that were damaged will just be rebuilt. Money may have been lost but wealth is of no issue. We are rich beyond measures, we just don't like sharing."

"You know who did it?"

"Yes," The President confidently stated.

"And you're not going to arrest them?"

"No, sir."

"You truly are a lunatic and I am so glad you cannot run again for President. You are tearing yourself and your own country apart," The Prime Minister spat, flabbergasted.

"Sir, I have been doing this for years. I know how to run America. I know how to handle the Moths and the people who worship them. They can try to change the system but the system will never change. Whether that's good or bad does not matter at all."

"You're babbling now and you know I don't care much for tedious logic. Tell me who is this Moth member who graffitied your walls?"

"Their leader, but he is not a threat."

The Prime Minister started laughing, "Oh, I hope your son is not as mad as you."

"My son?"

"Rumour has it he's hoping to take your job next year."

"Oh, that...Yes. Well, like father like son."
The Prime Minister rolled his eyes, "This is beside the point. The leader publicly humiliated you two years ago and he's done it again by breaking into your home. Have him arrested, not for you or me but for your people."
The President was the one covered in shock now, "You truly have no idea how I operate. Sir, my best friend ran the mafia and you think this is my first tango? I will not have the man arrested or killed. His fate rests in my palms and I know what I'm doing with it. All good things come in threes, thus I am waiting for their third strike before I play my part. Give it time, sir. Don't worry about what I know and what I do, worry about yourself and your own country."

"Maybe you should be the one arrested."
There was a knocking at the door and the men turned their heads to someone who was offscreen. A voice began to whimper.

"Excuse me, Mr. President," the mysterious voice echoed.

"Ah, Crane, come in," The President gestured to the lounge.

"I can only stay a minute."

317

The video cut out. I leant back in my chair. I felt like the life had been knocked out of me. The President *knew*. He knew about Phoenix or at least he appeared to know. Maybe he was just confused. Maybe he thought he knew but didn't really know. Maybe he was lying to the Prime Minister to get him off his back. I was trying to think about every possible situation which could be true other than the one staring me in the face.

Phoenix could be in danger. No, I was in denial. Surely the President was full of it... If he were really in trouble, Phoenix's secretary job could just be a set up and what were to happen on the day of the kidnapping? I could barely breathe. All the endless possibilities were oozing out of my mind and wrapping themselves around my neck like a noose. I was suffocating. Phoenix was my life now. I couldn't have Phoenix's fate parallel Daddy's. The thoughts of not trusting him were long gone from my mind. I had to protect him. I had to do something. I had to tell him. I had to tell the group. I had to watch more videos. I had to figure out who Crane was and if he had anything important to say.

xxxix. the rat

Death. *Noun*: The end of life for a person or organism.
Verb: to cease existence, to die.
Grief. *Noun*: intense sorrow especially cause by someone's death.
Verb: to grieve, to feel intense sorrow.
I had dreams of death and grief.

"Why have you gathered us here, Simon?" Nicholas asked.
I was pacing; anxious. Death and grief were resting on my chest and nothing could shake them. They were inside my head, cursing every thought that rattled through it. They were creeping into my tear ducts, ready to roll on out down my flushed cheeks. I was barely paying attention to anyone, anything. All I could hear was my own raspy breath.

"We've been sitting here for ten minutes, dude," Tara complained as Maria massaged her shoulders. Phoenix had been standing at the opposite end of the table, watching me pace and talk to myself. He was monitoring the situation, making sure nobody gave up and left. He was also making sure I wouldn't collapse at any given moment, either. I told them I had something important to share and I was wasting their time with my own mania.

"Simon," Phoenix muttered as he finally sat down at head of the table, as always.

His voice stopped me in my tracks. I felt my heart drop. I had to speak.

"The President... He knows..." I choked.

"Knows?"

I turned to face them. I had to find a way to explain it without bursting into tears, without appearing weak. After all, it might be an overreaction. There was no definitive proof the President knew who Phoenix was, it was all here-say. I was the one who heard it though, I was the one who believed it, I couldn't sit with the knowledge anymore.

"The Prime Minister of England and The President of the United States sat together in the White-House for a meeting two weeks ago. I was sent out of the room but luckily I found a video, the conversation had been filmed," I elaborated, "They were talking about the Moths... It wasn't the President's intent but the Prime Minister kept pushing to talk about it and so they did. The President said that we weren't an issue. He said he knew about Phoenix and that he wasn't a threat. He knows there's going to be a third Game, Christ, we could all be in some serious trouble but Phoenix... Oh, I just, I'm so sorry. I can't believe this is happening. Everything is ruined and I don't know how he knows."

"Simon," Phoenix shook his head, "Calm down."

I was outraged he wasn't taking it seriously, "I can't calm down! Your life could be on the line. All our lives could be…"

"Simon Sullivan, stop scaring everyone and shut the hell up," Phoenix hissed.

The life had been knocked out of me again, it appeared to be a reoccurring theme whenever Phoenix was involved. I dropped my hands to my side, my mouth slightly gaping. He was so needlessly enraged. I was scared, did he not understand that I was scared?

"Phoenix...?" Liam glared at the man of the hour.

Everybody seemed to be in shock except me. I wasn't just in shock, I was made of it.

"Phoenix, I don't mean to stir the pot... I'm telling them, you, what I know. I want everyone to be prepared not scared like I am. It is very likely something will go wrong during the kidnapping and so we need to be ready to-"

"Nothing will go wrong, Simon and if it does we're already prepared. We're not fucking amateurs, we've been doing this for a long time. We've been prepping for this specific Game since the very beginning of the Moths. So with or without your false claims, we're ready for whatever outcome."

"Phoenix Nathan Jackson," I snapped, the shock passing and outrage settling in, "These claims are not false."

"Then where's your proof?"

He knew I was bluffing, I had no idea if what I was saying was true. Again, I was repeating what I had heard, what I had seen. I was believing a man who had the reputation of being a liar. There were worse things, though, than being prepared for disaster.

"It was on that computer," I whimpered, sheepish now.

"I showed you so you'd stop freaking out about not being in the room, not so you can take the President's words out of context. You're so gullible, Simon, you'll believe anything. He could've just been saying that he knew me to get the Prime Minister off his back," Phoenix roared.

"You don't think I took that into consideration?!"

"Did he even say my name?"

I hesitated. For the first time since watching the video, I realised he didn't say Phoenix's name. He was only referred to as our leader. My epiphany must've been plastered all over my face because Phoenix cut me off before I could retaliate.

"I didn't think so. So not only could he be lying, he could be talking about a fraud. He could think he knows the culprit but it's someone who isn't me at all."

"What else did he say, Simon?" Maria enquired, trying to diffuse the tension between myself and the red-faced Phoenix.

"He... He... He said something about not arresting or killing the leader of the Moths. I don't remember if he meant at all or just yet. He's waiting until the third Game to do anything. Forgive me for freaking out but I have every reason to," I stammered with watery eyes, like a coward.

Phoenix continued to arrogantly groan and it worsened my stuttering.

"I don't want anybody to die."

"I won't *let* anyone die," Phoenix protested.

I rolled my eyes and folded my arms. Phoenix wasn't superman. He couldn't save everybody with the click of his fingers. If the President was telling the truth, death appeared a likely outcome. I was trying to look out for everyone, especially Phoenix himself.

"We know the routine. We go over it at least a thousand times a week. Simon secures the President in his office and locks the doors after. Sarah has come in with him, disguised as security and she deactivates the cameras and alarms. Maria and Tara are also disguised as security and whilst this is happening - are clearing a good getaway path so it's easy for the three in the room to sneak the President to the getaway truck which is disguised as a coffee shipment. Liam is driving, Nicholas is tagging along in case medical assistance is required at any given point... All the whilst Cillian and I hold down the fort, eager for your return. If something goes wrong we all know the procedures. Leave behind anybody who gets shot or wounded in some way and it's clear they're dead or don't have a chance. Phoenix is in charge of the President. If somehow the plan has been ratted out and there's gunfire, everyone must stop what they're doing and cover Phoenix so he can get away with the President. Even if that means staying back and fighting your way out of there and finding your own way to the cabin, it doesn't matter. You protect them. Look, I'm not even going and I know the deal. So let's not fret. I'm sure we've thought of every single possibility," Fetch explained, playing the parent of fighting siblings. The universe was weird. There were theories to our existence; God, the Big Bang, riding on the back of a giant turtle. I found it fascinating that we were all the recycled cells. We were atoms and stardust compiled into this human shape, believing we were of any importance at all which when put into perspective, was like if ants felt the same on Earth. We would live, then die and be recycled again. Whether or not there was an afterlife was beyond me. Life was what I really wanted to understand, our purpose and reason for being. I'd never know but I definitely knew it wasn't to say what I said next.

"What if Phoenix is the rat?"

"Excuse me?" Phoenix scowled at me in disbelief.

I ran with it anyway, "It is very possible you could be ratting us out. It could be the reason why the President knows you. You don't want to believe me. You don't want anyone else to believe me. You want me to shut my mouth instead of help you resolve the problem, super suspicious if you ask me."

"That is a very serious accusation," Nicholas snapped at me.

"Yeah, that's a little hot even for you, Simon," Tara frowned.

"You don't think that's wildly contradictory? Phoenix has been planning to kidnap the President since his first run ended tragically. This is his revenge. This is revenge for something the President did long ago. He has hungered for this since he was a teenager. You think he'd rat himself out? For what? Money? Security? There's nothing the President could offer Phoenix that's better than revenge," Sarah grimaced.

I swallowed hard. I was out of line. I had taken the Lord's name in vain at the church and now the worshippers were coming after me. I loved Phoenix. I didn't even know what I was saying or what compelled me to turn on him like that. I loved him. I loved him. I loved him.

"I'm sorry," I murmured.

My tear-swelled eyes were glued to my feet. My legs felt like jelly, I was going to collapse to the floor at any second. Guilt rotted away my insides. I bit down on my tongue, hoping it would snap off so I could never speak again.

"Sorry doesn't cut it," Phoenix growled. Phoenix stood up, his chair noisily scraping against the floorboards. He pushed passed me, our shoulders colliding on purpose. He angrily left the room and the tears streamed down my face. I couldn't look up. Everybody started to get up and shuffle out of the room without another word. They had nothing to say to me. I could feel their disappointment radiating off their bodies as they walked away. All I had wanted was to help. Liam was the only one to stay. He slowly approached me. He acted as if I was a grazing doe and if he was too loud, I'd be scared off. Eventually his arms enclosed around me and I folded into his body. My crying was obnoxious and the tears soaked his flannel but it felt so nice for him to rub my back and encouragingly whisper in my ear. Even if the whole world turned against me, I knew he'd always have my back.

"This is a big Game. Everybody gets stressed out. You're allowed to be manic, just watch that big mouth of yours, will ya?"

That night, upon trying to rest, I couldn't sleep at all. My thoughts were corroding my brain. I watched the ceiling fan, I observed the cracks in the walls and the stars outside the window but still my eyes were not shutting and my mind was not easing. I needed Phoenix. Phoenix was my codeine.

I took the risk. I rolled off my futon and snuck down the hallway. I walked on my tiptoes. I didn't want to wake anyone, not even myself. I got to Phoenix's door and took a deep breath. I twisted the doorknob and cautiously stepped inside. I softly shut it behind me and gazed over Phoenix. His back was to me and the blankets had been carelessly thrown off of his body. I assumed he was fast asleep by the rise and fall of his chest and his statuette nature. I had been so mad at him until now.

I very gently crawled into his bed, trying not to make too much movement. It was so much more comfortable than mine and triple the size. I made a mental note to sneak in more often. I inched closer and closer to Phoenix until my arm slithered around his side and one of my legs curled around his waist. I held on so tight with no intention to let go. I was safe. I buried my face into his skinny back and sighed. I thought it was a stroke of luck that he had not woken up, that was until I heard him sigh as well.

Phoenix couldn't get mad at me, though. In my initiation he strictly told me to creep into his bed when the nightmares were getting to me; my whole life was one big nightmare.

"If you're a rat, you're my rat."

We fell asleep together.

xxxx. unholy reunion

The *New York Times* crossword puzzle was one of my favourite pastimes back when I was a Bagman. I hadn't touched one of their papers since being dragged into the Moths but the President had one delivered to his desk every morning and he hated doing the puzzles. So I always stole it. I'd sit at his desk, a pen tapping my lips as I concentrated on my vocabulary. Doing the crossword, in my mind, wasn't a test of intelligence but rather honing in on the ability to read clues and solve problems. That morning I was sitting at the desk, as per usual, as if I, myself, were the President, wracking my brains for a nine letter word for 'vast quantity.'

"Atlas, I'm parched," The *real* President tore me away from my detective work.

"Any preference?"

"Coffee."

"Coming up," I sighed.

I dejectedly tore myself away from the crossword, wishing I had triumphed before having to put it down. He was sitting on the couch, pouring over papers for business I wasn't clued in on; no surprise there.

"I'm going to the bathroom first though," I grumbled and he chuckled.

The job wasn't at all what it was set up to be in the interview. I felt like I was getting nowhere with the President at all. Of course, I couldn't tell the

Moths that. Not that I could talk to them currently, after accusing Phoenix of being a rat. Being at the White House was starting to feel like a holiday. Here I was away from their awkward stares and whispering behind my back.

As I walked out of the Oval Office and through the corridor, I was still thinking about the crossword. The word 'plentitude' seemed to be the best I could come up with but it got in the way of another answer I had scribbled down earlier. 'Plethora' was another good word but one letter short. I almost walked right past the secretary desk without looking up but Phoenix got my attention.

"Hey, there's something I need to show you on our way home today."

I stopped where I was going and leant against the desk. I flashed him a curious frown which didn't last long because he was looking up at me with those pretty green eyes and smiling at me. I couldn't help but smile back and I shook my head, almost disappointed in myself.

"Fine! But it better not be too long a detour. We can't miss dinner again," I caved, "Oh and before I go, do you know a word for 'vast quantity?'"

"Numerous?"

"Too short."

"Are you doing those dumb crosswords again?" He laughed at me.

"Get back to work, *Vince,*" I teased him before he could continue teasing me.

Phoenix rolled his eyes and shooed me away and so I obeyed to his whimsical demand. I continued to the bathroom, still racking my brain for the answer. Phoenix thought they were a waste of time and I didn't have the energy to argue about it again.

I pushed open the door and strolled to a urinal, unzipping my pants and taking a piss. I sighed, looking around the eerily spotless bathroom decorated in tiles shaped like eagles and stripes and stars. I wasn't alone. On the other end was another man. The man had waxen skin, oily and almost combustible. His hair was down past his shoulders, tangled up in two box braids to keep out of his slick face. His face was host to clear-rimmed glasses and a scruffy brown beard, the same shade as his long hair. He looked old, not wrinkly or plagued with memory on his face, but perhaps a decade older than me. Tall, fit, not conventionally attractive but definitely pleasing to the eye. I had never seen him around here before. He had an air of importance to him, as if he was someone I should've known.

"Are you going to keep staring or are you planning on making conversation?" He said and it startled me.

He did a couple of shakes and fixed himself before flushing his urinal. I didn't say anything, I was a bright shade of red. I was so embarrassed, I looked back down, ignoring his gaze.

"Well, speak up," his grizzly voice sounded familiar but I didn't recognise the man at all.

"Just admiring your looks, if I'm being honest," I uttered.

I repeated his manoeuvre and joined him at the sinks. He laughed at my remark, beginning to wash his hands. I focused on myself, still refusing to look at him but we were in close quarters, so avoiding him would be difficult. When I turned on the tap and squirted soap onto my hands, I accidentally brushed against his shoulder. Anxiety was leering over mine.

"You probably think I'm letting these good looks go to waste then."

The stranger leant against the basin, with his eyes looking to his feet. I cautiously cleaned off my hands. Why wasn't he leaving? I worried I gave him the wrong impression, unintentionally flirting with the man when I was already spoken for.

"Why?" I amused him, finally looking to him again and drying my hands.

"Because I don't do boyfriends."

It was hard to breathe. I couldn't breathe. He looked up at me. I saw the purple in his eyes. I saw the sinful blue flecks. It stung. I was already beginning to cry. He shuffled forward. He caught the first tear. He grabbed one of my shoulders. He swept a rough hand through my hair. I couldn't stop the tears. I refused to believe this was really happening. This wasn't real. It couldn't be. I was still asleep.

"Well, say something," he encouraged, playfully squeezing my shoulder.

It didn't feel right. I didn't like him touching me. I struggled free. I stepped back. This wasn't how I pictured our reunion. It was too late to stop crying. It wasn't too late to speak.

"Are you going to ask me how Thailand was or…?"

"Simon..." He grunted.

"Yeah, it was good, I'm alive, I didn't get caught, thanks for asking, honey," I bitterly replied.

"Simon," he snapped and harshly grabbed my wrists.

I was held still and I couldn't help but reconnect with those haunting purple eyes again. They were purple. They were purple and blue. I was right all along. The one thing I remembered, I actually remembered correctly.

"Sparrow."

A film of poison curled around my tongue as I croaked out his name. It might as well have been poison because it killed me inside. It sure left a sour taste in my mouth.

"Not quite. I don't think we ever formally met," he rejected.

He released his grip on my wrists and extended out one of his arms. There was no way I was going to shake his hand.

"Last name is Crane, I'm S-"

"I don't want to know your name," I cried and hit his hand away, "I don't want to know you at all."

"Simon…"

"Stop fucking saying my name!" I growled. My face was drenched from the violent tears. I swallowed what I could. I gripped the marble bench where the sinks were, feeling dizzy. I tried to focus on my breathing. I wanted to teleport back to the President's desk, back to my crossword. My attempt at being civil was failing.

"You're still Sparrow to me. If you tell me your name then I separate all the good times I shared with you and what's happening now. You're not allowed to get away with this. I'm not allowed to believe you're two different people. You're the same man just with a worn in face. You're the man who loved me but hurt me too. I can't forgive just one side of you. I don't want to forgive you at all."

"I'm not looking for forgiveness," he scoffed, "I didn't come here for you."

His remark shouldn't have hurt me as much as it did. I was still face down in the sink, trying to regain my composure. He was standing behind me, watching, waiting.

"I suppose you work here."

"For the President himself," he confirmed.

"Same."

"Oh, I know. I know all too well," Sparrow suggested.

I turned to him. His arms were folded, unintentionally flexing his large biceps. His braids were becoming loose, a strand of hair had escaped them and was now dangling in front of his face in a perfect curl.

"You grew your hair," I breathed.

Sparrow's train of thought scared me too much to let him continue. I had to distract him the way he was distracting me. He couldn't reappear in my life and talk in vaguely threatening riddles, I wouldn't let him.

"I suppose I was bald last time I saw you," he said, looking at himself in the mirror.

"Brute of a man…"

"Excuse me?"

"That's what I called you... That day at the hotel... The first time we-"

"I remember… 'You're this big annoying brute of a man' yada yada, 'you've plagued my brain and I want you'... I remember all of it," Sparrow interrupted.

I couldn't believe he could recite my words like that, especially after so much time had past. I stared at him. Bewilderment had become me. Trying to decipher whether or not he had thought about me as much as I had thought about him felt

like a dangerous path to go down. My chest
tightened. I couldn't think straight. I couldn't look
away. He noticed my gaze and edged over. I
backed up against the wall. I was terrified of what
he'd do. I didn't know what would be worse; if he
kissed me or killed me.

"Anyway, your hair..." I gulped.
He was getting closer. His fingers brushed against
my waist and my spine straightened against the
wall. This wasn't right.

"What about it?" Sparrow whispered, "I got
glasses too, gonna comment on that?"
He was only inches away and he moved his hands
beside my head, pressing hard against the wall so
he could lean over me and trap me between those
bulging biceps. There was a knotting in my
stomach, was it butterflies or nausea?

"No, it's just your hair looks like Phoenix's only
straighter."
He frowned, "Phoenix, hey?"

"Phoenix," I repeated.

"He your boyfriend?"
I should've said Vincent. I could've told him he
was the secretary. Now I was really trapped.

"He's nobody," I shook my head.
When I said it, I felt horrible. He wasn't nobody, he
was everything. He was everything to me the way
Sparrow once was. Sparrow had thrown away his
chance, I didn't want him to believe he had another
one.

"So if I kiss you..." Sparrow mumbled, ducking his head down and closer to my mine, "He won't care?"

"Sparrow," I breathed, closing my eyes to stop the new tears.

I heard the door swing open. Our heads snapped around to look. Phoenix had the most inconvenient timing. If my heart wasn't broken already, seeing his break definitely did it. He couldn't comprehend what he was seeing, I couldn't comprehend how I'd even begin to explain the situation to him.

"This isn't what it looks like," I murmured, I couldn't even look him in the eyes.

"Oh," Phoenix barely choked out.

"I see," Sparrow smirked, putting the puzzle pieces together.

Sparrow tore himself off of the wall and off of me. He politely nodded his head to Phoenix before pushing passed him and departing from the bathroom without another word. Phoenix and I remained alone in the cold, tiled room. I still wasn't looking at him. I had done nothing wrong but I was ashamed. Phoenix hesitantly walked over and began to wash his hands and fix his hair.

"Who even was that?" He finally asked, aggressively snatching some paper towel from beside me to dry his hands.

"He was just some jerk who thought he could get to me," I shrugged.

It wasn't all a lie. Sparrow was being a jerk. He didn't deserve a kiss. He put me through endless hours of torment and self-loathing. He made me believe he didn't love me. He made me believe I wasn't good enough. He made me second guess myself. He made me who I was today.

"Looked like he fucking got to you," Phoenix hissed, knowing it was a piss poor excuse.

"Phoenix," I whimpered.
I brushed my fingers against his arm and made my way to his neck. I gently held it and tugged on it, pulling him down to kiss me. Our lips ever so softly touched and all I could think was how glad I was that I didn't kiss Sparrow. Phoenix broke away, removing all touch and shaking his head.

"You make it impossible for me to hate you."

"Then don't hate me."
A beat. He kissed me again and then my forehead and my cheeks and my nose and my ears and I laughed and he laughed and I loved him so much. He used to make me forget Sparrow even existed. Now he made me realise that even in a world where Sparrow did exist, I didn't need him. I didn't even want him, not when I had Phoenix.

"Simon."
It sounded so much better when Phoenix said my name anyway.

"My abundance of trouble," he chortled.

"Get outta here," I teased.

Another kiss and he left me alone. I wistfully stared at the back of the door for a while. I had only narrowly escaped a row with the love of my life and yet, I felt content. Abundance was the word I needed for the crossword. Phoenix would always have the answer.

xxxxi. spoils of the heart

Upon my return to the office, my mind was focused on my crossword. I was quick to enter, not paying attention to my surroundings, just grabbing my magazine and pen without a care in the world.

"You forget something, Atlas?"

On either side of the desk was Sparrow and the President, watching me fumble with my magazine in front of them. They both looked nonchalantly, holding paper cups of steaming hot coffee. I put the magazine down and straightened up, trying to act nonchalant too.

"Your coffee," I managed to say.

"Good thing Crane brought some upon his arrival. There's one for you too," The President bobbed his head towards the cardboard tray with said cup.

"I don't drink coffee."

"I had a hunch, cocoa though?"

I wanted to hate him. Every fibre of my being was repulsed by him. The mere fact he remembered I hated coffee wasn't enough to make me run back into his arms, if that's what he was thinking. So I didn't move. Sparrow took the hint but refused to let me win. He humbly got up out of his seat and brought the cocoa over to me. I glared at him as I reluctantly took the cup from his hand. He continued to leer over me until I took a sip. One point to him, nil to me.

Sparrow carelessly threw himself back into his chair like this was his lounge-room and not the Oval Office. I despised his causal behaviour. More so, I despised the fact I wasn't that close to the President when it was my job to be.

"Atlas, I believe you two have already met," The President said, looking between us.

"I guess we have," I bitterly replied.

"Crane has worked for me a very long time now and I'd find it best if you two would get along."

"What does he even do?" I snapped, jealousy and hatred getting the best of me.

"That wasn't very professional, Atlas," The President grimaced.

"It's okay, sir. I must not have made a very good impression on him earlier. Atlas, is it? Atlas, I guess you could say I work with profits and taxes."

"A treasurer?"

"Not quite."

I wasn't surprised that his role was as dodgy as he was. I didn't have to decipher his exact tasks to realise he was there to steal and extort money.

"How long has he been working here, exactly?" I enquired, cautiously taking another sip of my cocoa, "Before or after Daddy died."

"Before."

"Interesting... So, Mr. President, you know Crane worked for the mafia then?" I blurted. I was so angered by Sparrow's presence that I wanted to watch him burn. I wouldn't sit idly and let him intimidate me at work. He didn't deserve to work there, he didn't deserve spit. I wasn't sure throwing Crane under the bus like that would quite work as a tactic, seeing as The President also hired me and I was an ex-mafia member too.

"Yes, Atlas," The President grumbled.
I took another sip, scorching my tongue this time. The physical pain was better than how I had been feeling. I tried to savour the burning sensation.

"Funny that..." I muttered under my breath.

"Excuse me?"

"You knew he had worked for the mafia and you seem confident in him. Yet when I went in for my interview you were so pedantic about my past ties. Feels a little hypocritical."

"You got the job, didn't you?" The President argued, no time for the nonsense I was spouting. I bit my sore tongue, he was right. There was no point arguing. If I continued, I could lose my job and I didn't want to screw Phoenix over like that. I slowly drank my beverage, trying not to burn myself again. They were still staring at me. I wanted them to stop.

"Besides, he wasn't Daddy's nephew," The President mumbled and I restrained myself from making another comment, "Now, Mr. Atlas, considering you had so much to say, I assume you're full of energy. Crane and I were just finishing up. If you could take these files to their lockup, the secretary on duty will escort you. They know where to go."

I leant against the desk, waiting for him to sign them all off. This somehow evoked Sparrow to trace a finger up and down my leg out of the President's view. I glared at him. He wasn't allowed to touch me like that, not anymore. He mockingly put his hands up as if to surrender and I rolled my eyes. He smirked and I grunted, just in time for the President to hand the folder over to me.

"Quickly now," The President insisted.
Leaving the room felt like coming up for air after almost drowning. I clutched the folder so tightly, ready for my wrists to break. I approached Phoenix at his desk. He smiled like the angel he was. Soothing.

"Back so soon?" He teased.

"Shut up and tell me where to put these documents," I grumbled, still not fully healed.

"Someone's cranky."
He took the folder off of me and flicked it open to examine it. They were confidential but I had no energy to stop him.

"These are Nicola's files?" He mumbled, turning the pages.

"Oh," I pursed my lips.
I tried to get a glance at it but he snapped it shut and handed it back to me, "C'mon, follow me."

Phoenix gestured for me to follow and I obeyed, returning to cradling the folder close to my chest. I wondered what Sparrow and the President were doing snooping around Nicola's credentials. Everything about the day kept getting stranger and stranger. After a flight of stairs and a couple of narrow hallways, we found the lockup. Phoenix punched in a few numbers on the keypad beside it and pushed the door open.

"I'll wait out here, it's all in alphabetical order so it won't be too hard to find her slot."
I nodded and hurried inside as he kept the door open for me. I turned on the light so I could get a better look around but the light was blue and dim. Inconvenience always found its way to me.
I could see the outlines of the towering rows of documents that I'd have to weave in and out of. When I looked above my head I could see placards dangling on chains, with arrows pointing to each row.

"A to C," I read the first one aloud.
I continued to scan them until I found 'Q to S' and made my way down that row. Everything appeared to be in boxes labelled with somebody's name. I squinted at the name tags, wishing I had night vision.

"Ah!"
Nicola Smith. I grabbed her box and opened it up, placing the folder inside. I looked around inside out of curiosity but there was nothing of real

interest. She had no shady background, no reason for me to hate her, as petty as that thought was. I put her box back where I found it. I left the row and started heading back for the door when I thought of something.

"I'll be out in a second!" I called out, "Just having trouble with this light."
I could hear Phoenix's chortle as I quickly turned down the first row. I began analysing the boxes again.

"Chlaud, Christian, Ciril..." I mumbled the last names.
I went down further, frowning as each rolled pass.

"Cole, Connor, Cquari, Crah, Crakke, Crowe, Crüe... Hold on."
I double checked the last couple of boxes, my scowl only growing. I checked the shelf above it and below it, I checked behind me but there was nothing. There was no box for anyone named 'Crane'. Either Sparrow was using another alias or he didn't legally work here; neither surprised me. My concern for him ruining our Game though grew dramatically. I couldn't tell Phoenix.

"Atlas?"

"Coming," I barely spat out.
After I returned to finish my shift, Sparrow had fled. I was able to peacefully finish my crossword and have a humorous conversation with the President. He ranted to me about Britain again and his home life and I forgot about my own issues for

344

a while. He trusted me and I had to hope that was enough for the Game to pan out as planned.

When I broke out into the open air, Phoenix was waiting for me on his bike. I stole the helmet from the handlebars and put it on, my arms wrapping around his waist. He had a helmet of his own now, black with matching sunglasses, which made me chuckle every time. I was glad though, I wanted him to be safe for all of time.

"So what is it you have to show me?" I asked which came out a bit muffled.

"You'll see."

He took off and out of the carpark, onto the road. I wanted to think of the endless possibilities of what he was presenting me with but all I could think about was Sparrow. Even after an hour or so, I still hadn't deducted the reason for Sparrow's presence. Nothing was adding up. Was he there to provoke me? Evoke some sort of response from me? If that was the case how did he know I was working for the President and if he knew, did he know it was all a ruse? Was he aware I was involved with the Moths? Was he aware of the Moths at all? How did he get so close to the President? If he had buddied up with him before Daddy's death it only lead me to believe it was where he went while I was in Thailand. Every question I had seemed to raise more questions; it was exhausting.

Phoenix pulled into a curb and our abrupt stop yanked me out of my trance. I took my helmet off and looked around. The street was very suburban, all the houses were the same. They were the same size and shape, with stairs leading into a cement pathway that carried along the whole length of the street. The one we were in front of was tinted pink and had a fire hydrant out the front, the only reason it stood out from all of the rest.

"Where are we?" I asked.

He took off his helmet but didn't reply. He simply gazed over the house like there was a history there. The pink of the bricks looked faded but the front door and shutters looked like they had been treated to a fresh coat of white paint. The roof tiling looked old but sturdy, fitted with an old school chimney and the gutters attached to it were swamped with moss and mess. Phoenix stared at me.

"Phoenix...?"

He got off the motorcycle and I twisted my body to face him. He put his helmet under his arm and looked to his feet. The house was not as interesting as his reaction to it was. I patiently waited for him to respond.

"This is where your family lives."

"Phoenix," I uttered, not finding his remark funny.

"You're under the impression the President knows who I am and because of that something will go wrong during the Game..."

That wasn't the only issue now, not anymore.

"It freaked me out and I'm sorry. It lead you to believe that I'd be responsible if anything goes wrong and I don't want to be. I can't prove anything but I can prove I care about you. You're so paranoid about dying, you're worried about leaving loose ends…"

"I'm worried about you, Phoenix. I don't want *you* to die," I interrupted, my concern and stare sincere.

"My death is the least of your worries."
I glared at him as I hopped off the bike. I approached him, my fingertips brushed against his arms as I stood against him. He had no choice to look at me and my hand cupped his neck.

"It's my biggest worry."
He ignored me.

"I want you to see your family, make peace with them and tell them you love them. They need to know you're still alive and you care about them. If something happens to you, you'll never be able to do it again. You deserve to see them and let them know what's happening. I don't want to be the man responsible of keeping you from your family," he glumly continued his rambling.
His hand found mine and he held it against his own neck. I wanted to tell him I loved him. I wanted to tell him that if he died my whole world would be torn apart. It'd be so much worse than being ripped from my family or Sparrow's abandonment or Daddy's death. It'd be a hell I

never wished to conquer. Yet I knew too well that whenever he changed the subject, I shouldn't try to return to it.

"So you brought them here?" I said instead.

"When I knew we were taking you in, I asked Tara to go to Daddy's house and Maria to go to your family's. Tara grabbed Daddy's wife and child and Maria grabbed your mother and sisters. We put them here, altogether, so they could keep each-other company. Although Maria paid off the building and was more than happy to fund their lifestyles, your mother insisted she get a job which lead to Sakura following suit. They both work in a café and occasionally Michelle and Carol volunteer there after uni... Oh yeah, they graduated high school. Your other sisters are still in school and they treat Seikatsu as a sister of their own. She's grown up a bit now... They're grateful for all we've done despite Sakura's persistent grudge for what we did to Daddy and your mother's constant hassling of wanting to know about you. Maria goes once a week to check up on them and calls in every now and then too. They're safe and happy and breathing, Simon, but they miss you," Phoenix explained, "I know you miss them too. So go in, hug them, kiss them, apologise to the Gideons', tell them everything and let them tell you everything too… I have some errands to run, I'll be back in an hour."

I kissed him. With the force of a thousand suns, I kissed him.

"Thank you," I breathed.

There was no time to waste. I ran up the stairs. I knocked on the door. I held my breath. Heart in throat.

xxxxii. goodbye milkshakes

It was over. Drowning was never an option. I had kept fighting, pushing for the surface all the whilst ignoring the water's cold hands wrapped around my throat. Kicking for survival, I had made it through the last day at the President's side. For months, I had been suffering a near death experience every time I had walked into his office. I was free. Well, I was free until tomorrow when the abduction was to take place. Standing in the car-park, I continued my deep and savoured breaths. I tried to ignore the anxiety in my chest, imagining the horrors tomorrow would bring.
I waited at the boom-gate, my jacket draped over my shoulder as I looked around. Phoenix was meant to be taking me home. No sight of any motorbikes, just sad and lonesome motorcars. Some passed by me with no sympathy but there was one that inched closer; smooth, black paint with tinted windows from a ridiculously expensive brand. I felt it was stalking me. I'd take a step and the tires would take a step too. I let it catch up to me out curiosity and instantly regretted it when the window rolled down to reveal purple eyes.

"Need a ride?"

"No, thanks."

"I think you do," Sparrow laughed, almost mocking me.

He leant over and awkwardly opened the passenger door, expecting me to get in without a fight. I rolled my eyes, thinking he was pathetic to expect me to choose him over Phoenix.

"I'm waiting for Phoenix," I snarled, standing firm in my rejection.

"He went home, sick."

"How do you know that?" I scowled, not expecting his response.

"Saw him leaving. President said he was sick, I can give you a ride," Sparrow explained.

Bile crept into my throat. There were so many problems that arose with his supposed scenario. Phoenix going home sick meant I was left to fend for myself. I had no idea where the house was located, so even if it wasn't a violation to bring back a stranger to our secret base, I wouldn't be able to direct anyone there anyway. What really got to me, though, was the idea Phoenix had happily palmed me off to this man he saw tormenting me in the bathroom a few weeks ago. I was stranded. Phoenix had stranded me... Once again...

"So, need a ride?"

"No, thanks," I repeated.

Tears were starting to swell in my eyes but I quickly brushed them away. He didn't leave, staring at me like I was insane. Maybe it was a Game? Maybe I was being tested? Regardless, I pulled out my phone and hoped Liam could get me like the coward I was. My fingers trembled with terror and anger.

"Simon Sullivan, get in the car. I won't take you home if that's what you want, I'll drop you off at a diner or something so someone can come collect you but I want to talk to you. So just get in the damned car," Sparrow demanded, just as stubborn as I was.

I hesitated, looking around once more as if there'd magically be more options for me to take. Still angry and hurt, I surrendered. Phoenix had forced my hand. I couldn't see what harm having a chat with an ex could bring. The thought of him murdering me did cross my mind but then I thought Sparrow probably wasn't capable of killing the only man he'd ever loved. I hopped in the car and his greasy grin left me uneasy. I hated that he won but I needed to get out of the grounds, I needed to escape for a while. It wouldn't be that bad, it'd be a nice change of pace to my usual afternoons. Different face, voice, topics and if he was taking me to a diner, different food. Suddenly, I was excited. It had been so long since I had broken out of my Moth mould and was myself for a while. My true self that only a couple of people knew me as, one of them being Sparrow. I wondered if he remembered what I was like. I remembered him.

I buckled my seatbelt and he took off out of the carpark and onto the road. It was silent for a little while. I enjoyed the trip with the window rolled down and the cool air hitting my face. It was peaceful. Trees rushed past, boys on bikes, sun going down; on this day of stress, I found myself unwinding.

"I know what you plan on doing tomorrow."
I had spoken too soon. I couldn't speak.

"I know you're involved with the Moths," Sparrow continued.
I felt sick. Why was it when anything remotely bad happened to me that I wanted to throw up?

"I can't say it's as bad as the mafia but-"

"What do you care? What do you want?" I interrupted, panic had taken the helm.

"I don't want a goddamn thing," he growled and I shut up pretty quickly, "I'm looking out for you."
Looking out for me? I wanted to punch him in the face. The tears were coming back and my hands were twisting into fists.

"So you're *not* going to rat me out?" I scoffed, finding it hard to believe.

"Something is going to go wrong."
He avoided answering the question, cutting it off with some ridiculed hypothesis. I could only say that because I used to believe in it before I realised how well handled we were as a movement and how everything felt *right*. I had to trust my instincts, not Sparrow. These were empty threats meant to scare me away from the goal. Nothing would go wrong. *Nothing*.

"The President knows who Phoenix is, he knows he's Vincent the secretary. He's not stupid."

"He sure had me fooled," I retorted.

"Simon, this isn't the time for jokes. You're going to get hurt. I don't want you to get hurt. I thought I did but then I saw you in the bathroom and I thought 'oh wow, I skipped out on this?'. I still love you. I know that you love Phoenix now but I'm telling you, he's going to ruin you."

"What's that have to do with the President?"

"They're working together to hurt you."

He was full of shit.

"You're full of shit," I spat.

He had to be. I didn't want to believe otherwise.

"Something will go wrong and Phoenix is to blame for that."

"Sparrow, shut the fuck up," I roared.

My aggression grew, my cheeks became hot and red and my hands clammy. I couldn't take another word. This was absolutely insane. Nothing he said made sense. All he was doing was making my cheeks burn.

"Phoenix wouldn't do that."

"Sure," Sparrow rolled his eyes.

"You're not making any sense," I argued, "If something goes wrong tomorrow, it's not because Phoenix is a rat, it's because you are a rat. You're probably saying all these things to distract me. You're putting ideas in my head so I can blame Phoenix and run away from him and maybe fall

354

into your arms again. Well, it's not going to happen, Phoenix is the love of my life. I thought you were but he kissed me and everything changed. I trust him with my life. He wouldn't hurt me like this especially since he hadn't even met me when he started planning this Game."

A moment. Silence other than the tires on the road and the wind whipping past and my hot, short breaths. Sparrow's eyes were focused on the drive, ignoring me now as I fought back tears. He had a certain power over me.

"Please be careful tomorrow, okay?" Sparrow pleaded, admitting defeat.

Another moment. I forced myself to calm down, unclenched my fists, wiped my tears on my sleeve and took deep breaths. I ran a hand through my hair, deciding to avert my eyes to the road as he had.

"Yes, mum," I mocked, "How do you even know about any of this?"

"I'm the President's Bagman."

I should've seen it coming. After all this time I thought he had tried to escape me when really he had tried to become me.

A daydream in the passenger seat went by before we were pulling into a retro cafe off the highway. It was one of those places with Elvis posters on the walls and neon lighting. He stopped the engine but wasn't getting out of the car. I looked over to the brute of a man who was victim to his own daydreams.

"Are we going in?" I asked.

"You are. Call Phoenix, tell him to get you. I'll be on my way…"

"So this is goodbye?"

"This is goodbye."

"How long for?"

"Forever."

There was definitely sadness in his voice. I'm sure he never expected to have to say goodbye to me. He sure didn't do it the first time. I was finally starting to understand his pain. I paused, biting my lip and contemplating what to say.

"If it's goodbye forever, I think we deserve milkshakes," I smiled and nudged him.

"You sure?"

I nodded. Despite the years I harboured hatred for the disappearing bird, his final disappearance was one to be celebrated; not mourned. Milkshakes and burgers and laughter was the way I wanted to remember him. He smiled at me and I smiled back and thought to myself, we could've had it all once upon a time.

xxxxiii. the Game

"We'll be over soon."
Sweaty palms paired with shaky hands. The breath
in my throat got caught as Phoenix hung up the
phone. My vision was blurred. I wasn't sure if it
was illness or heavy sweat getting in my eyes. Dry
reaching felt like the best course of action but I
didn't have the time. I'd have to get over myself,
take deep breaths, count to ten or whatever it took
to walk back into that office.
I snapped the cheap, flip phone in half. Nothing
could be traced back to us. I placed the remains in
my pocket, leaving no evidence at the soon to be
crime scene. I rubbed the nape of my neck,
whispering sweet nothings to myself to get me
back into the mood. Wiping the sweat off my brow,
I re-emerged into the office. The President didn't
even look up. He sat behind his desk, drinking
coffee and reading a newspaper. The obliviousness
astounded me.

"Vincent will be here shortly, sir," I informed.
That's when he looked up.

"I don't remember that in my schedule?"

"You don't remember? He insisted I made the
appointment, yesterday, he was very adamant with
me, I told you as soon as it was scheduled."

"Hmm, alright," he shrugged and returned to his
papers.

Lingering by the door, I tried so hard not to look suspicious; although I kept taking glances over my shoulder. The President was too absorbed in the news to care. My mind was racing. I wondered what he was reading, what he had for breakfast, what he said to his wife this morning. I wondered when Phoenix would arrive, if he would be late, if he had a big speech planned...

Eventually I heard footsteps and a knock on the door. It was time.

I opened the double doors to see Phoenix and Sarah. It was the first time I had seen Sarah without a hijab. Although a devout muslim, she didn't want this Game to be branded as a terrorist attack - or at the very least, she didn't want to be smeared by the title of terrorist just because of her religion and the way she looked. I could tell she was uncomfortable exposing herself this way, it went against everything she believed in but she also believed in this cause, in the Moths and so she was pushing through. She was beautiful, with or without the headwear. In fact, she looked exactly like Fetch.

Phoenix had his porcelain mask strapped against his face already. It's shining nose nearly poking my eyes out as I had opened the doors. His eyes looked black, they were piercing mine, silently killing me. He seemed frustrated, ready to attack and I was getting in the way.

"Excuse me," he muttered and shoved passed.

358

Sarah reciprocated the concern on my face but she soon pushed passed too. I closed the door and locked it. I leant my back against the doors, my heart pounding rapidly in my chest. I was so frightened. I shut my eyes. I could hear Phoenix's loud footsteps as I imagined how he strode up to the President's desk and smirked at him, ready to give the most important speech of his life.

"Remember me?"
I heard the crumpling of the President's newspaper and the rolling of the wheels of his chair, "What is this? What is going on?"
I heaved a sigh, holding onto the doorknobs behind me. I opened my eyes and saw Sarah, she was disarming the camera in the corner and I assumed would make her way around the room to the others. The Game, it was really happening and I wasn't sure what to do. My job was simple, I had to guard the doors; that's all I had to do. Yet I felt the knobs burning my palms, as if they were branding me so I could look back in the future and remind myself what an atrocious idea this was.

"The definition of revolution is 'the forcible overthrow of a government or social order, in favour of a new system'. This is my revolution. You are the leader of the government. I am the leader of the new system. The definition of leader is 'a person who influences a group of people towards the achievement of a goal'. You have achieved nothing. You have reached no goals.

Time and time again I have seen you make selfish and harmful decisions that do not benefit your country or its people. You have worked with the mafia to keep your own skin. I have seen you rob your people blind and I have seen you befriend all the wrong people. You can't run a country. You're barely a leader. So, I'm here to take over," Phoenix threatened.

There was a shift in the atmosphere and a drawn out pause followed. The President was probably trying to evaluate the situation. I think Phoenix rehearsed those lines in front of a mirror every night so he could get them right for this moment. It was hard for me to evaluate how long he had been planning this, let alone the President.

"Phoenix Jackson, right? Stubborn little boy who was obsessed with my lawyer? You try to put a black bag on my head and you will get yourself shot. Pretending to be the secretary as if you and your schemes would go unnoticed... Please," The President retorted.

Before I had the chance to panic or burst into tears or be overrun with thoughts that this operation was a bust, Phoenix interrupted the President.

"You don't get to speak now, not for you, not for anyone. Your running mouth has come to an end. The black bag is your fate and you're coming with us," he had screeched, slamming a fist on the table. If only I could see it. My eyes were shut again. I wanted to see him screaming in his face and pointing out his flaws. I wanted to watch history happen but I couldn't bring myself to open my eyes.

"So either Atlas is working for you or you've killed him," The President sighed, "Neither of which I enjoy."

"I'm here," I awkwardly mumbled without thinking.

"Come forth, my boy," The President ushered.

"No," Phoenix hissed, "Stay there, Atlas."

"There's no harm in-"

"Stay there," Phoenix repeated through gritted teeth.

My movements were hesitated. I was unsure how to proceed.

"He has betrayed me. He has stabbed me in the back. The least he could do is have the common decency to look his victim in the eyes and admit to what he has done," The President spat back.

Guilt. Of all the things my brain chemistry could make me feel right now, it chose guilt. Guilt for a man who had never believed in morals, who had never seen right from wrong, who had been responsible for so many deaths in this country but never owned up to his faults. I didn't want to feel guilty for someone who was less than human and yet, I walked away from the doors and into his line of vision.

"Simon..." Phoenix breathed, staring at me.

"Simon Sullivan," The President grinned.

Phoenix shook his head in disappointment. I
assumed he didn't want me interfering but I
couldn't help but straighten out this crease. This
was my problem to bear, my own guilt to address,
I had to look the monster in the eye before he
decapitated it.

"I have to give it to you, you did tell me you
were working with The Moths," The President
said.

"You should've believed me," I shrugged.

"I never doubted you."

"I'm sorry," I muttered, looking to my feet.

"Simon, I hope you're kidding," Phoenix
growled at me, "This man is the enemy. He is the
fruit of evil and you apologise for bringing him to
his knees? Do you know what he's done? Do you
know how much this country will be better off
without him?"

"I know."

I felt bitter at Phoenix talking down to me.

"You don't understand. You don't understand at
all what I've gone through for this, for us."
Phoenix was yelling at me, as if I was the monster
in the room. We were all monsters.

"He doesn't understand at all," The President
sneered.

I was scared of what that meant. Phoenix held up a
revolver that he had been hiding in the belt of his
jeans, up to the President's face. His hand was

shaking, furious. I thought I could see tears in his eyes too.

"You need to shut your fucking mouth!"

"Feels good to say that after so long of wanting to, doesn't it?" The President teased, leaning back in his chair, "So do it, shoot me."

"This is a *kidnapping,*" Phoenix angrily explained, "But I will not hesitate if..."

"If what?"

"If you say something about or to Simon again."

"What if I shoot him?" The President asked.

"What?" Phoenix gulped, there were definitely tears.

The wind had been knocked out of Phoenix. He lowered his weapon and was just standing there, staring at the President. This retaliation was unexpected to him. It was almost as if a bond had been broken.

"I mean I don't plan to but Crane might."

"What do you-"

"Simon! Look out," Sarah cried from behind me.

I was confused until I heard the cocking of a hammer of a gun. I looked to my side and Phoenix looked back to me. Phoenix appeared paralysed. So did I.

The doors had been opened, somehow the lock had been broken and Sparrow had ever so quietly crept inside. He snuck up right beside me, he put a gun to my head and nobody had even noticed until now. The President was acting so smug, he was so happy he had his Bagman to the rescue. It reminded me of how I was with Daddy but I never killed anyone. It was always Sparrow who did the killing. That's when I knew that I was dead for sure.

"What did I tell you about being careful?" Sparrow said through his teeth.
I thought I knew him but apparently not. I took a deep breath, forcing the tears back. I had dinner with him. I trusted him. I thought I'd never see him again, we promised each-other that the last time was goodbye. Now he was ready to kill me. Daddy was right, I had always deserved better.

"So much for being the only man you ever loved," I harshly mumbled.
He impatiently pressed the muzzle of the gun into my temple with his finger firm against the trigger; a threat.

"Thanks for ratting us in like you said you wouldn't," I snapped, pissed off.

"Don't provoke him," Phoenix screamed at me, he was also pissed off.
Phoenix had fully turned around to face me. He raised his own gun to Sparrow's figure. He had tears drowning his cheeks and he was trembling with hatred. I must've meant a lot to him. I found the best in all of this, the truth of Phoenix and how he felt about me. He loved me.

"I think it's best you go now before anyone gets hurt," The President insisted.

"We're not leaving until you're in a black bag," I spat with sudden found confidence.

"Simon, shut the fuck up," Phoenix cried.
I had never seen him so vulnerable. It looked as if he'd drop his gun at any second because he was shaking so much. He was terrified, truly terrified and truly in love. He did not account for these feelings when planning the Game at all.

"Phoenix, this has been your dream for so long. Don't stop because of me," I insisted.

"You're my dream. You're my dream. You're my dream. You're my dream..."
Phoenix continued to babble on, repeating the same thing over and over. I was shocked. I couldn't stop staring at him, my mouth slightly agape. All I could do was watch him praise me as he sobbed uncontrollably. It was so out of character that even Sparrow lowered his gun for a second as well, observing this bizarre display of affection.

"Wow, you bagged a normal," Sparrow sarcastically muttered.
I would've elbowed him under different circumstances but unfortunately he was threatening to end my life and this was no time to act like friends. His colloquial manner was putting me off. I focused back on Phoenix who still was blubbering on about me.

365

"This is touching but this isn't an episode of Bold and Beautiful. Get the hell out of my office and never come back or Sparrow will kill him and I'll see you hanged," The President shouted. Phoenix simply nodded, wiping his eyes and putting his gun away. Sarah rejoined us, looking solemn and disappointed but she understood Phoenix in a way I couldn't. I could see it in her eyes. Still there was disappointment embedded in her chest, and mine, because we both knew what this breakdown meant.

We had failed.

xxxxiv. the Game (pt. 2)

Failure was not enough. As our harsh reality was being set in stone, it seemed accompanied by the sounds of heavy boots against the floorboards. The beat of security marching in, in their bulletproof vests and assault rifles cemented in their hands. They shut the door, trapping us, despite being just told to leave. Two of the men were dragging two women in by their hair. Their fists were full of blistering ponytails attached to the aching faces of the women. The girls' mouths were gagged, arms bound in front of them, knees bloodily scraping the floor as their mascara ran down their cheeks. They were in pain. They had been caught. They were our friends.

"Found these two killing our men," one of the brute's informed.

They threw Tara and Maria ahead of them, treating them like roadkill. I could hear Tara sobbing as she bowed her head in shame. All I could smell was vinegar.

"These yours?" The President asked Phoenix. Phoenix's despair quickly turned to burning rage. He had pushed passed the men who all raised their guns at him and raised his own to the President's head.

"Let the girls go," he demanded, clicking back the hammer.

"You're no fun, Jackson. You knew what you were signing up for when you walked through that door. Call them prisoners of war."

"Do not touch them again. They come with us or there will be hell to pay," Phoenix demanded, he was determined to take back control.

"No," The President snarled.
This would become the only gun I had ever researched; a semi-automatic pistol known as an AMT hard baller. Cartridge was .45 ACP, the bullet, in particular, that was released, in the same second the President was snarling, was a full metal jacket. Arcadia Machine & Tool were the company that manufactured the gun. They were set up in Irwindale, California, where they produced guns of stainless steel before going bankrupt and Galena Industries from South Dakota bought out the dying company. The hardballer had five inches of barrel and it weighed around forty six ounces, it was fed by an eight round magazine. It was the first entirely stainless steel 1911 pattern pistol. It was an impressive piece of machinery. If we focused on the bullet, the .45 ACP cartridge had a 230 grain bullet that travelled approximately 830 feet per second. The specific cartridge made for moderate recoil and low muzzle blast and flash. I felt obligated to know everything I could about that second, not just the specifics of the gun but the way the room stood still, the way the afternoon sun was reflecting in through the window and the look

on everybody's faces.

Sarah had tried to refute the despicable treatment of her two friends and in doing so, got herself shot. Smoke rose from the barrel of the pistol which stayed held in the air by one of the President's men. Sarah's stomach had been penetrated by the impulsive bullet and she fell backwards by the sheer blow of it. Down she fell, her knees buckled and her head harshly hit the floor. She clutched at her gaping wound, the blood pouring out of her and staining the carpet. Blood crept inside her mouth, peeking out of the corners and smudging her face. I didn't know if she was dead or alive. Fetch should've been there.

I didn't have time to comprehend what had happened before a reaction spurred inside the other Moth members. Without hesitation Phoenix turned around and shot at the man who had shot Sarah. His bullet was caught right between the piece of filth's eyes and I almost yelled 'timber' as he tumbled over. Revenge was sought but it wasn't enough. The other men began to fire their weapons at Phoenix, at the girls, at me. I was able to dodge their quick-fire but as bullets bounced around the room and smoke started spilling into the air, I was unsure where to go.

Suddenly Phoenix grabbed the scruff of my collar and pulled me into his body. He started to use his own body as a human shield between me and harm, his arm outstretched as he continued to

shoot at random and hoped he could save us all. I
didn't want him risking his life like that for mine
but when the room was filled with noise so loud, it
was hard to argue.

"Grab her!" Phoenix screeched above the
sound.
I thought he was talking to me before I saw Tara
and Maria had become unbound and un-gagged.
Being a couple made of a a spy and an assassin did
come in handy for scenarios like so. Though their
wrists were breaking out in rash and their mouths
were scabbed, they were not reluctant to grab what
was left of Sarah. Maria hoisted Sarah into a
cradle-like position and I made a mental note to
praise her on her strength when we got out of this,
if we ever got out of this. Tara covered her with the
hardballer that she had stolen off the man that
Phoenix had made a corpse. She made sure
nothing touched Maria the way it touched Sarah.
They quickly skipped over to Phoenix and I, as we
huddled in the corner.
More men kept flooding into the room, with
Sparrow leading the malevolent group. All the
President did was hide under his desk. Coward. We
were outnumbered and we were scared but we
didn't give up. Phoenix and Tara kept shooting our
enemies so we could make a path to the door. We
had to get to the van before someone else was hurt
or more men came to destroy us or the media got
involved.

Most of it was a blur to me. All I could remember was the deafening sound of guns, the smell of blood and smoke and vinegar, the tears that dampened my face and the breaths that were so hard to come by. I don't remember how we made it out that door alive, I don't remember how we escaped the guards and followed the route Tara and Maria had cleared for us prior to the van. I just remembered that we all survived, well, almost. When I had come back to reality, we were approaching the van and Phoenix had thrown his mask away. Liam had stumbled out and the colour had drained from his face when he saw ours had vanished too. He almost passed out when he saw a pale Sarah bleeding out on Maria's shirt.

"What the fuck happened?!"
Nobody could talk. We had all lost the ability to. We had to keep moving.
Phoenix shoved Liam into the passenger door, his gun was still in his hand and it jabbed into Liam's shoulder while Phoenix aggressively held him. I couldn't imagine the deranged look in his eye or the sweat that was dripping down his brow. Liam took this as a sign to get in the van and stop asking questions. When Phoenix moved away, Liam quickly obeyed. Phoenix raced to the driver's side and hopped in. Tara flung open the double doors at the back of the van and helped Maria delicately carry Sarah inside. Nicholas sat inside and although he was there for medical emergencies, I

371

don't think he ever expected one. Once Sarah was on the floor of the van, Nicholas at her side with Maria and Tara seated on either side, I jumped in and closed the doors behind me. I sat down, a cold sweat breaking out all over my body. All I could do was tremble.

Phoenix started the van and we took off. We were lucky that nobody was following us, at least we didn't think so. There were no red flags unfurling for us but it could've been we were so focused on Sarah. This wasn't actually meant to happen. We all talked about the potential of somebody getting hurt but we all believed we were untouchable.

"Sarah, can you feel my hand?"
Nicholas grabbed Sarah's hand and squeezed it. There was a cough and a slight nod of the head. Momentary relief washed over all of us despite her weak state.

"Can you speak for me, Sarah?"
There was a gargling sound but then she spoke with a rough, soft and croaky voice, "Yes... Yes I can."

"Tara, apply pressure to the wound. Sarah, you're going to need a blood transfusion. Simon, pass me my briefcase," Nicholas, although panicked, remained professional.

"No," Sarah croaked.

"Excuse me, Sarah? What was that?" Nicholas sincerely asked.

"No," Sarah repeated with the little strength she had.

"Sarah, without treatment you'll bleed out. You have maybe five or ten minutes before - "

"I was shot in the stomach. You know what that means, Nicholas," Sarah spoke with gentleness, placing a hand on his arm.

A bullet to the stomach meant bile and acid had leaked into her system. Even with the transfusion, even if, miraculously, Nicholas had the correct blood type to transfuse, it was more than likely Sarah would die of infection. She had come to accept her fate.

"Peritonitis," I muttered under my breath.

Sarah wheezed and started to cough. I tried not to stare at her as she spluttered blood over herself and Nicholas. Nicholas pushed her matted hair out of her face, rubbing her thumb over her forehead for comfort.

"I can't let you die," Nicholas gulped with tears in his eyes.

"Please," Sarah begged the way a child would, it all felt so wrong.

"What about Fetch?" I crudely asked.

"They'll know what to do," Sarah slowly explained, her voice growing weaker by the second.

"This is such bullshit," I yelped.

I punched the side of the van and started to cry, burying my head into my hands. Everything was falling apart. My anger was understandably ignored, everybody transfixed on Sarah. She was mumbling to herself something incoherent to the rest of us. I wanted to zone out, I didn't want to listen, I didn't want to know. I felt so out of place.

"What is she doing?" Liam bluntly asked from the passenger seat.

"She's reciting the Shahadah. It's a declaration of faith... She's dying. She's dying and Fetch isn't here. Fetch isn't here," Phoenix bitterly rattled on, "Tara cover her in a sheet once she's passed and face her towards Mecca and try not to touch her too much. In Muslim culture, they believe the body can still feel pressure after death and that the body should only be handled by someone of the same-sex."

"Can we not talk about her like that while she's still breathing?" Tara snapped.
Tara was profusely crying. Mucus and tears had formed a mixture that clung to her red, hot face. She was holding Sarah's hand as Sarah carried out the customs of her religion by herself. Maria was meant to be closer to Sarah than Tara but all Maria was doing was staring out the window. Grief made no sense to me.

"Isn't there something we're supposed to say when she's passed?" I asked, ignoring Tara's remark.
Sarah nodded, "Maria knows it."

Maria finally looked to Sarah. Sarah was pale, cold; composed mostly of sweat and memories now. Maria's fists were clenched and she fought the tears in her eyes as they continued to gaze at each-other. Sarah looked at peace. She closed her eyes but was still breathing. With all the strength she could muster, Maria ignored the world as she got on her knees to kneel beside her fading friend. She took a deep breath and leant down, her mouth aligning with Sarah's ear.

"Inna lillahi wa inna ilayhi raji'un," Maria whispered and stroked Sarah's hair.
With that, she was gone.

xxxxv. who is to blame?

As I stirred from my trauma-induced sleep,
Phoenix stopped the vehicle at the foot of our
cabin. I rapidly blinked as if to keep myself awake,
looking around the van to see what I had missed. I
was sorely disappointed. Phoenix shifted in his
seat to face us, disappointment becoming him as
well. His face dropped when he saw what I saw.
Sarah was covered in a white sheet and her body
had been rolled over. Tara wasn't holding her hand
anymore but had switched sides so she could rest
against Maria's shoulder. She had stopped crying,
she had probably dehydrated herself. Her eyes
looked more sore than her wrists.

"When did…?"

"A while ago," Maria bluntly answered
Phoenix.

"Okay," he defeatedly whimpered.
I couldn't breathe in there. I slammed open the van
doors and stumbled outside. I hurriedly inhaled as
if I had never tasted fresh air before and let out a
shaky exhale. I bent over and grabbed my knees,
my breathing only getting worse. People dying
wasn't my forte. Phoenix clambered out of the van
and I thought he was coming to comfort me. I
could barely stand up properly, my legs
uncontrollably shaking as dizziness took hold.
Alas, Phoenix helped Nicholas help the girls out of

the van and completely ignored me. Liam followed him, rubbing Maria's back in sympathy.

"Maria, I'm so sorry but I need you and Tara to move the body to around the back. We bury her *today*," Phoenix insisted.

Maria nodded but before she could proceed with her orders, we heard the front door open. Cillian and Fetch slowly descended from the house and onto the lawn. They looked concerned and they had every right to be. I wasn't ready for Fetch's heart to break but none of us had a choice.

"You're early... And you look like you've seen a ghost... What happened? Where's the President?" Cillian enquired, adjusting his glasses as if that'd help clarify the situation for him.

"Where's Sarah?" Fetch asked, as if they already knew the answer.

Liam sauntered over, stopping them from coming any further. They fought him for a second, shouting obscenities at his obscene actions. Twins had a heightened sense of reality when it came to their other half. Fetch could feel in their gut that something was off and Liam's brute force wasn't comforting them in the slightest.

"Look, before you look in the van, you have to know that it's what she wanted and that she loved you. God, she loved you so much but she loved us too. She wouldn't want you to be mad at us because she knows we have to look after you now, it's all up to us. Fetch, I'm so sorry but please just don't lose your mind and-"

"What are you going on about?" Fetch nervously laughed but I could tell they feared the worst.

Fetch defiantly pushed passed Liam and hurried to the van. Tara started to cry again and turned to rest her face against Maria's chest, hoping it would stop her tears. I stood back as Fetch gazed over the sheet and went pale.

"Please tell me that is the President and *not* my sister."

We all remained silent. Cillian had come to examine the situation too. Upon seeing the sight, he put a hand on Fetch's shoulder. They angrily shook him off, their hands rising to cover their gaping mouth.

"Please tell me that is *not my sister*!" Fetch repeated, their flurried words coming out muffled through their shaking hands.

Tara and Maria began to move the body from the van and when Sarah rested in their arms, Fetch impatiently peeled the sheet from her face. Fetch fell back, a loud yelp of horror escaping their lips as they came to their knees. Their hands came back to their mouth as they started to violently weep.

I couldn't describe what I felt. Maybe I felt torn, twisted, broken. Maybe I felt wrong, guilty, overwhelmed. Maybe it should've been me instead of the little one's twin. Fetch had just lost a piece of themselves. They grew up together, they were best-friends as well as twins, they rarely spent time apart and now there was only one. I would much rather I had died than Sarah, for Fetch's sake. It then dawned on me that it was all my fault.

I watched as Fetch convulsed and Liam tried to console them. Phoenix began barking orders, telling Tara and Maria to get Sarah's body around the back. Liam was to dispose of the van and weapons. Sarah was meant to deal with the media publicity of the event but the job was passed on to Cillian, who probably had no idea what to do. Phoenix kept rambling, yelling at everyone things that nobody could really understand. When he started screaming, I started walking. After a while, he went to give me orders but I was far away. I was still in the clearing but I was heading to the forest and I was almost at the brink of it. My arms were crossed as if I was cold but really, I was sweating. I was crying again and close to puking, as if in some sort of never-ending fever dream.

"Simon!" He screamed.

I flinched at my name but didn't stop moving. I had to break away. It wasn't until the second time I heard his angry voice that I felt compelled to stop. I turned around and stared at him. I had, unintentionally, gathered quite an audience. Everyone was there, huddled around Phoenix. Tara and Maria had returned from putting Sarah with the daisies and even Fetch had slowly stood up to observe my odd behaviour. Everyone was confused about my actions and they were waiting for an explanation.

"It was him, Phoenix. It was Sparrow," I admitted through gritted teeth.
They tried to make sense of my words but needed a bigger bite of the apple.

"I should've told you. I don't know why I didn't tell you. Fuck, if I had told you that the man from the bathroom was Sparrow, maybe we wouldn't have been in this mess! I should've told you because just yesterday he was telling me he knew about our plans and I still kept it a secret. He set us up and now - "
Without a beat to take a breath, Phoenix shouted back, "It's not your fault. Don't you dare say it is." His romantic involvement with me was tampering with his judgement. His could not right my wrongs or make it so my actions didn't have consequences. Tried as he might, I was still a horrible person and Sarah was dead because of me.

"I guess I didn't think he was a problem or I was worried you'd be jealous or mad. I don't know, I don't know anymore but I should've told you. I should've warned you, at least, that something would go wrong," I shook my head, beginning to slowly slink back to them, "It's all my fault."

"Simon, you told us time and time again that it'd blow up in our faces. It's my fault. I should've listened to you. I should've listened to you especially when you said the President knew who I was. I was such an idiot to soldier in there and expect everything to be perfect. We weren't prepared and I ruined it. Sarah's death is on me, not you."

Phoenix had unloaded his version of events but it was so hard to believe. Sweat was dripping in my eyes, my audience becoming an amalgamation of blurry colours. It forced me to close my eyes but the dark was terrifying.

"Sparrow... He knows everything about me. We shared so much. I thought he loved me until…"
My train of thought shifted from blame to panic, "Phoenix, he would know where to find me... Even worse he knows my family and he'd know where to find them. He was the best tracker in the mafia and he will stop at *nothing* to ruin me. I don't know what I ever did to him but he sure hates me... He's coming after me. I'm dead. I'm dead. I'm dead."
I stopped walking, close enough to the group to hear a whisper but not close enough to touch. I could hear Phoenix's heart longing to wrap me up and take me far away from here. His heart was echoing my own. I felt the twitch of his hand and it made me open my eyes again.

"He's not coming after you, Simon or your family. I won't let him," Phoenix hissed, a sudden rage effecting his composure.

"You won't let him?" I questioned.

"If he so much lays a finger on you, he'll have me to answer to," Phoenix growled but then suddenly his face lightened and so did his voice, "I love you, Simon. I'm in love with you."

"You're in love with me?"

It was everything I had been waiting for, granted not the time or place I had envisioned. It felt wrong to be having this conversation in front of the mourners. However, when he had said he was in love, his voice had trembled with fear and his eyes had darted away, as if embarrassed and I wanted to relive the moment, I wanted to relive it forever.

"Yes."

"Okay."

He looked into my eyes and I couldn't tell if I felt scared or safe.

"Let's get out of here," he said.

Phoenix walked over to me and wrapped an arm around my shoulders. I cowered into his body, still traumatised by the day's events. I knew I would be haunted by the ghosts of today for the rest of time but if he could make me forget the ghouls on my back, even for a moment, I would know that he was the one and that his words were true.

"Fetch, you can handle the burial. I don't know when we'll be back so don't wait for us," Phoenix informed them.

Fetch weakly nodded. It felt wrong to abandon the team after today's events but I was no longer an independent man. Under Phoenix's arm I was merely a shell of a man. I couldn't speak, I could barely even breathe. He would go, I would follow. There was no choice anymore.

xxxxvi. making love

"Have I ever told you why we call ourselves 'The Moths'?"
We had spent hours of riding out of the forest just to arrive at another one. We hadn't spoken the entire time, terrified of what might be said. Now that it was time for hiking, Phoenix seemed to think it was appropriate for at least some chit chat to fill the time.

"No, you haven't. Have I ever told you that you're obsessed with trees?" I teased.
He laughed and we left our helmets on the bike handles. He wandered over to me and took my hand in his. We started heading into the forest, something that I wasn't unfamiliar with when it came to him.

"Moths are ugly," he proceeded, ignoring what I said, "They're disregarded or deemed unimportant, sometimes even feared due to being disgusting. They're faded little creatures who aren't considered as good as butterflies... However, their one redeeming quality is always being able to find light. They find something beautiful to latch onto during their short, little lives. I guess you could say they find the good in every situation, if we regard light as good and dark as evil, that is. The idea was that we were always meant to be directing others to the light we had found."

"That's beautiful, Phoenix."

384

"Don't be so condescending," he scoffed.

"I wasn't! I genuinely like the idea," I shrugged, squeezing his hand.

"We're all just trying to find the light in our lives."

The rest of the way, we strode in silence until we came upon what looked like a ruin. The stones were faded, they looked as if they were slowly decaying. They were covered in moss and algae, as if Mother Nature had maliciously attacked them. She apparently, also, knocked them down and made rocks crumble. The stones were fairly large, mostly broken. The jagged marble and sandstone blocks didn't appear to make a building. They might've made walls or sculptures, maybe even beautiful carved attractions once. Most were ruined, they were severely weathered and the vines crept up them like winding snakes. Beautifully deprecated.

"We're in the depths of Rock Creek Park," Phoenix explained, smiling at my awe of the architecture, "In the war of eighteen twelve, the Capitol was nearly burned down and needed to be rebuilt. The stones you see now originate from there. They looked like this now not because they're so old but because there was a renovation in the late fifties. There was an agreement and these puzzle pieces were put here... Simon, this is my home."

385

My fingers brushed over the fuzzy moss and patterned marble. I wanted to be buried there, among history and nature and beauty. I wanted his home to be my home.

"Where do you sleep?" I asked.
Phoenix pointed roughly upwards and my gaze followed his finger. There was a treehouse a couple of metres away, looking high and mighty as it resided in an oak. I smiled, following the ladder down with my eyes before chasing after it.
Phoenix ran after me but I was faster. I hurried up the wooden planks nailed into the tree and after a few minutes or so, I scurried inside the makeshift house. After all that had happened this morning, it felt cathartic to have a play around.
I huffed and puffed but the polished wooden hut didn't blow down. There was carpet underneath my body and the room was tall enough for me to stand in but I stayed seated. It appeared there were multiple rooms, oak-carved bridges from one opening to another to get to different rooms dolled up in different trees. It reminded me of something you'd see in a movie. Phoenix was clever but I had no idea he was into carpentry or architecture.
Phoenix eventually caught up to speed and entered what I deducted to be the lounge room. Although there was no couch in sight, only an abundance of pillows littered the carpet and a cabinet that contained magazines and books. Phoenix crawled over to me as I was still lying down and didn't

hesitate to tower over me. He ducked his head down and gave me a kiss. He didn't move from his position, although one of his hands did move from propping himself up behind my head to stroking my oily, sweaty hair.

"Phoenix..." I breathed.

"Simon?"

"Sarah's dead," I croaked, my mind not at rest.

"I know."

"You know how I said you're the only person I've ever been scared of?"

"Yeah?" He frowned.

"Please help me to not be scared right now," I whispered.

Phoenix ducked down to kiss me again, his hair draping around my face as our lips gently brushed together. I brought a shaky hand up to his warm face and held it against his cheek. He continued to give me gentle kisses before suddenly he detached our lips. He began to leave a trace of delicate kisses along my jawline and I moved my hand down to his shirt. I clung to the fabric and shut my eyes. All I wanted to feel was his soft pink lips against my skin and the tug of his button-up shirt to know he was real and he was mine.

He started to kiss my neck, the kisses becoming firmer but sweeter. I let my fingers subconsciously undo the buttons on his shirt. I was in no hurry, my fingers patiently gliding with the plastic and the fabric as he continued tracing his tongue along my neck. When I had finished the last one, my hands travelled up to his shoulders and I pulled his shirt off his arms for him. I tossed it aside and he pecked my lips as a thank-you. I started to unbuckle his belt as our lips clashed together. I didn't feel like Oscar Wilde or Sir Francis Drake this time. This time I felt like myself. I was Simon Sullivan. I was Simon Sullivan and that's all Phoenix Jackson wanted me to be.

He kicked off his shoes and I reciprocated. My hand cupped his neck as his tongue gracefully slid into my mouth each time we kissed. I couldn't help but do the same, his flavour so familiar to me. We took off our trousers and Phoenix hungrily tore off my shirt. I lied half naked in a tree house with America's most wanted criminal. He had decided to start kissing my chest and let his wandering hands graze over my underwear. Nothing was bizarre to me anymore.

I curled my toes and licked my lips as his hand fondled my crotch and his tongue teased my nipple. I moaned in appreciation and he cheekily nibbled my nipple, making me buckle my knees. I grabbed a chunk of his knotty hair in my fist, his hand feeling for my stiffening cock through the material. He let his fingertips softly run up and down the length of it, his tongue getting bored of my chest so he started licking down my body. He let his tongue run down my chest to my stomach to just above my briefs where his hand was playing. I gulped hard when he removed my underwear and chucked it into the corner, out of sight and out of mind. My cock bounced up to my stomach, pre-cum already dripping from the tip. He licked it away and I released his hair, scratching at the carpet beside me now. He flourished with a wet kiss before moving away from me altogether. Phoenix stood up and I whined in agitation. He half-heartedly laughed and took off his hot-red underwear. I almost swallowed my tongue when I saw his dick. It was long and white and hard and his veins were pulsating radiantly through it. I had to stop myself from drooling. He shuffled to the cabinet and flung open the doors. He reached in and when he pulled out a condom and a bottle of expensive lubricant, I thought it was too good to be true.

"You bring a lot of guys up here?"
Phoenix rolled his eyes and shook his head. He came closer to me before getting down on his knees. He ripped open the packet and pulled out the condom, preparing to put it on.

"No, these are new, believe it or not."
I watched as he gracefully rolled the condom down his length. I noticed how he bit his lip and how his hair fell about his face and how the sun was coming in through the opening to shine a halo above his head. I had to stop falling in love with him.

"You were hoping to get me up here?" I raised an eyebrow, feeling particularly cocky.
He smiled at me before grabbing the lubricant and twisting open the lid. He squirted the blue substance onto his hand and started to lather the condom in it. He tried not to squirm at his own cold touch but his breath was rapid as he spoke. It made me want him more.

"Yeah," he shyly smiled, "I wanted to give you what you deserve."

"A good fuck?" I cheekily asked, enjoying this sensitive and open side of him.

"No. I want to make love to you"
I closed my mouth after that although my heart was wide open. He inched over and grabbed my feet. He kissed the sole of my left foot and then my ankle. He held onto both my legs as he continued moving towards me. My legs hung over his shoulders as his hands slipped down to my thighs.

"Keep your legs there," Phoenix breathed.
I nodded. Soon he was raising me onto his knees and his erection was getting closer and closer. I held my breath. It had been a long time since I was bottom or even had sex at all, but doing this with him, well, it made me truly understand the meaning of moths.

"I love you," I whispered as he slowly pushed inside of me.

"I love you too," he exhaled as if he had been holding his breath.

We spent most of the night making love. I used to think I would never forgive myself if I fell in love with Daddy's murderer but it had been nothing but a privilege.

xxxxvii. the past

High above the canopy of the trees, on a platform with no walls and only the navy sky and its sparkling stars as a roof, I was at rest. Phoenix had laid out a few blankets against the wooden planks and we found ourselves wrapped up in half of them. The quilts covered our naked frames as we lied tangled together. I rested my head on Phoenix's warm chest, my arm flung over his body and my fingers playing with his side. I huddled close to him as we looked up at the night and I couldn't help but audibly sigh with happiness. Sweet serenity.

"I think my backstory has been unlocked," Phoenix joked, running a hand through my hair.

"About time."

"I thought you would've put the puzzle pieces together by now."

"For the most part but I want to hear it from you. I've been dying to hear it from you," I confessed.

"Try not to fall asleep. It's not what you've been building it up to be," he jested.

"I'm sure it'll be more captivating than Tolstoy," I teased, my fingers tracing patterns across his chest.

Phoenix shifted slightly but tried not to disturb my drawings. He was wriggling because he was uncomfortable with the subject but I could tell he wanted to push through. He was really trying for me.

"After the stoning, I was critically injured. One had hit my temple and I would've gotten brain damage if it was not for Nicholas' miracle hands during my hours upon hours of surgery."

"Nicholas was your surgeon?" I asked with surprise.

"It's how we met. He's a wonderful guy, he is. During my recovery Jen, my sister, demanded I get a lawyer and sue. Sue or jail them, it didn't really matter, she just wanted justice. I'd do anything for my sister so I agreed to fight back. She decided she would hire the best lawyer she could find, an expensive top of the state lawyer whose never lost a case. I told her I could never afford it considering I was so young and had to pay medical bills and rent. She insisted she would pay, she always paid for everything when it came to me."

"You were sixteen, right?"

"Yeah, insanely young to be a part of such an attack," Phoenix shook his head, "So she found the best lawyer. She went and hired the *President's* lawyer. Christ, I have no idea how she did it or afforded it. So, on my last day in the hospital she brought him in and being as naive as I was I thought it was love at first sight. I met Zach and every time he talked to me or looked me in the eyes, I would blush. It was so embarrassing. I was just a kid."

Part of me wanted to smile, the thought of a young Phoenix fawning over an older man. Another part of me felt sick at the thought.

"He made me file to serve the Church the notice of Justin and Glenn's impending trial and the consequences of their actions that would follow. I don't think they were impressed but under legal obligations they were not allowed to communicate with me. Zach met up at our house regularly to go over our argument and evidence for the trial. I spent hours with him every week and although what had happened to me was tragic, I think falling for him was even more tragic."

"Was falling for me tragic?" I laughed.

"You have no idea."

I couldn't argue with that. He kissed the crown of my head and then proceeded.

"The thing you have to understand about the past, Simon, is that the President was fresh and new at the time and that made him a big deal. For anyone to share a lawyer with him, well, it was bound to be publicised. People found out we had teamed together and suddenly our faces were in the press. 'Presidential Law & Order' , 'The Stoned and The Ridiculed', 'Gay Government Vs. The Church'. It was horrible. They pinned him like a criminal when he was doing something heroic. When the President discovered Zach was working on this particular case, he threatened him. He said he'd fire him if he continued."

"What?! Why?" I frowned.

"The President was very good friends with the founder of the church. He made that very public in the media before the stoning. To have his dear friend's men be taken down by one of his own, by his very own lawyer, would be humiliating and would destroy the friendship entirely. Plus he'd be bombarded with the press about what the hell was going on. So he couldn't have it, not at all," Phoenix elaborated, "Zach figured he was bluffing. He'd never find someone better than him. So, he continued with the case. On the day we went to court, I told him I had fallen in love with him. I'm not sure why I did that. I should've waited until afterwards, I think I threw him off because we lost the case. I had never felt anything quite like that disappointment when I saw my attackers leave the court room unbound and their pockets full."

"I'm sorry, Phoenix," I whispered.

"My sister cried. It was a bad day. What made it even worse was that Zach got fired. He lost the case and he *still* got fired. I thought I'd never see him again but I soon found he had no-one else to turn to. He showed up on my seventeenth birthday and I thought that was the best present of all. We snuck out of the party to somewhere private so we could talk. He told me he was going bankrupt. He couldn't get a job anywhere in Washington. Nobody wanted him. I told him I wanted him but he shrugged it off. Kingdom State Banks wouldn't

395

give him a loan for his apartment and if he had tried another bank, he'd probably be penalised. His two best-friends, Fetch and Sarah, who were the reasons he took the case to begin with, just couldn't afford to take him in. He was close to giving up, so I offered him a room at Jen's. Jen didn't care, she quite liked him after all and she didn't know my inappropriate feelings for him. So he moved in and started renting out his apartment so he could get money that way."

"How long did he stay?"

"A couple of months. I'll never forget the day he left, I didn't even know he was leaving. He came into my room and pulled me onto my feet. He told me he liked my eyelashes, said they kept him from going insane and then he kissed me. For the longest time I thought something that beautiful couldn't have been as wrong as it was but then I met you and I realised what love was really meant to be like. Not a thirty year old man kissing a seventeen year old boy but this comfort, this stability, this relationship."

I sat up and curled my body around to face him. I ducked my head down and gently pecked his lips. I retreated and looked into his green, green eyes that were smiling without the need for lips. I understood him completely and felt sorry that his first love was such a disaster.

"So he's the reason you started the Moths?"

"I'd say so. Well a big part of it. I got a couple of people together; Cillian, Liam, Nicholas and we agreed to start a revolutionary movement. We foolishly tried to kidnap the President as our first act of revolution but that ended terribly. It was so, so bad. I'd say worse than today but at least nobody died. Fuck... Zach was practically a brother to Sarah and Fetch. I wonder if he still cares about them. He deserves to know of her passing but I have no way to contact him. It's been years."

"Maybe it's better he doesn't know," I shrugged.

"I wish *I* didn't know," Phoenix murmured,

"The second I met those twins, I was enthralled. They were so unique, there was no other way to describe the twins but as Sarah and Fetch. When I approached them about the Moths, they didn't even hesitate."

"I'm so sorry for killing her," I choked, holding back the tears.

"Simon, it wasn't you. Sparrow didn't shoot. Not once did he pull his trigger, did you see him? He loved you, he was just doing his job. I was the reason we got set up, The President recognised me from the stoning trials. I'm the reason Sarah is dead," Phoenix snapped, trying to defend my honour.

I didn't want to argue but I didn't want to let him think he had blood on his hands. So I stayed quiet, the tears swelling as I watched the stars instead of handling my problems.

"So what now?" I distracted him.

"What do you mean?"

"Well with the Moths, with me, with you… with us," I rambled.

"I have to leave for a little while," he sighed, "It's better if I go. Safer."

"Where to? How long for?" I questioned.

"I'm not sure and even if I was, I wouldn't tell you. I don't want you chasing after me. I need you safe and alive and well."

"They'll catch you," I gulped down hard.

"They won't catch me. They'll never catch me," Phoenix naively smiled.

Oh how I longed to hear him say that. Oh how I longed that it would be true.

"I need you to take over for me for a little while though," he added.

"As in take over the Moths? Phoenix... I'm not sure about this..." I mumbled.

"You need to. You need to for me."

He wrapped an arm around me and squeezed me tight, as if this hug was his way of saying goodbye.

"I'll miss you," I whispered, "Don't take forever."

"I'll try not to."

"Goodnight, Phoenix."

"Goodnight, Simon."

xxxxviii. alone

I woke up and he was gone.

It was early, the morning sun was blinding and hot against my face and back. I wriggled out from under the mass of blankets and I stood up on the platform. I stretched so I could kick into gear, get back to the cabin and the family I had become part of. The trees swayed with a soft breeze that tickled my bare skin. I grabbed a thin blanket and wrapped it around my naked body as I crossed the bridge to the kitchen.

The kitchen wasn't much but a bench, a cupboard and a small round table with one lonesome chair. When I approached the bench, I found my clothes folded neatly on top of each-other. Upon further inspection, I found a phone and a note to the side of my clothes. I grabbed the phone and the note, scanning over it.

There's an already paid cab waiting out the front of the forest for you for whenever you're ready. It's going to take you to your mother's house and Liam will pick you up from there at 6pm in the truck. You can thank me later for your brand new phone.
Love you - Phoenix x

I examined the phone and grumbled, missing him already. I quickly got changed and fixed my hair. I scribbled something on the back of the note and left it behind, strategically placing it among the broken condom packets, pillows and stains. He was sure to be back at some point and if he was anything like me, that spot would be the first place he returned to. I decided to take the blanket with me as a memento, it smelt like him.

I escaped the tree house, passed the ancient ruins and emerged from the forest. I found the taxi quite easily, hopping in without hesitation or doubt. The drive was quiet. I felt oddly alone in the rear seat but I couldn't stop myself from smiling every now and then when I thought of the night before. I could still taste him, smell him, feel him. I wanted to be smothered in it all day.

I spent time with my family, taking my sisters to the park. I watched shows with them, let them gossip about friends and school to me but when they asked me about my life, I wasn't sure how to answer. I joined the mafia for them, I was ripped out of the mafia and thrown into the Moths and I stayed in it for them, to fight for them and protect them. Yet when it came to discussing the details, I didn't know how to explain. Apparently Maria had ran her mouth off to them and told them about my fling with Phoenix. I hated that Maria spent more time with them than I did but I had a shining to the Moths that I couldn't tear myself away from. They kept interrogating me and I cracked under pressure, I even called Phoenix my boyfriend. My mum was so delighted, she didn't leave a millimetre of my face un-kissed.

The clock struck six and Liam had promptly arrived without a second to spare. He whisked me away in the truck and I waved my family goodbye. I'd miss them until I saw them next, if I ever saw them next. Things would be trickier since the gig with the President but I didn't want to think about it. I held tightly onto the blanket.

"How is everyone?"

"Fetch is, well... A Muslim tradition is that there's public grieving for three days after the death of a loved one and then the family can privately grieve. We keep telling Fetch it's okay if they want to take a trip somewhere or just spend a couple of days alone in their room but they insist on being with everyone. They want to be helpful. I think it'd kill Fetch if they thought they were just a moping puddle of mess and not useful," Liam explained, "Maria went to the shed and hasn't come out of it since the funeral. Cillian slept in my bed last night, I don't think he's ever seen a dead body that meant something to him, I think he's scared about the future too. Tara is holding together well, her and Nicholas are the only lively ones who want to cheer people up or at least distract them for a little while. It's weird because I've never seen them interact before now."

"Beginning of a beautiful friendship?" I smiled.

"Hopefully. I can't handle our members feeling sad and lonely."

"They're not our members, they're our family," I grumpily corrected but decided to go on, "Maria hates the shed, what's she doing in there?"

"She just lost her best-friend. It probably didn't seem like it to you but they spent a lot of time together, especially by the lake. I doubt she'll be going back there again."

"Neither," I said, I could taste the bad memories on the tip of my tongue, "But what about you? How are you?"

"I'm not sure how I feel anymore... about anything..." He sighed.
I placed a hand on his knee for comfort and his spare hand grabbed it and held it there for a while. We drove in silence the rest of the way. When we arrived at the cabin, I eagerly wandered up to the front door. I went to knock but someone had opened the door. I smiled when I saw the little one but it vanished as I remembered their predicament.

"How was your night with Phoenix?" Fetch asked.
They tried to smile but it was crooked and dry and half-hearted. Their eyes looked red, blotchy, scabby, sore and their cheeks were sinking in. I didn't want to reply, I didn't want to tell them I had the best night of my life while they were living in hell.

"Wonderful," I hesitated, holding up the small blanket with a smile.

They let Liam and I inside and as I went to walk down the corridor, Cillian popped out of one of the rooms and looked at me with such hope in his eyes. He was waiting for an answer to an unspoken question and luckily I understood because I would've asked the same. I shook my head and he gulped down hard.

Phoenix wasn't coming.

Suddenly there was a buzzing in my pocket and I yanked out my new phone. It was an unknown number and I was intrigued.

"We're going to go watch the news in the rumpus room, join us when you're done," Liam informed, implying I would take the call.

They shuffled out and I answered my phone, raising it to my ear.

I heard no words, I heard nothing comprehensible but I heard *pain*. There was simply a strangled cry over the line. It then began to beep, signalling the caller had hung up. I couldn't move, trying to figure out why someone would scream and pant and cry as if they were being tortured and only to let it go. It didn't take me long to realise Phoenix was the only person who knew this new number.

I didn't know what to do, I was leaping into a new state of shock and terror. I hurriedly tried to call back the number but it rung out and there was no voicemail, it was probably a public phone, maybe a telephone box? I didn't know, I didn't know, I didn't know. I could taste the bile at the back of my throat. I dropped my blanket in the panic and I ran down the hall, stopping at the entrance to the rumpus room. Liam and Fetch snapped their heads up at me from the couch after hearing my footsteps. They could see my grief stricken face and my trembling hand which held the phone. Both of them rushed over to me, worried by my sudden change of mood.

"Phoenix... I could hear Phoenix. It was Phoenix."

"What do you mean? Simon, calm down, explain."

"He was screeching. He cried out as if in pain and then hung up... The number... I don't know the number. I tried to call it again but... It couldn't have been Phoenix. Oh god, where is he? What has he gotten himself into? I should never have left him," I started to splutter, the tears flooding my eyes.

Fetch snatched the phone from my hand and investigated. Liam tried to console me as Fetch tried to call the most recent number, they seemed impatient. Nobody answered and they grumbled, examining the phone.

"I bet if Sarah was here, she could trace the call and find out who or where it was."

Maria had come into the cabin, just standing inside one of the glass doors and staring at us. She looked like shit and she talked like it to.

"Maria..." Liam fussed.

"No, she's right," Fetch shook their head, "But I'll try."

Maria rolled her eyes and crossed the room, throwing herself down on the couch.

"You can?" I stammered, drinking my own tears.

"Sarah taught me a thing or two. What, you'd think she'd go her whole life without showing her sibling a few of her tricks? No way," Fetch glumly smiled, trying to make light of the situation.

"Just find out if it was Phoenix, find out where he is or if he's in pain. I think I'm about to explode," I cried.

"They won't have to," Maria called, "I know where he is."

We all turned to her as she popped up from the couch. She pointed at the television, turning up the volume on the remote and when we came closer to the blue glow of the news, we all understood.

'Breaking news, the chase is over. The head of the terrorist organisation known as The Moths has been captured. The young male unveiled as Phoenix Jackson, who had been filed as missing by his family for some years now, was caught this morning outside of the President's office as what has been described as a solo kidnapping operation. Phoenix has since been captured and is currently being held at Washington State Penitentiary. I think we can all feel safe now that America's most wanted criminal has had his name

revealed and is behind bars, waiting trial. Here's what the President had to say...'
I didn't want to know what The President had to say. I didn't want to know at all.

xxxxix. come back home

A new Game was in order. We were getting
Phoenix out of prison and back into these arms
again.

Liam knew everybody working for the Moths. He
had complied everybody's files, even the ones who
were out of state and he found someone who could
help. Sydney worked as the main cook and food
distributor in Washington State Penitentiary. I had
met Sydney before, green haired and grey eyed
and willing to do anything for Phoenix; we hoped
even this.

We decided to give Sydney a call and I begged for
her participation in saving the love of my life from
a place where he was probably chained up and
isolated and getting illegally tortured by
government troops. There was a long pause before
she answered with "You had me at 'save
Phoenix.'"

She told us she lived with a couple of the guards
who regularly partied and since July 4th was
approaching and was on a Thursday this year,
they'd be out all week instead of working. It meant
their uniforms and passes would be left behind and
Sydney had an unsuspicious way to change the
roster. She said if we could produce three guys to
take their place and pretend to be her roommates,
we had a clear and easy path to Phoenix. There
was nothing stopping me now.

It only took a day to plan. I didn't rest at all that night. I laid in Phoenix's bed. All I could think about was him but then again when had things ever been different? However, this time filled me with such emptiness and left an ache in my side. I couldn't imagine what they were doing to him. I was with him just the other night and now he was in such a mess. It's crazy how quickly these things happened. I'd never take another night with him for granted, even if all we do is argue. Even if he killed Daddy, there was no denying it now, I was made to be with him. I was made for him. Morning came and I barely ate. I went over the plan with everybody again, except so far it was only Liam and I filling the shoes. It was Fetch's third and last day of public grieving and they insisted they accompany us.

"No," I shook my head, "No if something happens…"

"What? Can't handle the loss of both of us? Of both the twins? Well at least I'd be with her..." Fetch bitterly mumbled.

"I want Cillian to go," I stated and ignored Fetch's remark.

"What?" Cillian piped up.

"He always talked about how you and Liam were his closest friends in the world. *Are.* You still goddamn are... I want you there because I know he would," I persisted.

"I don't know... That night with Daddy was the only time I've ever held a gun... I'm not capable of killing anyone…"

"You don't have to. Walk through the prison like you own the place and stand by my side. Tara will drive the van outside the prison which we will escort Phoenix to once we open up his cell and pretend to cuff him. Fetch has made up some permission documents for Phoenix's, uh, 'transferral', so we should get by without a scene. I need you, the psychologist, to arrange the transferral."

Cillian hesitated. He looked around and then to me and then around again. Finally, he nodded and said he was in, he couldn't leave Phoenix hanging. I was thrilled. It had all come together so quick. I tried to ignore the tugging feeling at my chest that was telling me something would go wrong. Speed didn't outweigh success though, at least that's what I was hoping.

That night, we met up with Sydney. She dressed us up in uniform; giving the additional torch, handcuffs and prison passes. Tara made the inappropriate handcuff joke that we were all waiting for and though our nerves were high and I was sweating, muffled laughter echoed through the modern apartment. I wanted to relax, I really did but I needed Phoenix to be safe. I needed him to be with me.

Tara drove us to the Washington State Penitentiary. I couldn't get the title off the tip of my tongue. Sydney didn't come with us, as it was very late at night and distributors were only needed during the day. We had to go at night because we couldn't be seen. We needed the aid of the dark and the other cellmates asleep. Cillian was to deal with talking to workers and verbal confrontation, Liam was to deal with physical confrontation and an escape route of some sort if things went sour and I... I just had to deal with Phoenix.

We got into C block without any hassle. C block was atrocious. It was isolated and gloomy. There were barred windows with eerie shadows peering in that plastered against the cracked grey walls. The floors creaked, although they were cement and it felt like our souls had been left in the other room. The prisoners were illuminated in the dark with their bright orange numbered uniforms. They looked more like costumes, if anything. This was the block for the most dangerous of all people but they looked weak as they slept. I hoped none of them were like Phoenix, wrongly accused and their actions justified.

Phoenix's cell was all the way at the end. He wasn't asleep. He was lying on his bed, his tangled curls against the pillow as he tried to read the bible in the little moonlight available. I started to cry when I saw my angel locked up like that, even as peaceful as he looked. We carefully and quietly

410

strolled over, trying not to disturb the sleeping inmates. Liam tapped the bars and I grabbed ahold of them, the tears streamed down my face. Phoenix snapped his head up and his eyes widened to see us, his supposed three favourite people in the world. He put his book down and very, very slowly arose from his bed. It looked like he was trying to figure out if it was real, maybe he had fallen asleep while he was reading and didn't even realise. No, we were real. I was here and he was there. When he figured out this wasn't all a dream, he rushed over and our hands met through the bars.

"You twat!" I cried, resting my forehead against the cold metal.

"I told you they'd never catch me," he smirked. I wanted to punch him but instead I kissed him. He reached out and stroked my bristled face, he looked sadder than I did.

"We're getting you the fuck out of here," I exclaimed, voice trembling.

"We issued transferral papers with the front office who said he'd run it by the warden while we're waiting. Any minute now he's going to realise they're fake and we're fake and come after us, so we have to be quick," Cillian explained.

"I grabbed the keys while he wasn't looking, so let's do this," Liam insisted.

Liam shuffled closer and I tried to move away from the bars so he could unlock them but Phoenix pulled me back in. He stared at me with burrowed brows and a strict frown. His grip on my wrists was tight and unwavering.

"No."

"Phoenix…?"

"No, I won't let you do this."

"Phoenix, shut the fuck up," I growled, "We're doing this, we fucking need you. I won't let *you* do this, if anything."

"I'm not letting you jeopardise your safety for mine again. Get the hell out of here, for Christ Sake!" Phoenix demanded.

He let go of my wrists, trying to push me away. He went to go lay back down but I grabbed the back of his uniform and yanked him back into place. I held him by the scruffs of his shirt, anger and fear pulsating through me.

"We're unlocking this gate and you're coming with us. I'll handcuff myself to you if I have to," I snarled.

"Not how I imagined our first time with handcuffs to go..." Phoenix laughed but I wasn't in the mood for these jokes anymore.

"Phoenix Jackson, please."

"Simon Sullivan, I have a plan. I have a plan to escape that doesn't involve you. It doesn't involve anyone but myself and it's better that way. If anything happens it's all on me, there's no-one else to blame. So leave, please, I'm begging you. Just leave."

"How can I leave when I don't know if I'll ever see you again?" I choked, the tears returning. Phoenix wiped them away and he grabbed my flushed cheeks. Liam and Cillian stood behind me, unsure how to react or what to do. We had a time limit and I was ignoring it but it was so hard to remain focused. We had not prepared for a response like this, we all had assumed Phoenix wouldn't hesitate to leave with us. It felt like betrayal when really I knew Phoenix's intentions were the opposite.

"I'm going to get out of here and you're going to see me again, I fucking promise you. You will see me again, no matter what you hear or see. I will always come back for you. I love you," He insisted, sloppily kissing me through the bars, "Now there's something you need to promise me before you leave."

"What?" I sighed, closing my eyes and shaking my head.

"When I get out... After I'm gone for a little while... Promise me you'll marry me upon my return?"

I opened my eyes.

"Phoenix..." I shakily exhaled.

He smiled. I smiled.

"I'll marry you."

We kissed again, more passionately and more sloppily this time.

"Now get out of here!" Phoenix demanded, merrier than the last time.

"I love you," I uttered before retreating from the bars of the cell.

"I'll see you when I see you," he smirked.

"C'mon, Simon."

Cillian wrapped a shoulder around my trembling self. I didn't know whether to laugh or cry. He guided me out of C block and out of the barbed wire prison altogether, with Liam circling us in defence. We broke away without any trouble, the warden didn't chase after us or send a bunch of manic guards to kill us due to the stunt. We managed to get into the awaiting van just fine, despite the fact we'd never be able to show our faces there again. I didn't think any of us planned to though.

"Where the hell is Phoenix?!" Tara panicked, twisting in her seat to face us.

My stomach wrenched. I felt the same. Where was he? I regretted leaving him the second we stepped out but there was nothing else we could've said or done. He was so stubborn. Liam told Tara to drive, he said he'd explain later and I buried my head in my hands. We had left him behind but as Phoenix would say us Moths can find the beauty in ugliness. My next thought was that we didn't just leave Phoenix behind… We left my *fiancé* behind.

xxxxx. the Fourth of July

1776.

"The second day of July, 1776, will be the most memorable epoch in the history of America. I am apt to believe that it will be celebrated by succeeding generations as the great anniversary festival. It ought to be commemorated as the day of deliverance, by solemn acts of devotion to God Almighty. It ought to be solemnized with pomp and parade, with shows, games, sports, guns, bells, bonfires, and illuminations, from one end of this continent to the other, from this time forward forever more."

John Adams was wrong. He wrote the quote in a letter to his wife Abigail in regards to a resolution of independence being approved by the Second Continental Congress to legally separate the thirteen colonies from Great Britain. America was to be free, independent. Yet, he was still wrong. The second of July is rarely heard of, overshadowed by its successor the fourth. 240 years ago Benjamin Franklin, Thomas Jefferson and John Adams sat down in Philadelphia, Pennsylvania to sign the Declaration of Independence. They formed the United States of America, abolishing them of the rule of the Great British Empire. The declaration was a formal explanation as to why the vote on the second had been reached, more than a year after it had been proposed, mind you.

Adams was wrong in his letter because we don't celebrate the second of July. Nobody has a family reunion on the second. Nobody has a barbecue on the second. Nobody has a picnic on the second. Nobody participates in parades on the second. Nobody attends a baseball game on the second. Nobody, nobody. We celebrate the Fourth of July because it was official, it was legal on the Fourth of July and that was something to celebrate.

It was now the Fourth of July and it was a time of celebration. It was a time of freedom. It was a time to be alive.

He wasn't, though.

I wanted to get married on the Fourth of July. Liam thought I was crazy to think Phoenix would be back in time and I guess he was right. I never slept. It was the reason for my erratical behaviour and expectations. The bags under my eyes resembled the ones they put on people's heads. I was twitchy and my beard was growing and my knuckles ached and my lips were cracked and I must've stank. I sat on the couch in the rumpus room just watching the television, waiting for a news update, waiting for contact. I barely got up, it was just for bathroom and coffee breaks. I hated the taste of coffee but I wanted to stay awake. I didn't eat, I didn't sleep, I didn't even blink. I was wasting away.

On the Fourth of July, instead of setting off
fireworks or sneaking me off to a bonfire like he
usually did, Liam sat with me. He cuddled up next
to me on the couch and he made me a hot cocoa
and made me eat something and we watched the
news all-day. Numbers began to multiply, Liam
had started a trend. When Tara came into the cabin
she found us and didn't hesitate to join, curling up
on the floor. Maria eventually joined her, playing
with Tara's hair as we all sat in silence. Nicholas
brought his laptop over and sat in his usual one-
seater and silently browsed. Around noon, Cillian
crawled out of his cage and was almost astounded
by our little gang but cuddled up right next to us.
Liam held his hand.

I wasn't expecting Fetch to come out. They were
meant to be privately grieving. After we had told
them Phoenix was still in prison when we returned
that night, they said nothing. They turned away
and retreated to their room, we hadn't heard a word
since. So when Fetch came out, for food no doubt,
with owl like eyes and faded hair to match their
fading personality, I was thinking they'd just turn
away. Yet, upon seeing such a sight of unity, they
couldn't help but join. They leant on the armchair
of the lounge and folded their arms. They didn't
say anything but they shared a quick glance with
me that said it all.

This was my family and it always had been. So
when the news report that spoke of Phoenix's death

417

was viewed, I was glad that they were there with me.

"This just in, Phoenix Jackson, head of terrorist movement The Moths, attempted to break out of Washington State Penitentiary earlier this evening. Since his escape, the police had been out for his re-arrest until eventually the search was called off. A body was found on Pennsylvania Avenue, just outside the White House and has been identified as Phoenix Jackson. The police have deducted he was going to pay the current President a visit on his motorcycle before he crashed right in front of the gate, taking a tumble into his own grave. Images and video footage have been sent in, though I must warn you, what you're about to see is disturbing… Seen here is his out-of-shape vehicle and the cracked porcelain mask he was often seen wearing during his heists. We watch as his still warm body is taken away… As we celebrate the Fourth of July, we can also celebrate another victory for America, the death of its biggest enemy. The Moths will surely be laid to rest."

I watched the coroner load the sheet-covered body into the back of an ambulance, waving an arm as it drove away. It was that simple. He was dead. He was gone. Everybody was silent for a while. They either had nothing to say or they were out of breath. I was out of breath.

The warmth of Liam's body left me as he slowly lifted himself from the sofa. He was just standing

418

there, staring blankly for a while. We watched him as he suddenly turned to me, a glimpse of hope in his eyes.

"They're lying! They have to be lying!"
I almost mistook his expression for a smile.

"What?" Fetch frowned.

"The media always do this to minimise fear or threat. It's totally totalitarian! They're faking it. Besides Phoenix said he had a plan... He said no matter what you hear he's coming back... There's no way…"

"What if he's not?! What if the greatest man we've ever known has died and we're part of the fucking reason?!" Cillian snapped, standing up and aggressively grabbing the onto Liam's collar, "We left him there in that cell because we thought he had it under control."

"He always has it under control, how were we to suspect this?" Liam shouted, pushing Cillian away.
I stood up from my position and walked around them as they fought. I made my way to one of the glass panels of the rumpus room. I folded my arms and stared out at the dark forest. I didn't want to listen but my ears betrayed my mind.

"Besides he does have it under control, he's still alive!" Liam exclaimed in denial.

"Liam, Phoenix is fucking dead! You're making this worse. Think about Simon right now!"

Tara had jumped up and pushed Liam away from Cillian, screeching at him. Maria shortly had her back and not before long, everybody was standing up and arguing amongst themselves in a crowded, steaming group.

"Phoenix is immortal" Liam scoffed, "He always comes back…"

"Liam, say he's still alive one more time and I might punch you in the face," Fetch growled, "He's dead. He's with Sarah now."

"Then what about us?" Liam blubbered, beginning to cry.

Everybody stopped screaming after that. Nobody was used to Liam crying, it was an unusual event but not impossible. Cillian pulled Liam into his body as he sobbed against his chest. They all just looked at each-other, hoping someone would find the right words to say.

"What do we do now?" Liam continued.

"What do you mean?" Cillian gently asked.

"Without Phoenix, what are supposed to do?"

"We keep going."

Now I was in the spotlight. I turned around, their curious eyes darting to me. I was made of stone.

"Phoenix wouldn't want us to disband over this. The Moths is his legacy, it's his pride, it's his baby, it's all that's left of him. If he's really dead, if he's not coming back then it's up to us to take over the world for him. He might not be here but you still have a leader. Why do you think he trained me?

Why do you think he got *all of you* to train me? I'm what links you and Phoenix together. I'm parts of you and I'm a parts of him. He knew something like this would happen, it's why I'm here. I don't know why I never saw it before. I am his little prodigy. If that's who he wanted me to be, then so be it. I'm taking over in his name and we're going to keep fucking going. We're going to plan new Games, we're going to upgrade our weapons, we're going to find new targets and we're going to be *better*. We're going to get the President like Phoenix never did. That's what he wants us to do. In fact that's all rebellious leaders want, is to be avenged and not let their deaths be in vain," I insisted, more determined than I'd ever been in my whole life, "Phoenix told me we're all fighting for something in this movement and if there's one thing worth fighting for, it's Phoenix. There is nothing, *nothing* more worthy than him."

Liam's tears had dried and my hands had balled into fists. Something changed inside me. I was killing off all the people I had been and creating a messiah. I would not tremble. I would not weaken. I would not be powerless. I would not let Phoenix's legacy die with him. I learnt a lot from him, I owed it to him to share that knowledge with the world.

"Simon..." Liam breathed, unable to say more.

"Call me Atlas."

"Simon?" Cillian frowned.

"Things have to change around here. I can't be Simon without Phoenix, so I won't be. Just like we can't be the Moths without Phoenix, so we won't be. I am David Atlas and we are Osiris and we will win… We will win."

On the Fourth of July, both Phoenix Jackson and Simon Sullivan died and the smell of vinegar went with them.

To be continued…